The Vulgarization of Christ's Church

The Vulgarization of Christ's Church

Combating Progressivism's Damning Influence upon Christian Thinking and Preaching

RONNIE W. ROGERS

Foreword by R. Alan Streett

RESOURCE *Publications* · Eugene, Oregon

THE VULGARIZATION OF CHRIST'S CHURCH
Combating Progressivism's Damning Influence upon Christian Thinking and Preaching

Copyright © 2017 Ronnie W. Rogers. All rights reserved. Except for brief quotations in critical publications or reviews, no part of this book may be reproduced in any manner without prior written permission from the publisher. Write: Permissions, Wipf and Stock Publishers, 199 W. 8th Ave., Suite 3, Eugene, OR 97401.

Resource Publications
An Imprint of Wipf and Stock Publishers
199 W. 8th Ave., Suite 3
Eugene, OR 97401

www.wipfandstock.com

PAPERBACK ISBN: 978-1-5326-1633-4
HARDCOVER ISBN: 978-1-4982-4005-5
EBOOK ISBN: 978-1-4982-4005-5

Manufactured in the U.S.A.   04/05/17

Readers should be aware that Internet Web sites offered as citations and/or sources for further information may have changed or disappeared between the time this was written and when it is read.

I dedicate this book to my grandson, Winston Augustus Crosby. I know that your great grandfather is honored that you bear his name as I am honored as well. I know he would be equally desirous as I that your life would so reflect Christ that the name Winston would always remind people of Jesus. I love you Winston Augustus!

Contents

Foreword by R. Alan Streett | ix

Acknowledgements | xi

Introduction | xiii

1 How the Modern Church Mind Was Contaminated: The Subversive Influence of Progressive Education upon the Contemporary Church | 1

2 The Fading Christian Influence in American Life and Christ's Church: Understanding State Education's Scandalous Hostility toward Christianity | 33

3 What the Church Must Do to Stem the Tide of Progressivism: Countering the Corrosive Influence of State Schools upon Culture and the Church | 60

4 Progressivism's Attack upon Faith through Sociology, Psychology, and Law: Protecting the Church from Culture in Order for the Church to Penetrate Culture | 98

5 Scientism, the New De Facto Public Religion: How Naturalism Is Replacing Christianity in America | 135

6 The Peril of Trusting Science Too Much: The Strengths and Weaknesses of Science | 150

7 A Call for an Equipping Model of the Local Church: Restoring the Spiritual Vitality of the Local Church | 172

Appendix A: Signing of Stem Cell Executive Order and Scientific Integrity | 193

APPENDIX B: SOUTHERN BAPTIST CONVENTION RESOLUTION ON REMOVING CHILDREN FROM THE PUBLIC SCHOOL SYSTEM | 195

APPENDIX C: EXAMINATION OF THE CHALLENGE TO THE CLAIM THAT AMERICA HAD A SIGNIFICANT CHRISTIAN POPULATION IN 1776 | 197

APPENDIX D: THE LETTER OF THE DANBURY BAPTISTS TO THOMAS JEFFERSON | 199

APPENDIX E: JEFFERSON'S REPLY TO THE DANBURY BAPTIST ASSOCIATION | 201

APPENDIX F: COMPARISON OF FOUR TEXTS—JEFFERSON AND DANBURY BAPTISTS | 203

APPENDIX G: PHRASES THAT RELATE TO GOD OR RELIGION IN OUR FIVE MOST SIGNIFICANT FOUNDING DOCUMENTS | 205

Authorial Definitions | 209

Bibliography | 215
Name Index | 225
Subject Index | 227
Scripture Index | 229

Foreword

In "The Vulgarization of Christ's Church" Ronnie Rogers tackles the issue of *progressive education* and its negative impact on American culture in general and on the Church in particular. Tracing the development of education from the turn of the 20th century until the present, this book shows how the classroom has devolved from a hallowed sanctuary of sacred and classical learning to a study hall of profane and modern scholarship.

Emphasizing a utilitarian, child-centered and felt-needs approach to teaching, progressive educators have abandoned truth for a relativism that rejects both revelation and the verities of life, upon which classical education is based. Offering a system intended to match the needs with the "modern man," progressive educators have actually thrust Western society into a new "dark ages."

Should the reader be leery of the author's conclusion, consider the following incident. As I pen this *Foreword*, the Denton Independent School District in Texas has embraced a radical child-centered methodology of testing its sixth to twelfth grade students. No longer will a student receive a zero for missing an exam or be given a failing score when flunking one. Rather, he will be allowed to retake the test numerous times until the teacher is satisfied the student has reached the highest score possible. If a student fails to submit a term paper or turns one in late, instead of receiving a zero or being docked points, he will be allowed to write it at his convenience and receive full credit.

When questioned by reporters, a Denton School official said, "Zeroes indicate that no content mastery has been achieved. Using zeroes for missing or incomplete work gives an inaccurate reflection of a student's knowledge or improvement toward mastery of content."

Another official remarked, "A student's grade should reflect his/her mastery of the content. Allowing students to retake an exam or test, lets students reflect on what they have learned and demonstrate their increase in knowledge of the content covered."

One wonders how these students will survive when they graduate and enter the world of reality.

Ronnie Rogers not only exposes the consequences of progressive education in society, but shows its negative effects on the contemporary church. Seeker-sensitive churches are a case in point. Many have embraced man-centered, felt-needs, market-driven, and "I'm okay, you're okay" models of ministry, that reflect the basic principles of progressive educators, and in turn, leave doctrine, discipleship and church discipline in the dust. We might add that the principles of macro-evolution and natural science have also infiltrated the pews and influenced the pulpits of these churches.

Fortunately, the book does not end in despair. Rogers calls for the church to adopt an equipping model of ministry as a deterrent and counter measure to progressive education's penetration into church and culture. The solution, he suggests, is to restore spiritual vitality to the local congregation. This involves a commitment to studying the Scriptures doctrinally, apologetically, evangelistically, and in their historical-grammatical context. No easy task, but necessary and worthwhile! Those equipped in this fashion will go forth as salt and light into a decaying and dark world, and serve as the antidote to the ever-spreading virus of progressive education.

Reading this book is like auditing a college course. When you complete it, you will understand that progressive education is not benign, but a pernicious attack on the revelation of God. We must oppose it until that day when "the earth will be filled with the knowledge of the glory of the LORD, as the waters cover the sea" (Hab 2:14).

R. Alan Streett, PhD
Senior Research Professor of Biblical Theology
Criswell College
Dallas, Texas

Acknowledgements

My story began with contemplation of what others might owe me one day, but God's love has ever shown me that there are none who owe me, but I am everyman's debtor and my greatest debt is to him. Anything that others might graciously feel they owe me is truly owed to God and his grace in teaching one of the most obtuse, meanest, and sinful humans one could know; this so that others may be helped rather than hurt by the old me. He has both used the unmerited love of many, and the desire of my demise by others to mold me. Thus, I will be deeper in debt to more people on the morrow than I am today.

I thank Gina, my wife of forty years, who has through her unique giftedness and unwavering love for Christ and me, influenced me more than anyone else other than my Lord Jesus. She has modeled a divine faithful love toward me as we have followed Christ; we have celebrated the great moves of God as a pastor and his mate, joys unspeakable, and we have wept together in the bizarrely confusing and harrowing times as well. Through it all, she has never left my side; if she had, I would not be.

I also want to thank Larry Toothaker and Billy Wolfe who have with loving fastidiousness selflessly proofed my manuscript; Anita Charlson for her sedulous and unfathomable oversight and editing of the manuscript, without which the project would have been too dismaying to even consider; Sommer Buss for her splendid work on the cover creation; JR Crosby for his creative insights and caveats; the elders for their unwavering support of my commitment to study and their untiring encouragement to equip the saints and write; as well as my brothers and sisters at Trinity Baptist Church whom I have been blessed beyond measure to serve for over sixteen years. You have loved me without measure and provided me the greatest opportunity for spiritual growth. My longevity as your pastor is a testimony of your Christ-like gracious and generous forbearing love towards me. No man could deserve such a life of being loved, but none so little as me.

I will always be indebted to all of you for your love and support.

Introduction

IN THIS BOOK, I primarily seek to elucidate and demonstrate the incalculable and deleterious influence that progressive education has had upon preaching and the understanding of what a local church is to be and do, as well as the ability of Christians to think Christianly. I provide both current and historical evidence of progressive education's undermining of the mission and message of the church. I refer to certain ideas as tsunamic, by which I mean ideas that spawn, empower, and perpetuate additional and consequential ideas. Often and unfortunately, many see the consequences of such substratal ideas as the real threat while they (although important) are actually emanations from the truly constitutive philosophical idea. It is this basal idea that must ultimately be understood and addressed.

Progressive education began at the turn of the twentieth century and is a tsunamic idea. Progressive education replaced classical and academic education with what is purportedly a science-based education. This seismic shift in public education has not only affected what we learn but how we think, both of which are, in many ways, contrary to classical and biblical thinking, e.g., existence of absolutes, importance of history. Tragically, this educational transformation has affected most Americans, and to the degree that its influence remains undetected or underappreciated by the church, the church is concomitantly infected. In order to enable the church to protect herself and be equipped by the progressive revelation of God, to help Christians think more Christianly and the church to be more faithful to Scripture, I seek to highlight some of the underlying intolerable essentials of progressive education and demonstrate how they are contaminating preaching and thereby the church.

I also provide some basic methods the church can employ to counter this substratal influence enabling us to be the church Christ desires us to be. While I believe there are many styles of local churches, I believe the biblical model is what I refer to as an *Equipping Model*. The equipping model is based upon Eph 4:11–16 and carries out the mission of the church as given by our Lord Jesus Christ in Matt 28:18–20.

The companion book to this one, *The Equipping Church: Somewhere Between Fundamentalism and Fluff*, primarily focuses upon contrasting the *equipping* model of the local church with other local church models, with clear reasons why the equipping model is the most biblical and how it encompasses the complete New Testament teaching for the local church. It gives clear biblical and practical steps for building an equipping New Testament church. I believe that the only way to disabuse the church of being guided by progressivism, gauzily clad with select verses, is to become aware of the pervasiveness and particulars of progressivism in order to detect and reject it outright; the next step is to replace progressivism with the progressive revelation of God. This can most thoroughly be done in a biblical model of the church that is molded by the full weight of the Word of God.

I use three terms throughout both books to distinguish the various genres of churches in America today. I use *traditional* to refer to an array of church models that, for various reasons and in varying degrees, commonly consider certain traditional practices as biblically superior to more contemporary approaches. I use *contemporary* to encompass various models that include a common commitment to contemporize church ministry without compromising the message of the gospel.[1] These genres have styles within each that are more or less consistent with the biblical model. *Equipping* is the term that I use to describe the biblical model that is based on Eph 4:11–16 and Matt 28:18–20. Even the equipping model consists of varying styles of churches.

Secular progressive education is undermining Christian education in the church and is actually undergirding much of the contemporary approach to church ministry, which ultimately leaves Christianity weak and anemic, merely driven by each new cultural wave and generation of culturati. The influence of progressive education upon the church has transformed much of the contemporary church into being driven more by science and scientism than Scripture, albeit at times unwittingly. The church must view its educational responsibility as paramount because if the church fails to grasp the educational nature of the church, she will fail at her mission.

---

1. I recognize that each approach, such as church growth, emergent, etc., may dislike being grouped together, but I do so for the sake of simplicity, allowing me to focus more on clearly contrasting some modern and traditional approaches with the biblical model as it is laid out in the New Testament; additionally, in contrast to liberal models, the ones I am considering are *generally* considered evangelical and claim to believe in the inerrancy of the Scripture or at least biblical authority.

1

How the Modern Church Mind Was Contaminated

The Subversive Influence of Progressive Education upon the Contemporary Church

OFTEN PEOPLE DO NOT recognize how enormously they have been shaped by the less obvious influences in their lives. This is particularly true when it comes to education. This is not to say that people do not recognize that education has an impact upon their lives, but rather they do not appreciate the profound influence that the philosophy of their education has on their life and thinking about life.

When I left my first church to go to Criswell College for theological training, a dear friend and member Marzell Kingry said to me, "I hate to see you go to school because I have watched many good preachers go to seminary and lose their passion and beliefs." Several years later, after my schooling, I went back and preached a funeral at that church, and she told me, "Well, I'm glad to say that you did not lose your passion and beliefs when you gained an education." I told her what I came to realize is that it is not education that strips a man of his passion and biblical beliefs, but rather it is the *kind* of education that makes the difference.

My goal is not to challenge us to become more aware of how taking a particular class—math, history, or biology—influences a person's life, for that seems quite obvious. Rather it is to challenge us to become more aware of the philosophy that determined the content of the subjects, how they are classified, their importance to overall education, when the subjects are offered, who takes them, why other subjects are not offered, how each subject relates to the other, how they are taught and in fact what defines education and learning. It is the guiding philosophy of the education, and its almost subliminal effect upon people that concerns me.

This veiled influence may not be as obvious to a person as the unmistakable content of a given subject—in literature they may have learned about Huckleberry Finn—but it becomes glaringly pronounced through what I call generational infection. Simply stated, this refers to people imbibing at the cistern of a quite different philosophy of life and thought than what they initially believe; then through continued exposure to the undergirding and driving philosophy they gradually begin to think, evaluate, and communicate more and more consistently with the new system of thought while remaining largely unaware of the subtle shift.[1] Public education demonstrates this well. People are exposed to certain ideas they do not like or are uncomfortable with, and so reject them. However, the underlying premise of the public education, which may or may not be mentioned or fully understood, results in one becoming intellectually befouled with some of the ideas that *seem* to coincide with one's own worldview; on a deeper level, they unknowingly become tainted with an underlying premise, or worldview, which through generational infection will eventually either change their current worldview or strip it of its uniqueness or coherency.

Therefore, generational infection is where fundamental beliefs and the coherency of one's worldview are eroded to the point where successive generations are willing to accept what previous generations rejected categorically because in accepting certain proposals, they also accepted certain modifications of their philosophy of life even though they were either marginally or totally unaware of them. It is only detected by evaluating where a person is and who one is in light of more than one's own experience or culture because phenomenologically the two ideas may look very similar or compatible, but philosophically they are irreconcilable. Generational infection is only detected by stepping outside of our normal thought processes and evaluating them not merely phenomenologically but biblically, philosophically, and comparatively. Then and only then can we begin to see the influence our education has upon us and upon the church through us.

For example, I grew up in the sixties. I am, in large part, a product of the sixties and seventies. By anyone's estimation, these were years of cultural revolution. Robert Bork, former professor of law at Yale Law School, said of the sixties, "The revolt was against the entire American culture. The United States, it was said, was engaged in an immoral war only because the

---

1. See Authorial Definitions for a more thorough definition.

United States itself was deeply immoral, being racist, sexist, authoritarian, and imperialistic."[2] However, even though I grew up during that tumultuous time and was aware of the war protests, rock music, and hippies, I did not realize the seismic cultural shift that was transpiring; for how could I objectively evaluate that of what I was in fact a noncontemplative participant. Only years later, through becoming a Christian and studying for many years, have I come to understand that of which I was a part. This example helps to highlight the fact that generational infection is much more sinister than other more obvious cultural enticements, because it is far more difficult to detect and correct.

I believe the most influential agent in shifting American culture to a more culturally liberal society is progressive education. Progressive education began around the turn of the twentieth century[3] and has dominated state education ever since. It stands as the most significant vehicle for changing the ideas of culture changers and disseminating those ideas on a massive scale. My setting forth of progressive education as the principal vehicle for transforming modern American culture, and to an alarming degree the church, is not to say it is the only or even the swiftest influence. Obviously any given culture is a supersystem and therefore not totally the reflection of any one particular cause.

Just consider the fact that almost all adults—including preachers, evangelists, missionaries and Christian leaders—have attended state schools.[4] In addition, about ninety percent of all children attend state schools kindergarten through twelfth grade.[5] They do this for approximately eight hours a day, nine months a year, for twelve or thirteen years. Also, college enrollment has grown significantly. "In 1930, as Seymour Martin Lipset noted, there were about 1,000,000 students in [colleges or universities] . . . But in

---

2. Bork, *Slouching Towards Gomorrah*, 32.

3. Although there were progressives prior to this time, the latter part of the nineteenth and early twentieth centuries seems to be the time when the wars over what type of education would dominate America began to intensify. "The progressive movement in education began in the 1890s," Ravitch, *Left Back*, 53. "In the early twentieth century, there was a decided split between those who believed that a liberal education (that is, an academic curriculum) should be given to all students and those who wanted such studies taught only to the college-bound elite. The latter group, based primarily in the schools of education, identified itself with the new progressive education movement and dominated the education profession in its formative years," ibid., 15.

4. At times, I use the term state schools, as opposed to the term public schools to distinguish between schools owned or controlled by the state or federal government, and schools that can be open to the public that are not controlled by the government.

5. "About 9 of every 10 students in kindergarten through grade 12 . . . were enrolled in public schools in 1993," Bruno, "School Enrollment," pg. 17, col. 1, ln. 5–10.

1970, there were 7,000,000 students."[6] Nearly eighty percent of all college students attend state schools[7] and over twenty-one million are enrolled in state colleges today.[8]

Although the media, with its brazen images and mass dissemination of political demagoguery, clearly drives us faster and faster to error being accepted as a form of truth, I intend to demonstrate that the underlying problem is the philosophy of progressive education, which has forged our culture, and to a large degree our churches, into non-thinking institutions. Progressive education has created a culture whose learning process is conducive to images, sound bites, and demagoguery rather than well-informed, analytical, linear thinking. My major concern is what it has done to the church, or better said, what the church has allowed it to do. This is not to play the blame game, but rather to identify this subversive influence for what it is and how it has infected the church, and to challenge the church to rise up and be what God called her to be.

While people are keenly aware of the power of more visible influences like modern media or advertising, seldom do they probe beneath the obvious to investigate the reason or cause. Why are so many so susceptible to ideas that once were so repugnant? For example, while it is obvious that the entertainment and social media—television, movies, music, internet—vastly increase the dissemination of detrimental ideas upon the American public, that does not address the origin of the plethora of rancid ideas and the reason people have become so accepting of them. Where did the ones who determine the content of movies, music, and news get their ideas? In other words, who influenced the influencers and what happened, and continues to happen, to much of the church that makes her so vulnerable and even quick to embrace each new wave of ideas? Why has this happened to the church, and how do we build churches that remain faithful to the Scripture and are thereby able to thrive in hostile environments without retreating into traditionalism or supping at the table of modishness? That is what this book and this chapter in particular is about.

While I recognize that evil ideas ultimately originate in the heart of Satan and fallen man, my concern is why the promulgation of that evil has become so prevalent, and why much of the church is not only acquiescing but also embracing things that even thirty years ago were categorically

---

6. Lipset, *Rebellion in the University*, xxxix-xl.

7. "Nearly 4 out of every 5 college students were enrolled in public schools in 1993," Bruno, "School Enrollment," pg. 17, col. 1, ln. 7–10.

8. At the college level, 13.9 million students were enrolled in 1993, ibid., pg. 16, col. 3, ln. 7–9. For enrollment figures for 1993–2010 with links to stats for 2016, see http://nces.ed.gov/fastfacts/display.asp?id=98.

rejected? The church has not only been swept up in the tide of the progressives, but she has actually, in disconcerting measure, become complicitous in the propagation of progressivism, albeit wearing different attire. Remember that I am not considering the liberal wing of Christianity, but rather those known as conservative, evangelical, or neo-evangelical. In addition, my emphasis is not to merely attack the progressive influence on the church growth movement and extol fundamentalism or legalism, for they are as much a part of the problem as the contemporary model, only in a different way. The contemporary model does not counter progressivism because it actually embraces many of its underlying concepts, albeit often unwittingly. Traditionalism fails to counter it because its intellectual spirituality is measurably disengaged from the century in which it operates. That is to say, traditionalism emphasizes an isolationist model rather than biblically equipping Christians to engage the modern world.

The contemporary approach was right to reject traditionalism as a model for the church because it was not biblical and therefore was increasingly irrelevant, but it seriously erred in replacing traditionalism with an equally inadequate contemporaneity, which is often predicated more upon the ideas of progressive education than progressive revelation. The church growth movement has not demonstrated sufficient prudence or shame for its dependence upon secular growth models, marketing, and non-Christian experts even though some of their own more recent research indicates the failure of such secular ideas to produce spiritually mature believers.[9] However, I believe they would be ashamed if they understood that the premise of much of their innovation is based more upon ideas that are antithetical to Scripture than based upon Scripture itself. Church growth adherents are inherently and relentlessly, although at times imperceptibly, undermining and eroding true biblical Christianity, which they seek to live and spread. The force that I am talking about is, of course, progressive education.[10]

First, my comments are not intended to be a critique of all public school teachers. There are many dedicated Christian teachers in the public

---

9. See the self-study publication *Reveal,* by Hawkins, Parkinson, and Arnson,

10. Progressive education has always been made up of a complex series of related ideas and movements (see Ravitch, *Left Back,* 54) and continues much in the same fashion today; however, as in the past there is still a congruence of ideas warranting the term progressive education. John Dewey believed "the advance of education depended on the application of the social sciences, particularly psychology to education. The school, he said, 'must represent present life' . . . children should understand what they learned as it applied in real life," ibid., 57. Progressive education basically describes an underlying philosophy of education that is antithetical to classical and academic education and includes various changes in curricular titles, superficial promotions, and other changes. See Ravitch, *Left Back* for other movements: 327, 453, 462.

school system, for which I am very grateful. Some of them understand the fundamental problems in progressive education and are actually a force against its advancement. Sadly though, many other fine Christians are not fully aware of their complicity in advancing the core principles of progressive education. Secondly, the church growth movement has influenced most churches in America, and some of that influence has been for the good. The detrimental effect upon the church is from church growth movement principles that undermine or marginalize biblical mandates, thereby consigning churches to trendy shallowness.[11]

The challenge is to examine everything through the lens of Scripture and to think substantively about ideas, philosophies, and long-term ramifications of core concepts—none of which are characteristics of the church growth movement or of the progressivism that significantly undergirds the movement. This seems to be a deficiency of the church growth movement and its uncritical enthusiasts, which in my opinion, potentiates dispossessing the church of its spiritual power derived from being a church operating *under* God's instructions. For that reason, I want to explain the underlying premises of progressive education and then demonstrate how these are also, albeit unknowingly, some of the premises of the church growth movement. I am aware of the numerous name changes or emphases that take place in education like outcome based or constructivism,"[12] and the like, but the basic premises that I will lay out have undergirded state education for the last century and still do.

THE DETRIMENTAL EFFECTS OF PROGRESSIVE EDUCATION

In the early 1980s there was a palpable sense throughout the country that our educational standards needed immediate attention and improvement, and I would say they still do. To this end, the Reagan Administration commissioned a study, and a report was made by the National Commission on Excellence in Education. "That report was a galvanizing event; the report was entitled A Nation at Risk. It was a call to action; it said in part, 'Our nation is at risk . . . the educational foundations of our society are presently being eroded by a rising tide of mediocrity that threatens our very future as a Nation and a people . . . If an unfriendly foreign power had attempted

---

11. See my book, *The Equipping Church*, chapters three and seven.
12. Common Core, Next Generation Science Standards

to impose on America the mediocre educational performance that exists today, we might well have viewed it as an act of war.'"[13]

Today the church is at risk of becoming what she preaches against. The mandate for the church is to transform the culture, but with each passing generation, the reality is that the culture is transforming much of the church. I am speaking of evangelical, conservative churches that hold to the Bible as the Word of God, who have a passion to reach the lost and transform our culture. There is a rising tide of mediocrity and superficiality within the church that threatens the very future of the local church. The modern threat is hosted and inculcated into society through progressive education.

Because progressive education began in the latter part of the nineteenth century, flourished in the twentieth century, and dominates twenty-first century state education, it is safe to say that virtually every American has been influenced to some degree by the tenets of progressive education. Only by coming to grips with that reality and how it is affecting our churches can it be truly countered. It has to be done in the local church where the people are equipped by shepherds feeding the flock with the meat of the Scripture. The following seeks to delineate some of the essential ideas of progressive education and demonstrate its profound and deleterious influence upon the church as well as the detrimental impact it is having upon our Republic. I will spend sufficient time explaining each of the concepts educationally. Then I will demonstrate how each concept is undermining the work of the church *in the church*.

Progressive education rejected mental discipline

Speaking of *mental discipline*, Educational Historian Diane Ravitch, in her book *Left Back* says, "Most parents and educators believed in that doctrine . . . because they assumed that the purpose of education was to 'train' the mind and 'discipline' the will. Mental discipline . . . held that the mind was composed of specific 'faculties' or powers, such as reasoning, memory, will, observation, judgment, and imagination, and that these powers could be trained and strengthened by vigorous effort."[14] Consequently, subjects like Latin not only taught you Latin but trained the mind to judge and reason, and it developed the student's will power. Therefore, the content of the subject may not be immediately or ever directly applied to a student's life, but the mental training that he gained from it could be transferred to other areas. This concept is at the heart of classical, academic, and biblical education.

13. Ravitch, *Left Back*, 411–12.
14. Ibid., 61–62.

Therefore, "the reformers knew that they had to dethrone the academic curriculum and that they would not succeed unless they were able to break the tenacious hold of the doctrine of mental discipline."[15] Concerning the progressives, Ravitch says, "These psychologists sought to demonstrate that training in one activity did not transfer to other uses, either in other subjects or outside the school. This turned out to be a crucial issue in the history of education in the twentieth century."[16] Thus, Latin was good only for learning Latin, and that was only good if you were going to teach Latin or use Latin in some direct way.

Later, "Psychologist Edward L. Thorndike . . . a founder of educational psychology and a leading figure in the progressive education movement . . . acknowledged that transfer sometimes occurred but in limited situations."[17] Other studies also disproved the conclusions that transfer does not take place.[18] "In the late 1950s, Walter B. Kolesnik of the University of Wisconsin surveyed hundreds of studies of transfer of training and concluded that 'it is now generally accepted as a sound principle that under certain conditions and to a certain extent transfer can and does take place.'"[19] Whereas the classicist valued training the mind and the will through interdisciplinary studies, which may or may not have either immediate or direct application, the progressives' rejection of mental training led them to promote vocational learning—learn only what you will directly use. It shifts the emphasis of education from broadly based research, lecture and memorization to learning by experience and activities.[20]

Now as a result of a failure to appreciate mental training, we have continued devaluing the classical approach to education—studying of the classics and history and learning to read phonetically—and placed an undue emphasis upon curricular differentiation at earlier grades and disproportionate learning by experience and observation.[21] Curricular differentiation is the idea that different students require different curriculum—doctors and lawyers need different curriculum. The point of contention between the

15. Ibid., 61.
16. Ibid., 63.
17. Ibid., 63–65.
18. Ibid., 67–69.
19. Ibid, 69.

20. Academic, classical, or biblical education does include learning by experience and activities, and progressive education includes some lecture and memorization, but the issue is the change in priority and emphasis.

21. Other things like utilitarianism, the scientific approach to education and life, and other principles of progressive education still to be discussed have played a part in this as well.

progressives and the classicists was at what point the differentiation needed to start. The classicist had long held that there are certain core subjects that every student in America needs to learn, certain facts everyone needs to know, and therefore curricular differentiation comes later. The progressives, who emphasized hands-on learning and vocational learning, believed that either there did not need to be any core curriculum or if there was one, it was minimal and curricular differentiation should come early.

Consequently, some of the results from the progressives' rejection of mental discipline include the belief that learning in one area either does not help you at all in other areas or the benefit is marginal. Learning also should not be academic, but specific, practical, and related to everyday real life. Therefore, subjects like history, languages, and the like are only for the specialist and have little relevance in the real everyday life of people. Many do not realize that the debate between phonics and the look-say method is not merely about which is the best way to learn to read, but rather a debate about the philosophy of education because what a person is going to read determines in large part which method should be used. The phonics method of learning to read was rejected by the progressives from the beginning because of the very nature of progressive education as defined by them.

In other words, if you are going to teach a child to read the classics, history, and other subjects that provide a good academic curriculum, then phonics is the best way to learn to read information that is beyond one's own experience. However, if it is true that children need only to learn from their immediate experience, learn what they want to learn, and learning must always be fun (as progressives insist), then the look-say method is great. This is the problem with even debating studies about which method is the best because in classical or academic education, phonics is clearly better, but in child-centered progressive education, look-say may be as good because it is easier and more fun to learn. Consequently, when some argue that students do better with the look-say method, that it is easier to learn, and it does not hurt their learning of the present curriculum, they may well be right. Of course this is to miss the real issue of what is education, which is much deeper than a comparison of reading methods.

The influence of progressive education can be seen in the church when we are told that pastors are not supposed to teach Bible history or encourage Scripture memorization. People do not need to know deep theology or really be taught in-depth about the abstract nature of God or other such abstractions that will not help them in real life—meaning in part that knowledge is not transferable. That is material for the scholars, preachers, and specialists but not for the people in the pew. People need what is relevant to their lives and addresses problems in everyday living, like how they are to cope at work on Monday. While it is definitely true that people need to learn the teachings of Scripture that deal with obvious problems in everyday living as a part of teaching all of the Scripture, preachers should be able to say with Paul, "For I did not shrink from declaring to you the whole purpose of God" (Acts 20:27).

That being the case, the same argument holds true to declare the truths about the deep things of God. Moreover, we should categorically reject the notion that deep knowledge about the nature of God, man, etc., is not practical. Progressive education ridicules and mocks memorization by referring to it by such pejoratives as rote memorization, which sneering has found supporters even in the church. Now if one is going to practice Scripture memorization, he should know the context and only recite it as it truly applies, but that is not a word against memorization. Actually, what is often viewed as non-practical, meaning deep theology—predestination, God's nature, and the like—are in reality even more beneficial than the down to earth pragmatics of the practicalist. The very question of utility, does it work or is it relevant, is somewhat meaningless without the follow-up question, relevant to what? Far too often the what for the contemporary church is will it increase numerical growth.

David Wells, in discussing the professionalizing of the ministry and its impact on training, and how a shift from theology to task—which often includes an overemphasis upon pedagogy—affects the place of theology in training ministers, says, "Whereas the unity once lay in the theology that was taught, it now lies in the needs in the church that the minister will have to manage. There is not, therefore, a conceptual link between what is studied in theology and what will be practiced in the church, but simply pragmatic rationale that asks only what specific help theological knowledge can offer for the needs that arise. When the tasks of ministry provide the criteria for what should be studied, then the alienation of theology becomes almost inevitable."[22]

Leadership Magazine is one of the foremost leadership magazines for evangelical leaders. A study was conducted that evaluated the articles in the magazine. Between 1980 and 1988, articles were written covering a wide range of personal challenges and problems encountered by clergy, along with numerous articles concerning techniques for managing the church. All of these are issues that the Scripture speaks to clearly, repeatedly, and definitively. However, "less than 1 percent of the material made any clear reference to Scripture still less to any idea that is theological."[23] Furthermore and

---

22. Wells, *No Place for Truth*, 243–44.
23. Ibid., 113–14.

obviously, this eliminates true expository preaching because not everything in the Bible is vocational or experiential. The sway of progressive education causes us to view the Bible as a how-to book or a book of proverbs. Strategically important is to remember that while the Bible contains a book of proverbs, the Bible is not merely a book of proverbs or principles. Rather it is a divine revelation about God, man, and God's world, plan, and work that unfolds in simple and complex truths and stories.

In *Rediscovering Pastoral Ministry,* Richard L. Mayhue, senior vice president and dean, Master's Seminary, offers a valuable perspective regarding the balance. "The statements of this chapter are *not* a call for a *user-unfriendly* church, a culturally *ignorant* church, or a seeker *insensitive* church. We have no desire to . . . promote an irrelevant dinosaur of a church. On the other hand, neither do we want to substitute the latest theories in sociology and psychology for the truth of theology. We do not want to confuse the common sense benefit of demographic statistics and analysis of culture with the far more important understanding of God's will for the church . . . We ardently desire to let the important consideration of God and His revealed will in Scripture be the major focus."[24]

Progressive education embraces utilitarianism[25]

English philosopher Herbert Spencer, a social Darwinist, exercised profound influence upon American education. Historian Lawrence A. Cremin described Spencer's book on education as "probably the most widely read in America."[26] Spencer asserted, "Utility was the measure of all things," and the most worthwhile knowledge was "knowledge for self-preservation."[27] Spencer's emphasis in education discounts the afterlife.[28] In his order of importance regarding the kinds of knowledge on which to premise education, he lists first "activities which directly minister to self-preservation" and secondly "activities which . . . indirectly minister to self-preservation."[29] Neither these, nor the remaining three in his list, include knowledge regarding eternal life. Accordingly, he says regarding the value of history, "The

---

24. MacArthur and The Masters Seminary Faculty, *Rediscovering Pastoral Ministry,* 15.

25. I am not referring to the full-blown philosophy of utilitarianism but rather to a more populist utilitarianism, practicalism.

26. Cremin, *The Transformation,* 91.

27. Ravitch, *Left Back,* 27

28. Spencer, *Education,* 17–18, 31, 44.

29. Ibid., 18.

only history that is of practical value, is what may be called Descriptive Sociology."[30] Consequently, the value of knowledge is determined by its usefulness in this natural life. The most valuable kind of knowledge is that which helps you in this life or vocation. Does it work, is it or will it be useful, or is it immediately meaningful? If so, it is right and good, which means that it accomplishes certain ends.[31]

Consequently, this emphasis on utility, which is seen in the progressives' rejection of classical education, involves two inextricable components. First, what is learned must be practical—useful in ordinary this life activities. Second, what is learned must be valuable now, or at least in the very near future, otherwise it fails the test of being practical in one's experience. So the question of progressive education becomes, does the material being taught have immediate practical value for *real* life? Consequently, subject material is deemed worthy of a person's time only if it is *obviously* useful to him or her now or in the very near future. Again, this just reinforces the rejection of mental discipline or learning anything that is not perceptibly implementable in this. Therefore, if a core curriculum exists, it is minimal. This concept provided a basis for the vocational training and real life argument: what will help a farmer farm, what will help a person get a mate, what will help a person cope on Monday. Needless to say, the distant future is beyond consideration, and the eternal is useless religious jargon. One should not choose whether a student should learn a subject based on some abstract notion of what education is, for education is observation and experience. It is for today in the real world.

Based on utilitarianism, which results in educating at the lowest common denominator, blacks were not challenged. Jean Jacques Rousseau (1712–1778), born in Geneva, was a French philosopher and social reformer who profoundly affected modern western education, including men like John Dewey. Speaking of a Negro, Rousseau says, "It seems also as if the brain were less perfectly organized in the two extremes. Neither the Negroes nor the Laps are as wise as Europeans."[32] The same can be said for the poor. "The poor man has no need of education. The education of his own station in life is forced upon him, he can have no other."[33] For the progressives, Intelligence Quotient (IQ) testing played a large part in determining which

---

30. Ibid., 62.

31. The actions that take precedence over all others is that by which "we secure personal safety." This present natural life is the context of valuable knowledge both in his explicit statements and by his neglect or derogation of eternal knowledge. Ibid., 18.

32. Rousseau, *Emile*, 19. His book *Emile*, published in 1762, is his theory of education; Negro is the term that was used for blacks until the mid-twentieth century.

33. Ibid., 20.

child should be taught what. The IQ test revealed what they would need based on their supposed ability, and the progressives were "dedicated to the idea of social adjustment rather than social advancement, the schools in the 1940s and 1950s prepared children to fit into society as it then was."[34]

The ubiquitous influence of utilitarianism upon the local church's teaching and preaching ministry is too obvious to deny.[35] In the church, preachers evaluate the message by whether it had an *immediate* and *observable* effect—did people respond? The listeners evaluate it based on the answer to the question, "How does this affect my life *today?*" If there was no immediate and perceptible change in the hearers, and if the listeners did not see immediate relevance, then try something else, and do so quickly for time is of the essence. Forget that it is the Word of God. Forget that Psalm 119:65 says, "You have dealt well with Your servant, O Lord, according to Your word." Forget that every word of God is a treasure, because tawdry immediacy reigns.

The avant-garde would admonish pastors to spend little time preaching the history and theology of the Bible and devote their attention to only those things that are practical, meaningful to people and immediately so, because the immediate benefit of a message determines its value. Messages focusing on such things as depth, history, theology, difficult concepts, and intellectual aspects of Christianity, are seen as irrelevant, passé. This infection dooms the equipping ministry of the church to the lowest common denominator. There is no depth beyond perceived ability, need, and station in life or society as it is. The church mimics the progressives who want to "ensure that each child got the curriculum appropriate to his needs and future occupation."[36] Like progressive educators, the question for the viability of a topic or message is "Does it function?"[37]

Christianity is missional by nature. It is about knowing God and making him known to the world. It is living for eternity in time; however, based upon the progressive's model, everything is to be based upon felt needs, being relevant—which translates to only what is germane to the here and now of natural life. Many times, even talk of the eternal is valued only if it is communicated in such a way as to be relevant to a person's immediate life (make him feel better NOW). That is to say, the comfort drawn at the moment is more important than the reality of a future with God. We need to be

---

34. Ravitch, *Left Back,* 377.

35. Warren "Contemporary Approaches," #20 and #25. This is from a talk given to leaders of Saddleback Valley Community Church.

36. Ravitch, *Left Back,* 101.

37. Ibid., 102.

reminded that utilitarian immediacy proved to be a fatal flaw in progressive education because it was shortsighted, saw only the immediate, the status quo, and did not consider that things might drastically change, as they in fact did. They did not see that subjects like algebra would be needed for the farmer as well as the doctor, that people might create new technologies that would alter what people needed to know for daily living, nor did they see that the black may break out of his culture. They could not imagine that one day farmers might become doctors or that the percentage of people going to college would greatly exceed their expectations.[38]

The pervasive utilitarian approach in the church results in even greater tragedy. We should remember, as the song so aptly says, "When others see a shepherd boy, God may see a king."[39] We have no idea how God is going to use someone in the future. When we equip people only for their life today, we ignore all of biblical history and 2000 years of church history, where God does extraordinary things with ordinary people and does not leave people where they are. When we prepare people only for present needs, oblivious to what God might want them for later, it dooms us to seeing only a shepherd boy and training him to be nothing more.

Progressive education emphasizes pedagogy more than content

The rejection of classical and academic education by progressives was also a result of their desire to make education a science. Progressive education from its inception has placed an inordinate emphasis on methods of education as opposed to the academic approach, which emphasized the content of education. The progressive's curriculum contains more emphasis on *how* children are to be taught than *what* children are taught. The teacher becomes more of a facilitator of learning rather than a teacher of knowledge.

Emphasizing how one learns over what one learns is classically modeled in Rousseau's book *Emile*. Emile is a fictitious character that Rousseau uses to teach his pedagogy. It is important to remember as previously mentioned, Rousseau's ideas influenced progressives including John Dewey, known as the father of progressive education. With regard to learning by experience, Rousseau says, "Give your scholar no verbal lessons; he should be taught by experience alone; never punish him, for he does not know what it is to do wrong; never make him say, 'Forgive me,' for he does not know how to do you wrong. Wholly unmoral in his actions, he can do nothing

---

38. Ibid., 106, 331.
39. Boltz and Millikan "Shepherd Boy."

morally wrong, and he deserves neither punishment nor reproof."[40] Note the deemphasizing of content or moral instruction. Consequently, with Emile there is neither training of the mind nor molding of the will.

Ravitch, with regard to the lack of content in some states' history books says, "The states that ignore content are very prescriptive about the skills that students must learn. They call on students to do research, use technology, evaluate information, discover relationships, solve problems, work in teams, communicate, and exercise minutely specified 'critical thinking skills' or 'applied learning skills.' But they leave blank the historical knowledge to which these skills should be applied."[41] Carl Rogers was a humanist thinker who believed that people are basically good and he is the founder of client-centered (sometimes referred to as person centered) counseling. He was one of the most influential psychologists of the twentieth century and his client-centered approach is still used extensively. He said students only needed to learn "'the processes by which new problems are met' . . . He asserted that students needed to learn how to solve problems but did not need to study the origins of problems or how people had solved them in the past. In his ideal system, teachers would not teach but would be 'facilitators' of 'self-directed learning.'"[42] In light of these, one can see that there is a very prominent and precise plan of developing curricular methods, but curricular content is significantly less important. In December 2004, my wife received her Bachelor of Science in Elementary Education from the University of Oklahoma. She was taught only the constructionist view of education and rarely was the content of *what* the students had to learn discussed, but rather it was four years of *how* to teach students.[43]

Accordingly, the shift from classical education to progressive education is in fact an immoderate shift in emphasis from *what* is taught to *how* to teach. Therefore, according to the progressives, the most important thing that teachers can know is how to teach children rather than what to teach children. It is style over substance. As Rogers' point emphasizes, what they know about the past, or anything outside of their life experience, is either minimally or totally unimportant; all they need to know how to do is solve problems, which is called critical thinking.[44]

40. Rousseau, *Emile*, 56.
41. Ravitch, *Language Police*, 139.
42. Rogers, *Freedom to Learn*, 303–7.

43. Constructionist education is just another development or refinement of the basic idea of progressive education. The disseminators of constructionism are as disparaging of the characteristics of classical education—actually their criticisms are against caricatures—as they are proponents of method over content approach.

44. Progressives often extol the emphasis upon teaching children to think *critically*

This type of critical thinking takes place often without necessary knowledge of the past, exposure to the great ideas emanating from the great minds of the past, or even having adequate knowledge of the historical facts of the subject about which one is supposed to be thinking critically. This is not an overstatement. According to the leading progressives, there are no absolute truths to be passed from generation to generation, little or no core body of knowledge that every American child needs to know in order to contribute to the Republic, and history is of little value for most because the past is no guide for tomorrow and history cannot be known objectively but only subjectively thanks to the unbridled acceptance of deconstructionism, multiculturalism, and a scientific view of life.[45]

In the church, pedagogy is queen. Jesus is still king, but second only to him is method. It is style over substance. Contemporary church literature overflows with methods; there are numerous books on the local church, which are light on the content of the theology and message of the church, but contain boundless information on what works—how to *do* church. Further, a method's utility is its value. There is far too often simply an uncritical acceptance of what works seemingly legitimized by their unimpressive emphasis upon Jesus using different approaches, or quoting of Paul saying, "I have become all things to all men, so that I may by all means save some" (1 Cor 9:22). Rick Warren's paper on the contemporary approach to ministry evangelism and organization (CAMEO), which lists thirty-three characteristics of that approach, does not contain one doctrinal requirement of a church or member.[46] Os Guinness quotes one well-known proponent of the church growth model as saying, "I don't deal with theology. I'm simply a

---

or to solve problems on their own rather than merely teaching facts, which sounds wonderful and is readily accepted by a naive public and church. However, the truth is that a part of critical thinking and resolving problems is having sufficient knowledge and facts, which they deem to be unworthy of being sufficiently learned. Additionally, one needs an adequate knowledge of the subject to which to apply *critical thinking* skills.

45. Deconstructionism refers to the philosophical movement that began in the 1960s, which rejects the idea that language actually has the ability to convey reality. Multiculturalism refers to the ideology that "sees all cultures, their mores and institutions, as essentially equal." Of course this usually excludes Euro-American cultures with Judeo-Christian underpinnings, which are often condemned. History is not really studied as it was, but rather as one wants it to be. In addition, "cultural differences are highlighted and maintained," and "our shared story and unity are destroyed." Also, multicultural methods emphasize the sins of Euro-Americans and magnify any contribution from minority groups. Schmidt, *The Menace*, 3, 11, 57.

46. Warren, "Contemporary Approaches," #10 requires agreement with the "church's philosophy of ministry" but no biblical doctrinal minimum is listed. Both ten and eleven leave a person with a negative impression of doctrine.

methodologist."[47] Guinness goes on to note, "Theology is rarely more than marginal in the church-growth movement and discussion of the traditional marks of the church is virtually nonexistent. Instead, methodology, or techniques, is at the center and in control. The result is a methodology only occasionally in search of a theology."[48]

Thus the ubiquitous mantra "the message stays the same but methods change" is in many circles rarely questioned. And at first glance, it is irrefutable, for the Bible and history bear out the reality that Christianity, the church, has and does employ different methods at different times and places. However, it is not the concept itself that is wrong or needs refuting, but rather the uncritical acceptance of methods, as long as they work, and the notion that methods are neutral, both of which lead to a superficial evaluation of methods, which will result in inevitable corruption or alteration of the message. This is true whether one applies this uncritical acceptance to pre-modern, modern, or post-modern methods. Os Guinness says, "Thus, when the church growth movement relies on the insights and tools of modernity for its 'new ground,' it does not rely on something that is neutral or entirely benevolent. At the very least, there is a gigantic paradox in the relationship between modernity and the Christian faith . . . modernity simultaneously makes evangelism infinitely easier, and discipleship infinitely harder . . . we modern Christians are literally capable of winning the world while losing our own souls."[49]

Although great truths of Christianity are believed—as they are understood—they are usually explained superficially or selectively, or a general understanding of them is assumed. Worse is the idea, though usually not clearly stated, that much of theology is irrelevant, and what people know or believe beyond elementary and immediately applicable ideas about God is not as important as simply believing and living it out in real life. Of course this is contrary to any notion of biblical Christianity, and reason for that matter. Moreover, the assumption that everyone knows the basics of Christianity, or that is in fact all that they need to know, is unfounded and spiritually corrosive.

Progressive education is child-centered

This is at the heart of progressive education, and the next two points, learning by experience and learning must be fun, are directly related to this idea.

47. Guinness and Seel, *No God But God*, 155.
48. Ibid.
49. Ibid., 163.

At first glance, it seems obvious that education ought to center on the child, understood as meaning focused upon educating the one you are trying to teach. Most parents are thrilled to hear that the educational philosophy of their child's school is child centered. Parents and many teachers think that means that "children are our business" as the saying goes. We do everything for the children to learn and become all that they can be. Parents believe their children are being taught all they need to know—skills, knowledge, facts, truths, as well as developing their mind and will—in an age-appropriate way. Therefore, most parents are delighted that the focus is upon the children, but they probably would be less excited if they knew that child-centered education to the progressive pedagogue means a very different thing than it means to most parents.

What the progressive pedagogues mean by "child-centered education" is that the content, structure, and goal of education are determined by the child and not by the teacher or sages of the past or present. Children are to learn according to their felt or immediate needs. Without understanding this, it is impossible to understand the dumbing down of modern education, and I believe, the child-centered fixation of the contemporary church. Under classical, academic, and biblical education, children—students—are central in the sense that they are taught at their level and in a way they can understand. Under progressive education they are *only* taught what they want or feel a need to know—practical in this life, now. They, on the basis of scientific studies of behavior and future projections, are only taught what they need to know for their own personal benefit.

Again, this is clearly laid out in Rousseau's *Emile*. "Nature provides for the child's growth in her own fashion, and this should never be thwarted. Do not make him sit still when he wants to run about, nor run when he wants to be quiet."[50] Note the freedom: the will of the child determines not only what he will learn but how he will learn. Concepts like right and wrong are not to be taught or demanded of the child. "The very words *obey* and *command* will be excluded from his vocabulary, still more those of duty and obligation."[51] Of course this view arises from considering man to be essentially good and not corrupted by inward determinants or influences; consequently, he will choose what is right for him. Note the place for values clarification arises out of this scientific view of man, that there is no right or wrong for everyone—a conclusion that science truly cannot make—and man is capable of deciding on his own.

50. Rousseau, *Emile*, 50.
51. Ibid., 53.

Therefore, the child, and only the child, actually determines the curriculum. G. Stanley Hall, who was the first American to earn a doctorate in psychology at Harvard, taught psychology at Johns Hopkins University where one of his students was John Dewey. According to Ravitch, he was a leader in the child-centered education movement and he "believed teachers were wrong when they thought 'their primary responsibility was perfecting the art of imparting knowledge,' when they should be learning from the child . . . Education should be based on a child's own nature and needs, not on subjects that existed outside the child's immediate experience. He held that scientifically trained educators exhibited 'a willingness to fit the school to the child rather that child to the school.'"[52]

In 1901, Hall addressed the annual meeting of the National Education Association. His statement, "Health, growth, and heredity, a pound of which is worth a ton of instruction"[53] implied that instruction is not worth much. He went on to say, "The guardians of the young should strive first of all to keep out of nature's way, and to prevent harm, and should merit the proud title of defenders of the happiness and rights of children . . . We must overcome the fetishism of the alphabet, of the multiplication table, of grammars, of scales, and of bibliolatry."[54] Along with this was the "integration movement," which sought to replace academic "subject matter with experiences tied to either pupil interests or community problems, or both."[55]

"In 1934, the NEA's Department of Secondary School Principals, which presumably spoke for the nations' high school leaders, endorsed the idea of replacing subject matter courses such as science and history with 'fundamental categories of genuine student experiences,' thereby reorganizing the curriculum to 'start with the student rather than with items of subject matter."[56] Of course parents were outraged and in 1937 complained that their children couldn't read, and were incensed that the class spent an entire day "learning how to make nut bread."[57] This complaint was in spite of the fact that the superintendent had explained that "baking nut bread was a very good way to teach mathematics."

The Progressive Education Association commission "suggested that the transformation of the high school from an academic institution to a custodial institution based on the 'needs of youth' was essential to preserving

---

52. Ravitch, *Left Back*, 71.
53. Ibid., 73.
54. Ibid.
55. Ibid., 262.
56. Ibid., 263.
57. Ibid.

'the living tradition of democracy in American life.'"[58] Only a small number of experts needed to be trained in academics or works that had contributed greatly to civilization. The 1939 publication by the National Association of Secondary School Principals published by B.L. Dodds, *That All May Learn*, as summarized by Ravitch, says "Their curriculum should be based on their needs and interests, giving particular attention to problems such as how to dress, how to make friends with the opposite sex, and how to get a job."[59]

The Open Education Movement of the sixties was modeled on the "activity movement of the 20s and 30s."[60] According to Ravitch, "An open school emphasized projects, activities, and student initiative. Its teachers were 'facilitators' of learning, not transmitters of knowledge . . . affective (or emotional) learning was prized more than cognitive (or intellectual) learning."[61] This led the director of The National Council of Teachers of English Commission on Reading, who supported whole language reading and an expansion of the look-say method of the 20s, to say in 1990, "Teaching the mechanics of reading would actually interfere with children's ability to read. The best way to teach reading . . . was to let children read whole texts, 'even if they can't read all the words.'"[62] This is in spite of "a 1985 report from the National Academy of Education (called Becoming a Nation of Readers), which said that 'on the average, children who are taught phonics get off to a better start in learning to read than children who are not taught phonics.'"[63]

With regard to purging complexity and unpleasant reality from history and current events in order that students see themselves in everything in school, Ravitch says: "How utterly vapid to expect that adolescents want to see themselves in everything they read, as if they have no capacity to imagine worlds that extend beyond their own limited experience, as if they will be emotionally undone by learning about the world as it is. How tedious it is for young people to find that school is an exercise in narcissism rather than an opportunity to discover the mysteries of time, space, and human nature."[64]

In the church, the ideas of consumerism, preaching to felt needs, making congregants comfortable, avoidance of difficult concepts along with

58. Ibid., 274.
59. Ibid., 280.
60. Ibid., 395.
61. Ibid., 396. This model is built on the British "activity centered infant schools," ibid., 395.
62. Ibid., 446.
63. Ibid., 445.
64. Ravitch, *Language Police*, 159.

developing the curriculum of the church, the preaching calendar and methods employed according to the wishes of the people are all too common.[65] In progressive education, an emphasis upon content is reserved for those who will use it, such as experts, resulting in a general dumbing down of the population. In like manner, the church's resounding message is keep it simple and do not teach difficult concepts or deep truths of Scripture, but reserve that for the experts. John Dewey promoted this very idea. "Dewey's writings encouraged those who thought that education could be made into a science: those who wanted to create child-centered schools based on the interests of children rather than subject matter; those who believed that learning by doing was more valuable than learning from books."[66]

Children—some spiritual and others just old (unsaved) children—are determining what can be taught and how it is taught in much of the contemporary church. Everything has to be directly and obviously relevant to their life. This does two things. First, it lowers Christian education to the lowest common denominator. So we often hear such pronouncements as people will not come if you teach the deep things of Scripture or people want to hear things relevant to their life *today*. Determining what is taught by those criteria makes Christian education limited to what people—and often not-so-spiritual people—think is important. The church often criticizes public education for its lack of discipline, dumbing down, and holding back those who really desire to learn; yet the church does the very same thing. Why should we expect anything different, when she often follows the same model? Just because we sprinkle our teaching with Scriptures does not make it any less child-centered. Often, the Scripture becomes the illustration of the message rather than the message.

Second, it limits what people can learn. When children's school curriculum is chosen based on the child's experience, it severely limits what the child can learn. In the same way, once the church decides that the messages have to address the felt needs or be immediately relevant to everyone and cannot be too deep, then she has severely limited *what* can and will be taught—objections notwithstanding. This is not to say biblical teaching does not have context, address felt needs, or speak to things that are relevant at the moment; of course we are to do that. But it is a categorically different approach to seek to teach the whole counsel of God and apply those truths to today's listeners, knowing that some of the great truths will be applied by the Holy Spirit in the days to come in their life's journey and the results will

---

65. This is quite different than making people feel welcome and loved.
66. Ravitch, *Left Back*, 59.

be very different for each person; this compared to making every concept or doctrine pass the felt need or utilitarian test before it can be taught.

In addition, child-centered education teaches the child that he is the center of life, not necessarily because of the content—although that may be a part of it—but primarily it is communicated through the philosophy of education. We should not be surprised that children grow up to be more selfish and less willing to give for the common good or to others who cannot reciprocate, much less care about deep spiritual concerns. That is why much of giving, sacrifice, or helping others is promoted not for the good it did for those in need or because it is right, but rather because it makes the doer feel better. To wit, do for others primarily for what it does for you.

That some are not corrupted by coming through the systems of progressive education in our schools or churches is not proof that this is not happening on a massive scale. There will always be some who excel and some who come forth shining in spite of deprivation. Basing learning on a person's experience means that they will never have the chance to see if they can thrive in other genres of learning, leading, reading, or working. For example, we are told repeatedly that "people do not read anymore" or "this is a visual generation" which is to say that teaching and learning will not be accomplished by reading but by using visual aids. I am all for using visual aids. The fallacy is the way the idea is framed and promoted.

First, it is simply not true that people do not read anymore. Millions of books are read each year in America: people, even young people, read for school as well as reading magazines and blogs. It is true that people do not learn *exclusively* through reading any longer. However, even that does not answer whether teachers *should* be emphasizing reading or not. To acknowledge a fact is quite different than granting it one's endorsement. I for one believe that the church is committing a fatal error in acquiescing to the overgeneralization that people do not read anymore. To add visual aids to learning is good, but to replace reading with pictures is regression into primitivism.

Second, that a person does not read does not mean that he should not be made or encouraged to read, nor does it mean that he will not become a reader if encouraged. I am forever thankful that my first pastor, Sam Whitlow, did not follow the child-centered philosophy. I became a Christian at the age of twenty-five. I had never read an entire book—especially for such noble causes as learning or pleasure. I faked my book reports all through school. However, as Sam discipled me, he kept giving me books to read. I would take them and struggle through them, and eventually grew to love reading. I have now read thousands and thousands of books, magazines, journals, and electronic sources. Thank God Sam did not use my past to determine my future. We need to place the challenge before them, extol it, let God determine if they will be a reader or not, and stop videoing people into dumbness. We are to seek the best methods of educating people in the truths of Christianity rather than spiritualizing the failed progressive model.

Child-centered ministry will forever ban expository preaching from the pulpit. It is no accident that CAMEO churches preach insubstantial topical messages and shun the very mention of exposition. Exposition is built upon the idea that God has revealed what is important, and it is more important to teach than to speak on what man thinks is important.[67] I realize that contemporary communicators do not accept that their messages are insufferably shallow when compared to exposition, but if they preached expositionally for a time, they would be ashamed of their theretofore depthless talks.

The truth is that much of the Scripture does not contemporarily address a person or group of persons specifically. For example, Scripture records what God said to Israel, but it was not said directly to you or me; further, Scripture speaks of many things that are not immediately applicable to everyone listening, and this is particularly true with regard to the lost person or the carnal believer (1 Cor 2:14; 3:1–3). Therefore, the child-centered listener and speaker will avoid those places or read them as though they were spoken directly to them—bypass interpretation in order to conjure a relevant instant application or, even worse, a misapplication. For in child-centered education, the child is center, not just in how he is taught, but also more importantly and damningly, in what he will be taught.

Progressive education unduly emphasizes learning by experience—projects rather than subject matter

"Dewey wanted schools to concentrate on problems and processes rather than academic subjects . . . In one of his famous lectures, he chided those who favored a course in zoology over a course in laundry work; he said that either could be narrow and confining, and either might 'be utilized as to give understanding and illumination—one of natural life, the other of social facts and relationships.'"[68] Ellwood P. Cubberley's *Public School*

---

67. By exposition I refer to the practice of preaching messages that arise from serious study of the passage under consideration through the process of prayer, observation, interpretation, and application. The passage determines the message, and the message should be substantial in content and principally related to the passage rather than superficially connected to the passage. This does not necessarily limit extended application drawn from the passage.

68. Ravitch, *Left Back*, 59.

Administration, published in 1916, served as the primary text for school administrators for many years. He contrasted two curricular approaches: "'the knowledge curriculum' which he described in highly pejorative terms . . . The opposite of this dreary approach was 'the development type of course' in which 'knowledge is conceived of as life experience and inner conviction, and not as memorization of the accumulated knowledge of the past.' Using this approach, school would change from a place in which children prepare for life by learning traditional subjects to one in which children *live life*."[69] (italics added) In other words, education is all about what the child needs at that time, right for that child.

The problem with an overemphasis on learning by experience is that it severely limits what a person can or will learn. When education is limited to a child's experience, they remain limited. *No one* can experience history, the wisdom of the sages of the past like the Founding Fathers, or the details and complexities of events and thought like zoology. While it is true that one could reenact the Civil War, stage a production where people play the Founding Fathers, or go to the zoo and play with the animals for the zoology lesson of the day. It is equally true that someone still has to read the history in order to create a play about it or read the works of the sages to recite their wisdom. In addition, while a day at the zoo is a fantastic zoological experience that should be afforded to all children if possible where they may even see how the polar bear eats his food; they will not gain an understanding of the digestive system of the bear from a day at the park. Nor would they want to climb in the cage with the bear to experience the violent way the bear gets its food in the wild.

One simply cannot experience everything that brings pleasure, knowledge, context, and meaning to life, nor can he experience them with sufficient complexity and specificity. The academic approach is based on the belief that there is a body of knowledge, wisdom, and experience that lies outside of one's feelings, personal experience, or time in history, which are essential to know in order to become all that one could or should be. The progressives devalue the need for every person to know a common body of knowledge that lies outside of the individual's experience or interest. This is due in large part to progressive education being scientific, and in science, very little that lies outside of the context of the experiment is necessary for the experiment.

Now I do not want to position Christianity as either exclusively in-depth verbal knowledge or personal experience, for that is a perversion

---

69. Ibid., 98. The emphasis on spontaneity, lack of defined curriculum was later criticized by Dewey, ibid., 199. Of course it was his writings and lectures that fueled excessive emphasis on the practical and earlier curricular differentiation.

extraordinaire. However, in the church growth movement, the emphasis is almost entirely determined by the experience of the listeners. Far too often they reach people where they are but fail to take them where they need to be. The truth is that people not only need to be saved, they need to grow in the knowledge of God in all of his complexity and fullness, 2 Pet 3:18. The excessive emphasis on speaking to people's felt needs, getting on their level, meeting them where they are, and speaking to today's needs is excellent for sharing the simple gospel; however, it is disastrously insufficient for carrying out the Great Commission to make *disciple-makers*, by teaching them "to observe all [Christ] commanded" (Matt 28:18–20).

It is not that there is not a place for all of those things (speaking to felt needs, meeting people where they are, learning by experience, etc.) within the equipping church (Eph 4:11–16), for there certainly is. However, it is an elementary part of learning and not the sum of what disciples are to learn. People must be stretched, challenged, and pushed in their cognitive understanding of Christianity, not just challenged in their living, or else we have simply a *progressive* Christianity where the *felt* needs arising out of the experience of the listeners determine what and how preachers and teachers teach. This places man's experience at center stage and thereby usurps God's place and plan. While Scripture admonishes us to be "doers of the word and not merely hearers only" (Jas 1:22), that does not diminish the necessity of being a hearer but rather it emphasizes living what we hear. Unfortunately, and far too often, the spiritual culturati's disproportionate emphasis upon living either undermines mature understanding of Scripture or has the practical outcome of promoting the absurd idea of living out a faith that remains unlearned. Imagine what learning by experience does to the ministry of teaching in the church. Much of Christianity is propositional truth to be learned, known, and taught to others. We are to live our faith, but we cannot live such realities as the Trinity, creation, or what God did with Abraham.

The emphasis upon experiential and immediately practical learning, taken to the degree of progressive education and incorporated into the church growth movement, extols the process of living out what has been learned, but not learning for knowledge or content that may be used much later, or knowledge that simply makes one a more thorough and wiser Christian. Now some of the emergent church has taken this to a whole new level where not only does one not need to know or believe very much, but what one believes about cardinal doctrines is little different than a preference or non-essential opinion. However, the truth is that Christians do need to know the Scripture for themselves, but they need to know far more than what they may deem important for themselves because we are to "make disciples" of others.

Today, as a result of this type of excess, expository or substantive teaching has been decentralized, and center stage are small groups, where experience quotidianly dictates what is learned and how it is learned—each one sharing what the particular passage under consideration means to him based on his experience—which makes the church nothing more than a constellation of quasi-spiritual, experiential jam sessions. The leader of the group is no longer considered a teacher but rather a leader, facilitator, or guide. Learning is said to take place through the group experience, more than through the teaching of a teacher or a mentor. The dire consequence is that the teaching and training of the church is limited to the lowest common denominator—what polls show that everyone needs or wants. While fellowship and sharing groups are a vital part of church life, they do not constitute the church nor are they biblical alternatives to pastors equipping the saints in the full counsel of God.

Progressive education requires that all learning must be fun

Phonics is connected to learning history, and the look-say method is linked to the child's present experience. Phonics includes memorization and academic knowledge that will be applied and useful in the future when one transcends the present boundaries of his own experience through either living or reading. However, the look-say method is fun because it is easier to learn, immediately relevant, and pragmatically gratifying. Therefore, because learning parts of speech, the alphabet, grammar, and memorization is not fun, and because learning must be fun, out with phonics and in with look-say. One should only be challenged to learn by what he can immediately relate to like, Dick and Jane went up the hill; forget the classics, the Gettysburg Address, wisdom and experiences of the ages, for that might intimate that the child is not the center of the universe and that is not a fun thing to learn.

Often parents wonder why their children are not good readers, and the answer is that there is not a high value placed on reading. We have experienced this at our Here I Grow Child Development Center.[70] We teach children to read in kindergarten. Parents who then enroll their children in state schools complain that their children are too far ahead and are therefore bored. Some of the public school teachers have told these parents that children really do not need to learn to read until the third or fourth grade. This de-emphasizing of reading is nothing new. G. Stanley Hall said, "It would

---

70. Here I Grow Child Development Center is a learning center operated at Trinity Baptist Church for infants through kindergarten.

not be a serious loss, if a child never learned to read."[71] The wars over the value of reading have and do continue unabated.

Horace Mann, known as the founder of the modern public education system—mandatory state schools—referred to the repulsive learning of the alphabet and its letters as "skeleton-shaped, bloodless, ghostly apparition"[72] and argued against teaching the alphabet saying, "When we wish to give to a child the idea of a new animal, we do not present successively the different parts of it . . . but we present the whole animal, as one object."[73] In response to the decline in reading ability and promotion of only the whole word approach, Rudolf Flesh wrote his best seller, *Why Johnny Can't Read*, in 1955. This modern teaching approach rewarded little effort and transformed schools in certain areas to what Kenneth B. Clark condemned "as a shift from teaching to custodial care."[74]

The results of the idea that education must be fun and experiential can be seen in "another study by researchers at the U.S. Department of Education in 1984 comparing high school graduates in the classes of 1972 and 1980. They found that over this eight-year period, test scores in verbal and mathematical skills had fallen, the amount of time spent on homework had declined, and grade inflation had increased. The percentage of seniors taking an academic curriculum had fallen from 46 percent in 1972 to 38 percent in 1980 and the percentage that had to take remedial mathematics in high school had grown sevenfold during this period from 4 to 30 percent. Nearly three quarters of the students thought their high school should have put more emphasis on basic academic subjects. But despite this array of negative indicators, the graduates of 1980 had 'higher self-esteem' than their peers in 1972 and were more likely to believe that they had the ability to complete college."[75]

I do not believe that learning should be intentional drudgery, but to say it must always be fun severely limits what can be learned. In addition, and in some ways more importantly, this principle teaches children to live for pleasure and never pursue what is not fun—work, responsibility, and selfless sacrifice. I love to study, but quite a bit of what I study is not fun, of which progressive education is a stellar example. Yet, I along with others benefit. Part of being mature, and yes even becoming mature, is doing

---

71. Ravitch, *Left Back*, 72.

72. Ibid., 356.

73. Ibid., 357.

74. Ibid., 381, talking particularly about the way blacks were under challenged in schools because of assumptions about their IQ and low expectations from their teachers.

75. Ibid., 405.

things that are not fun but necessary. Paying bills is not fun, sometimes being responsible is not fun, preaching certain topics I assure you is not fun, and most would say that it is not fun to listen to them. Nevertheless, mature adults and Christians know that there is more to the meaning of life than me or my immediate pleasure; moreover, some of the best things in life and eternity come through difficulty.

Now I believe that the modern quest for entertainment, for everything to be fun and self-fulfilling, has been, in large measure, inculcated into us through the education process. This has given fertile ground to the televangelist's message of health and wealth. It just seems more fitting that if the progressives loved the children and wanted what was best for them, and the best was always fun, self-serving, and determined by the individual, then if God really loves us, he will want the same. A message of sacrifice, taking up the cross, and living for others is not only unacceptable; it is often not even understood. Perish the thought of messages that concern something outside of your immediate experience, on top of not being fun. In the contemporary church, the idea of relevancy generally means that the message is about you and explains how to make you better in a feel-better way, not some abstract or eternal way. It has to affect all or at least the vast majority of the listeners, lost or saved, spiritual or carnal, once again operating at the lowest common denominator. The call to follow God solely because he is worthy is nonsensical to the progressive Christian. Messages are so constructed that they superficially appear to place God at the center and man in his rightfully subservient role, but they are far too often centered on man with God as the all-willing servant.

It is this emphasis on fun and a high view of self that heightens the popularity of churches like the Crystal Cathedral,[76] where David Wells refers to Robert Schuller's teaching that "Sin . . . is not what shatters our relationship to God; the true culprit is the jaundiced eye that we have turned on ourselves. In the Crystal Cathedral, therefore, let the word *sin* be banished, whether in song, Scripture or prayer. There is never any confession there."[77]

Schuller said, "Reformation theology failed to make clear that the core of sin is a lack of self-esteem."[78] Schuller's emphasis on man and self-centeredness causes him to turn biblical Christianity on its head with statements like, "This is not to say that self-indulgences are always sinless. Rather, it is to say that at the deepest level the heart of sin is found in what

---

76. After having filed Chapter 11, the Crystal Cathedral was sold to the Catholic Church in 2011. http://abcnews.go.com/blogs/business/2011/11/bankrupt-crystal-cathedral-sold-to-catholics-for-57m/, accessed 12/3/16.

77. Wells, *No Place for Truth*, 175.

78. Schuller, *Self Esteem*, 98.

it causes us to do to *ourselves*. The most serious sin is the one that causes me to say, 'I am unworthy' . . . For once a person believes he is an 'unworthy sinner,' it is doubtful if he can really honestly accept the saving grace God offers in Jesus Christ.'"[79] (italics added) Of course, the heinousness of sin biblically is that it is an act by a created being against his creator, the thrice-holy God.

The largest church in America presently is Lakewood Church in Houston, Texas, and Joel Osteen is the pastor. He preaches to approximately 25,000 people each week. Osteen says of his church's message that his goal is "to give people a boost for the week . . . we believe in focusing on the goodness of God."[80] The goal is not to make authentic followers of Christ, to preach "the whole counsel of God" but to give people a boost by focusing on the goodness of God. Thus, his method has severely altered the message—the content—for if it is not fun or will not lead to fun in the here and now, it cannot be preached—and I use the term preached rather loosely.

He goes on to say, speaking of Lakewood church, "It's not a churchy feel . . . We don't have crosses up there. We believe in all that, but I like to take the barriers down that have kept people from coming."[81] We have truly come a long way from removing words like invocation and benediction, because they were obstacles, to now removing the cross for the same reason. They still believe in it, but just not enough to say it if it is going to offend. How different this was with Jesus, who told the truth about the cross even when it offended and confused, John 6:52–66. Christ rejected their desire to make him their political king; they rejected Christ's teaching that he must die for their sin, and they must believe and partake of him—referring to the Lord's Supper.

Jesus made the cross central to his call to salvation, and he was saying to them all, "If anyone wishes to come after Me, he must deny himself, and take up his cross daily and follow Me" (Luke 9:23). The very thing Jesus made essential to salvation and discipleship, Osteen has removed. Jesus repeated this claim several times. The cross is central to Christianity, as the old hymn says, it is "the emblem of suffering and shame," and that is not fun.[82] The cross reminds us of our sin and God's holiness, our hate and God's love, our evil and God's purity, our inability and God's power, what our sin cost another, and none of that is fun, not to mention that it does not give a boost to the idol de jure, self. For to follow Christ, one must "deny himself" and that is not just a condition that Jesus decided, but rather it is

79. Ibid.
80. Sims, *"Religion Gets Supersized,"* 2–3.
81. Ibid., 3.
82. Bennard, *"The Old Rugged Cross."*

essential for one to follow—he must deny himself—or else he would follow himself. Jesus called disciples to take up his cross *daily*, yet Osteen considers the cross a "barrier" (stumbling block), and in reality, it is. It is a stumbling block to pride, self-esteem, self-sufficiency, self whatever, but without it, no one comes to God. The following sums up the child-centered, fun approach. "The curriculum must take into account students' 'wants, wishes, inclinations, and desires . . . problems, feelings, aspirations, foreseen and desired achievements. The student must not be required to make up lacks that he himself does not recognize.'"[83]

When the stumbling blocks to church growth embody the essential truths of Christianity, church growth has gone awry. Yet over and over, based on the premise that learning must be fun—ostensibly relevant—we are discouraged from teaching in-depth Christianity. The common refrain is because people will not come or people will not understand—meaning it will not be fun or uplifting to know there is something they need to know or that Christianity is more than just clichés. Consequently, we become centers of positive thinking, positive confession, or focusing only upon the truths of Scripture that even the lost distortedly find uplifting, but not centers that equip the saints of God to do the work of God.

Progressive education devalues preaching

Progressives de-emphasize teaching, a teacher teaching facts, for that implies that the teacher knows more than the student does, that there are absolutes, and that there are essentials that need to be passed from generation to generation. The progressives exclaim, "What teacher can claim to know what is best for every student?" Thus teaching and preaching are degraded while facilitating and guiding are treasured. Rousseau, in referring to the teacher as facilitator, said, "I prefer to call the man who has this knowledge master rather than teacher, since it is a question of guidance rather than instruction. He must not give precepts, he must let the scholar find them out for himself."[84] The U.S. Office of Education described the modern elementary classroom as "one where learning occurred spontaneously . . . In this natural, noncompetitive, progressive classroom, the teacher remained in the background, facilitating but never instructing."[85]

---

83. Ravitch, *Left Back*, 274. This is actually a report by Progressive Education Association's commission on the Secondary School curriculum, which pressed to make "the needs of youth" the central purpose of secondary curriculum.

84. Rousseau, *Emile*, 19.

85. Ravitch, *Left Back*, 359.

Years ago, a friend of mine with a seminary degree from one of our Southern Baptist seminaries used to tell me how preaching did not work anymore. He told me how studies demonstrated that it is not the way to learn; how lecturing is not the way to teach. Now, I believe there are times that interaction and hands-on activities do teach, and that they are a valuable part of learning. However, that was not his message because, although he did not know it, his message was the message of progressive education in the church. He was quoting the data, but of course the data was built upon a progressive view of education that rejected, or unduly minimized, mental training and a certain body of knowledge that everyone must know, both of which are essential to Christianity. You see, if children are basically good and will learn what they need to learn when they are ready, and facts outside of their experience or direction are irrelevant, then teaching is preaching and that is condescending and repugnant.

In much of the church today, there are many who classify themselves as evangelical and believe the Bible undermines and degrades preaching. We have all heard statements like "I don't want to be preachy," "preaching is passive"—meaning of little value, "people need to apply what they already know," "people do not remember what you said but what you did for them"; all of which have a very subtle but powerful influence on downplaying the biblical place of preaching. Thus, the quest of the church growth movement has always been fewer services where Scripture is preached, and the fewer messages are shorter, and the shorter, fewer messages are shallower, and the shorter, fewer, shallower messages must be peppy, uplifting, and immediately applicable to the listener's life.

John Dewey spoke in no uncertain terms about his view of what must happen to Christianity for democracy to thrive. He said, "I cannot understand how any realization of the democratic ideal as a vital moral and spiritual ideal in human affairs is possible without surrender of the conception of the basic division to which supernatural Christianity is committed."[86] In other words, it is one or the other, for they are, in Dewey's mind, mutually exclusive. Who will usher in this new era and be the voices of what culture needs? Dewey proclaimed in 1897 that "the school was the primary means of social reform and the teacher was 'the prophet of the true God and the usherer in of the true kingdom of God.'"[87]

The hostility of state education against the very tenets of Christianity as well as the Christian approach to education is not merely one of style or preference but rather it is systemic. Thus, the underlying philosophy of

---

86. Dewey, *A Common Faith*, 84.
87. Dewey, "My Pedagogic Creed," 80.

progressive education undermines Christianity and yet the startling reality is that the principles of the church growth movement seem to be based more upon progressive education than the progressive revelation of God. We dare not sup at the table of progressivism. For the church to do so is not only to dine with mediocrity, it is to dine with death.

2

The Fading Christian Influence in American Life and Christ's Church

Understanding State Education's Scandalous Hostility toward Christianity

The philosophy of progressive education that has dominated state schools in America for the last century has not only had a detrimental impact upon the local church as demonstrated in chapter 1, but understanding the nature of progressive education also explains the hostility of state education to supernatural religion in general and Christianity in particular. Progressive education displaced not merely classical education but also Christian classical education. Education in America had always been built upon a theistic view of life, more specifically a Christian view of the world. This is not to say that the ideas streaming out of the Enlightenment did not play a significant role. It does mean that the unifying principle of everything was God, as revealed in the Scripture, and as taught specifically by Christianity. To put it succinctly, Americans were taught and believed that science had a very important role to play in the world created by God.

The shift from Christian classical to progressive was a shift from a Christian view of education, the world, and science to a scientific view (actually a scientistic view) of education and the world, and Christianity as well as religion in general. The progressives were intent on making education at least ostensibly scientific. One of the four significant ideas of progressive education "was the idea that education might become a science and that the methods and ends of education could be measured with precision and determined scientifically."[1] This meant the application of social sciences, particularly psychology, sociology, and things like mental testing—the IQ test. This would allow educators to scientifically determine what kind of education every child needed rather than giving all children an extensive necessary core education based upon wisdom of the past and truth revealed by God, along with knowledge gained by science. Moreover, everything like morals, purpose, value, etc., would be ultimately explained by science—material processes—even man's belief in God.

This was the beginning of transmogrifying not only education but also our culture, from one where Christianity was the common unifying idea and science played a prominent role to one where Christianity has been all but removed from state education and is being methodically removed from public life, particularly the public arena of imposable knowledge and developing the public mind.[2] This removal is both systematic and necessary if science is to be the basis of all *real* publicly valuable knowledge. The reason is not that religion allows no room for science, but rather that science, expanded to scientism, allows no room for supernatural religion. By scientism, I mean the view that believes the assumptions and methods of physical and biological science are equally essential and applicable to every area of life because all of life is either physical or epiphenomenal (emanating from the physical), and that it is the most reliable form of knowledge for public considerations. Succinctly, scientism is naturalism enveloped in the cloak of respectable science.

Now, once science is seen as *the supreme* way to learn and as either the *only* or *supreme* real knowledge, and is applied to all areas of life, then belief in the supernatural or immaterial is just that, a *belief* but not knowledge; therefore, it should have no influence in developing the public mind or in educational philosophy, other than token comparative religion courses, etc. Consequently, rightly understood, the debate is not about the clash between religion and science; it is about the clash between supernaturalism and naturalism, Christianity and scientism.

Science proper is both powerful and weak. It is powerful because it works. Science has given us longer, easier, and better lives in many ways. Therefore, science is seen, and rightly so, as a good thing. It works, solves problems, and finds cures; it exposes false claims made in medicine and other vital empirical areas. It is weak and pessimistic because it seeks only to solve problems and is limited in that it is utterly incapable of addressing the

---

1. Ravitch, *Left Back*, 60.

2. Knowledge and ideas that are permitted to influence law, education, and society. See my book *The Death of Man as Man*.

great questions of life—where did I come from, why am I here, where am I going, or who am I? Its strength is weakened and its weakness exposed and accentuated when science is transformed into epistemic naturalism (scientism). To wit, whatever can be known can be known through science and the five senses. This of course, reduces life to a meaningless set of unrelated empirically detected particulars, man being merely one of the particulars, but man as a special and unique being ceases to exist. In a scientific world, there is no place for man as created in the image of God, intrinsically sacred, or superior to the rest of creation. In a merely scientific world, everything, including man, is just another experiment or means to an end.

Here is the problem that arises when science is expanded beyond its domanial authority—dealing with the material phenomena of reality. When science claims to deal with all reality, then the conclusion is inescapable; man as more than matter does not exist and there is no immaterial reality beyond what is epiphenomenal. God does not exist in this scenario. As a result, man's behavior, thoughts, and actions must all be explained by matter or having their genesis in matter—even his belief in the immaterial. Man who loves, chooses, and acts with valor is non-existent because man who can be reduced to being scientifically explained simply mates, acts, or assists others because he is determined to do so by material antecedents, which is not what such concepts as love, choice, valor, or heroism are understood to actually mean. Even the loyal naturalist does not live as though he is a product of determinative antecedents but rather as a free will being who makes real choices between two accessible options. In the world created by God, these (love, valor, etc.,) are acts of free otherwise choice, which are inherently meaningful and noble because man could have chosen otherwise; however, in a purely material world, man is reduced to being a part of nature and nothing more. He acts a certain way because of the unstoppable evolutionary process, which is neither noble nor ignoble; it just is.

When two people love each other, what makes it so meaningful in God's world is that they could have chosen not to love each other, and they can choose to continue to love or not to love. Consequently, it is romantic and life changing to hear the words "I do" quotidianly spoken at weddings. However, in a world explained solely by material processes, those beautiful words are reduced to meaning, I am freely making a predetermined decision because of some unstoppable powers of nature over which I have no control. This explanation is an ominously dark contrast that strips life of meaning, purpose, love, and everything that makes life worth living. Humans are merely deluded in thinking they possess otherwise choice and actually. Laconically, outside of some delusional therapeutic benefits for individuals, God has no meaningful role to play in a purely scientific world. He is man's creation rather than man being his creation.

Additionally, evangelism is an artificial need since man is not biblically sinful, redeemable, or eternal. Correspondingly, the super-inflated role of scientism in public education and the public square has a direct toxic impact upon not only the church's sense of need to evangelize but also how much freedom to do so will be granted by an ever-increasing scientized culture as well. Americans are not merely gospel hardened (heard the gospel too much), they have been reeducated to believe in the supremacy of scientific man, that he is merely matter, and therefore the value of Christianity is peripheral at best. The intelligibility of Christianity for many who linger long at the deep dark well of progressivism is limited to something of material origin and of only therapeutic value and that only for *some—the weak*. Without a biblical response as well as a widespread and thorough understanding of the influence of progressive education upon the mind of the church, and upon the public mind about the value of Christianity and the church, the present hostility toward Christianity will inexorably move beyond a mere devaluation of the church as being unnecessary to viewing her as dangerous. This latter phase justifies secularism's hostile persecution and eradication of Christianity.

MAN SEARCHES FOR A UNIFYING PRINCIPLE

Although there has been antagonism between Enlightenment and Christian views of the world, in the history of America, the Christian worldview has clearly dominated in private, educational, and public life. The change in education to an exclusively Enlightenment view of the world has eliminated any meaningful place for anything that cannot be explained scientifically—naturally—and any other theory of reality is *a priori* excluded from education except for courses like comparative religion and psychology of religion.[3] Even these are most often approached with a bias toward science; to wit, scientific processes determine their reality or value. In an educational system premised upon the scientific approach to all of reality, religion can

---

3. By Enlightenment, I am speaking specifically of the European intellectual movement of the seventeenth and eighteenth centuries that elevated reason and the scientific method to the status of being the determiner of truth, and by such ideas sought to transform society. This Enlightenment perspective is built upon rationalism and the scientific method, which eventually degrades into scientism. An Enlightenment view of the world progressively applies science to all of life. The conflict between Christianity and the Enlightenment is not the use of reason, but rather the place of reason in learning and also the reality of revelation.

no longer be allowed to be the unifying idea of the world or education. Therefore, the antagonism that state education and public life are displaying toward Christianity is not incidental. It is not a series of issues scattered somewhat haphazardly along the concourse of educational and public life. It actually necessarily arises out of a shift in education from classical to progressive, which is built upon and promotes a scientific liberal culture. By scientific liberal culture, I mean a culture whereby publicly imposable knowledge is governed by science (see chapter 3 and Authorial Definitions for a fuller explanation).

For example, if science is the source of all truth (or the best way of knowing), and science by its very nature deals with matter, it can never speak absolutely; consequently, concerns over such controversies as values clarification are not really dealing with the substratal issue. Values clarification fits well with a scientistic view of reality. In such debates, most Christians think we are debating about the viability of philosophical relativism, but if science is king, there simply is no debate because relativism is intrinsic to a scientific worldview rather than a separate philosophy of life. Subjects like history are also demoted to a less prominent position in progressive education than they once held in classical education. As Bryan Appleyard notes, "The truths of science do not require the wisdom of the past. A computer scientist need never have heard of Newton, he need only know of a thin film of recent knowledge to be able to master his art. Scientific progress is so radical that, at every stage, it is able to throw away almost all the baggage of its own history."[4] With regard to relativism, it is easy to see that it is inextricably bound to the scientific method. No experiment can be absolute, for with science the possibility of refutation must always be possible. Appleyard again says, "To sustain its effectiveness science insists upon a universally open-ended view of the world that accepts and embraces the permanent possibility of change and progress. At any one time scientific man can only regard his knowledge as provisional because something more effective might come along. He may construct private absolutes of faith or morality, but in public, he must inhabit a fluid, relative world."[5]

Resultantly, there simply can be no *real* place for, or objective reality to, the immaterial world in a scientific education. The damnable thing about this is "science is perfectly capable of marginalizing believers without actually stripping them of their belief."[6] People of faith can teach in a progressive educational system. They may even stem the tide toward full-

---

4. Appleyard, *Understanding the Present*, 223.
5. Ibid., 10.
6. Ibid., 10.

blown progressivism, but in the end, unless the underlying philosophy of naturalism is corrected, religion will be utterly displaced in education and public life because there simply is no place for the immaterial in an exclusively material view of reality.

It is important to understand that man is always in a quest for a unifying principle of life. In the history of America, that unifying principle was God, particularly Christianity, in both private and public life. The Founders saw no problem in teaching belief in God or morals derived from God in public education; as a matter of fact, they saw it as essential, which I will demonstrate in chapter 3. Moreover, they considered it essential to private as well as all of public life. It is only in the last approximately sixty-five years that we have seen a large-scale erosion of respect and acceptability of religion in public life—even though the progressive machine was set in place at the turn of the twentieth century. This erosion is mostly due to the ubiquitous philosophical and pedagogical shift in education from the unifying principle of God to the unifying principle of science or Darwinian evolution (although technology has contributed massively to both the rapidity and pervasiveness of its dissemination). It must be recognized by Christians that Darwinian evolution, Darwinism, is held to be far more than a theory of how biological life came to be what it is today because if Darwinian descent is true, then its tentacles reach into every area of life whether it is politics, penology, psychology, sociology . . . or even faith.

At this point it might be helpful to clarify what I mean by science proper. Science proper is the systematic study of the physical nature, relationships, and interactions of physical phenomena. Biologist Jonathan Wells offers some vital clarifications concerning evolution and Darwinism. He notes, "Evolution means change over time" and of course no one doubts that.[7] "But Charles Darwin claimed far more than any of these things. In *The Origin of Species* he set out to explain the origin of not just one or a few species, but *all* species after the first—in short, all the diversity of life on Earth. The correct word for this is not evolution, but Darwinism."[8] He then gives three distinguishing characteristics of Darwinism: "(1) All living things are modified descendants of a common ancestor; (2) the principal mechanism of modification has been natural selection acting on undirected variations that originate in DNA mutations; and (3) unguided processes are

---

7. Wells, *Politically Incorrect*, 2. "Change over time" "cumulative change through time" "a change in gene frequencies over generations." Even Darwin's phrase "descent with modification" is OK in a limited sense; "Even hypotheses that some closely related species (such as finches on the Galapagos Islands) are descended with modification from a common ancestor are not particularly controversial," ibid., 2–3.

8. Ibid., 3.

sufficient to explain all features of living things—so whatever may *appear* to be design is just an illusion."[9] Darwin's theory specifically "applies only to living things. Darwin speculated that life may have started in 'some warm little pond,' but beyond that he had little to say on the subject."[10]

Science proper is not a problem or threat to Christianity. This explains why there have always been countless scientists who are Christians or theists, and why Christians can rightfully be enthusiastic about science. Even evolution, meaning change over time, is not the problem. The problem is secularists' faith in Darwinian descent and their constant equivocating with the terms evolution and science. One moment they use evolution to mean change over time or micro-evolution, then without signification they use it to mean macro-evolution or Darwinian descent. This same equivocation is found in their use of the word science to mean science proper (limited to explaining empirical reality) at times and then in the next breath using it to mean scientism (capable of explaining all reality because all reality is empirical).

Now I want to demonstrate the long-standing hostility of state education to Christianity and religion by quoting some important voices, and then give five reasons why religion is minimized in state education. The removal of religion from state education is due to the nature of an education built upon scientism, and that is the direct intention of the progressive founders and the elite. For the church to counter progressivism's influence within the walls of the local church (members have been influenced to varying degrees, but almost always more than they realize), and American culture's marginalization of Christian influence in areas of public importance, the church must grasp public education's intrinsic hostility toward supernaturalism in general and Christianity in particular.

The importance of this influence can be seen by historical contrast. Historically, both private and public education were built upon the premise that Christianity, Scripture, is true. Consequently, Christian parents were correct to see public education as bolstering, or at least accommodating, the faith of their children. Science was taught as an important component of learning in a world created by God where the reality of the material and immaterial world coexist. The material world existed within the greater immaterial and eternal reality. Thus, the influence of school and church worked synergistically to mold the mind and spirit toward God. With the change in public education to progressivism, the premise changed and science became either the only way or best way of knowing and learning. Eventually, if

9. Ibid., 2.
10. Ibid., 4.

education is to be science based (as the progressives argue) then science will necessarily be transformed into scientism, which is antithetical to the coexistence of material and immaterial reality, at least in any meaningful public way like education. Consequently, God and any god-talk was increasingly marginalized and ultimately banished from public education.

STATE SCHOOL'S HOSTILITY TOWARD RELIGIOUS FAITH

G. Stanley Hall said, "We must overcome the fetichism of the alphabet, of the multiplication table, of grammars, of scales, and of *bibliolatry*."[11] (italics added) In 1901, sociologist Edward A. Ross called the free public school "an engine of social control."[12] In other words, the purpose of state schools was to conform the people to the needs of society—today known as social engineering. He was well aware of the ultimate displacement of religion and predicted "the disestablishment of religion would be followed by the establishment of the school as the guarantor of social order."[13] Such were the thoughts of the progressives concerning education at the turn of the twentieth century.[14] While primary and secondary schools, out of fear of a lawsuit, often fail to represent religion appropriately and even shun the subject, many state colleges and universities are openly antagonistic toward and denigrating of religion.[15] They particularly direct their focus toward Christianity, specifically those within Christianity known as fundamental, conservative, or evangelical—who are often indiscriminately, pejoratively, and I might add erroneously, lumped together as the 'Religious Right'.

Following are examples of the seriousness of the problem. Stephen L. Carter, William Nelson Cromwell Professor of Law at Yale University, said, "On America's elite campuses today, it is perfectly acceptable for professors to use their classrooms to attack religion, to mock it, to trivialize it, and to refer to those to whom faith truly matters as dupes, and dangerous fanatics

---

11. Strickland and Burgess, *Health, Growth, and Heredity*, 25.
12. Ravitch, *Left Back*, 80.
13. Ibid.
14. To see more of the thinking behind the Progressive Education Movement in the U.S., read *Left Back* by Diane Ravitch.
15. Often the fear of being sued and losing are without warrant, but the potential of costly litigation has led to an inordinate fear about teaching religion in public schools, often infringing on students' First Amendment rights. See websites http://aclj.org/ and https://www.adflegal.org/issues/religious-freedom/overview.

on top of it."[16] Huston Smith, who taught for thirty years at several prestigious universities including Berkley, in reference to the attitude of some prominent scientists who are unwilling to limit the scientific method in determining truth, says, "This is the kind of misreading of science that got us into the tunnel in the first place, for it belittles art, religion, love, and the bulk of the life we directly live by denying that those elements yield insights that are needed to complement what science tells us."[17] He also states very candidly, "The modern university is not agnostic toward religion; it is *actively hostile* to it."[18] (italics added)

The NEA's disregard of Judeo-Christian values is well documented, be it their equation of sexual orientation with race, representing homophobia as the only alternative to endorsing the homosexual lifestyle, opposing a moment of silence in schools, as well as promoting things like biological sex education and values clarification.[19] Concerning the deleterious impact of diversity and multiculturalism on the value of Christianity, Alvin J. Schmidt, professor of sociology at Illinois College, says, "Most diversity is considered diverse only insofar as it departs from Judeo-Christian principles and morality."[20] Sociologist Alan Wolfe, Director of the Boisi Center for Religion and American Public Life at Boston College, says of himself, "I am not, and never have been, a person of faith."[21] However, he is quite candid about the hostility of academicians toward religion, when he says, concerning his own book, "Yet nor do I write out of the kind of hostility to religion that has characterized so many academics, especially in the humanities and social sciences, who feel that they have an obligation, evangelical in its own way, to dismiss any kind of faith as hopelessly wrongheaded and anachronistic in a skeptical age."[22]

When sociology views religion through the lens of science or scientism, it will always seek to explain it as a social or psychological construct; merely the "product of individual choices."[23] If religion is viewed as having no reality beyond a person's choice, then it will never be treated with the same respect as humanism or naturalism; thus, social scientists, educators, and

16. Carter, *God's Name in Vain*, 187.

17. Smith, *Religion Matters*, 187.

18. Ibid., 96.

19. These and other ideas found in the article "Some NEA Resolutions Passed at 2002 Convention in Dallas."

20. Schmidt, *The Menace*, 6.

21. Wolfe, *Transformation*, vii.

22. Ibid., viii.

23. Ibid., 246.

others of the same mindset will never fully understand the driving force and importance of religion in the lives of people that result in the changing of cultures and the world. They will preclude themselves from understanding or correctly representing people of faith, and thereby consign their students to a mediocre understanding of the human experience.

In the past, deep devotional faith was seen as a valuable character trait, but according to Professor Carter, that has changed. He says, "One sees a trend in our political and legal cultures toward treating religious beliefs as arbitrary and unimportant, a trend supported by a rhetoric that implies that there is something wrong with religious devotion. More and more, our culture seems to take the position that believing deeply in the tenets of one's faith represents a kind of mystical irrationality, something that thoughtful, public-spirited American citizens would do better to avoid."[24] Logically and actually, it is a short step from an educational system that precludes religion from real knowledge—appropriate for teaching to citizens as knowledge that is educationally, socially, or publicly meaningful—to excluding religion from any meaningful place in the public life of a culture. This can be demonstrated by considering how one's view of epistemology frames the kind of education one gives and therefore the kind of culture one produces.

Epistemology is an "enquiry into the nature and ground of experience, belief and knowledge. 'What can we know, and how do we know it?'"[25] Epistemology answers the questions of what is the nature of knowledge, what can we know, and how can we know that we know. Although epistemology is often thought of in terms of relating only to a philosophy class, it is actually something that everyone is engaged in every day. For example, when a person plans to fly somewhere, he seeks to find out such things as when the plane is leaving and arriving, the cost, and whether the pilots are qualified. This is everyday epistemology, in which several forms of knowing are combined in just one activity.[26] Since education is predominately an endeavor to teach knowledge, or how to acquire knowledge, the answer to the question of what we can know and how we can know will determine the type of education the state will offer. If the epistemic approach is unnecessarily limited, it will result in limiting knowledge. If the approach is limited severely enough, it can become propaganda, social engineering, or state religion as opposed to genuine education.

---

24. Carter, *Culture of Disbelief*, 6–7.

25. Lacey, *Dictionary of Philosophy*, 56–57.

26. See Esther Lightcap Meek's book, *Longing to Know* for an excellent work on how everyone employs epistemology every day.

State education is for everyone; accordingly, it should not be guided by the social engineering of an elite group that is built upon an unnecessarily limited view of knowledge, which at this writing is also still contrary to the beliefs and values of the majority of Americans.[27] However, this is exactly what has happened in the American public education system. Following are five ideas that have negatively affected teaching religion in state schools. Although these ideas are built upon the larger idea of progressivism and a naturalistic—scientific—basis of education, breaking them down may help demonstrate the utter disdain toward a public role for Christianity and the march toward trivializing all religion; preparing our culture to willfully stop, limit, or at least guard children from becoming victims.

First, emphasizing pedagogy more than content

When the emphasis in education focuses on social engineering and pedagogy more than learning facts, history, standards, and intellectual development, the place of religion is necessarily minimized, and there is a toxic effect upon education in general.[28] Consider the following: "American 12th graders rank 19th out of 21 industrialized countries in mathematics achievement and 16th out of 21 nations in science. Our advanced physics students rank dead last. Since 1983, over 10 million Americans have reached the 12th grade without having learned to read at a basic level. Over 20 million have reached their senior year unable to do basic math. Almost 25 million have reached 12th grade not knowing the essentials of U.S. history."[29]

The situation does not seem to be getting better. For example, "According to the 2009 PISA, U.S. students ranked fourteenth in reading, twenty-fifth in math, and seventeenth in science compared to students in other developed countries."[30] This seems to correlate directly to a study showing that "Only 38% of U.S. public school teachers majored in an academic subject in college. 40% of public high school science teachers have neither an undergraduate major nor minor in their main teaching field and 34% of

---

27. By social engineering I mean the intent by some to educate people to take their place in society, for the good of society, as defined by the elite, rather than educating people to be their best, encouraging them to excel individually, and giving them access to the past and all areas of knowledge.
28. Ravitch, *Left Back*, 459–62.
29. "Twenty Troubling Facts," points one and two.
30. Crotty, "7 Signs," point one.

public high school math teachers did not major or minor in math or related fields."[31]

The decline in teachers being degreed in a subject is consistent with the proposal of "Neil Postman and Charles Weingartner [who] recommended a series of steps that would have disrupted the transfer of knowledge from generation to generation. Every class should be an elective, they proposed, and all subjects and requirements should be abolished. They recommended that teachers should be assigned to teach subjects they had never studied ('Have English teachers teach Math, Math teachers English, Social Studies teachers Science, Science teachers Art and so on')."[32] Additionally, Postman and Weingartner said, "One of the largest obstacles to the establishment of a sound learning environment is the desire of teachers to get something they think they know into the heads of people who don't know it."[33] Although Postman recanted these views ten years later, state education still seems to find merit in them.[34]

Similarly, based on a rapidly changing world, Carl Rogers says students only needed to learn "'the processes by which new problems are met' . . . He asserted that students needed to learn how to solve problems but did not need to study the origins of problems or how people had solved them in the past. In his ideal system, teachers would not teach but would be 'facilitators' of 'self-directed learning.'"[35] In other words, gathering all the facts or knowledge about the facts and engaging the great minds of the past concerning perennial issues was of little value.[36] This is consistent with a scientific view of the world as noted before; history is of little importance as far as scientific advancement is concerned, and in a purely enlightened world, that is the only kind of advancement desirable or possible.

Progressivism's disproportionate emphasis on pedagogy versus communicating a certain body of truth is based on a scientific view of life, which does not require being well acquainted with general history and knowledge

---

31. "Twenty Troubling Facts," points thirteen and fourteen.

32. Ravitch, *Left Back*, 391.

33. Postman and Weingartner, *Teaching As a Subversive Activity*, 116.

34. Ravitch, *Left Back*, 514, footnote 37, says Postman recanted these views a decade later in his book, *Teaching As a Conserving Activity*.

35. Rogers, *Freedom to Learn*, 303–307.

36. According to Ravitch in *Left Back*, this is a continuation of the failed child-centered education of the past century; see pages 59, 71–74, 175–79, 310, and 392. Among other things, the book actually chronicles the child-centered movement in America, and to some degree abroad, demonstrating the deleterious impact it has had on learning.

from the past.[37] Therefore, the subject matter is not determinative but rather the child is determinative of the subject matter. As previously mentioned, Rousseau provided the genesis of child-centered education, which he illustrated by educating a fictitious pupil named Emile. He transformed the teacher into a facilitator, concerning which he says, "I prefer to call the man who has this knowledge master rather than teacher, since it is a question of guidance rather than instruction. He must not give precepts, he must let the scholar find them out for himself."[38] To wit, the child's experience is the determiner of the content learned.

Diane Ravitch, in her book *The Language Police*, goes into great detail demonstrating how political correctness from the right, the left, and multiculturalism are distorting history and undermining the education children are receiving.[39] She says, "The textbooks sugarcoat practices in non-Western cultures that they would condemn if done by Europeans or Americans."[40] In reference to bias guidelines imposed on publishers she notes, "So long as books and stories continue to be strained through a sieve of political correctness, fashioned by partisans of both left and right, all that is left for students to read will be thin gruel."[41] Ravitch succinctly spells out the loss from such non-academic education.

The flight from knowledge and content in the past generation has harmed our children and diminished our culture . . . We do not know how these trends may yet affect the quality of our politics, our civic life, and our ability to communicate with one another somewhere above the level of the lowest common denominator. The consequences can't be good . . . Intelligence and reason cannot be achieved merely by skill-building and immersion in new technologies . . . Not only does censorship diminish the intellectual vitality of the curriculum, it also erodes our commitment to a common culture . . . We are not strangers, and we do not begin our national life anew in every generation. Our nation has a history and a literature, to which we contribute. We must build on that common culture, not demolish it.[42]

---

37. This is not to say that science does not require a review of relevant literature in a particular area of study, but rather that a scientific education or view of life does not require or even value knowledge of the past such as academic, classical, or biblical education does. See Ravitch *Left Back*, 127–28, 341, 350–51.

38. Rousseau, *Emile*, 19.

39. Ravitch, *Language Police*, shows how publishers favor the left more than the right, 87 and 92.

40. Ibid., 142.

41. Ibid., 96.

42. Ibid., 164–65.

In the transformation from classical to progressive education of the last 120 years, both the prominence and reality of religion, as well as other facts of history and life, have been expunged.

Second, expanding science beyond its domanial authority

This is really at the heart of the transmogrification of education and culture. For that reason, it is critical to understand this indefensible expansion and where it is ultimately headed if left unchecked. This is not to say that one day there will not be a public place for religion (although that is possible), but rather that there cannot be a meaningful place for public influence by religion in a culture where science is the source and guardian of all public truth.

Science, properly understood, is the study of the natural world, empirical data. In this realm, the scientific method provides a process for separating the true hypothesis from the false one. Science's domanial value is significant and has benefited humanity enormously. However, when scientists conclude or teach that the material world is all there is, it is all that we can know about, or they expand science to be the final arbitrator of truth or knowledge in all areas of life, then science is stealthily transformed into the philosophy of naturalism—scientism. Once that happens, any talk of the supernatural, or life outside the natural, is *a priori*, categorically rejected because naturalism by definition excludes the supernatural. Therefore, scientism does not eliminate religion in state schools, but rather it replaces supernatural religion with non-supernatural religion—philosophical naturalism.

Huston Smith cogently distinguishes between scientism and science when he says, "Scientism adds to science two corollaries: first, that the scientific method is, if not the *only* reliable method of getting at truth, then at least the *most* reliable method; and second, that the things science deals with—material entities—are the most fundamental things that exist . . . Unsupported by facts, they are at best philosophical assumptions and at worst merely opinions."[43] The consequence of the acceptance of scientism as science is monumental. William Dembski, one of the leaders in the Intelligent Design movement, elucidates how the Darwinists have defined science to

---

43. Smith, *Religion Matters*, 59–60. He gives as an example Freud's statement, "Our science is not illusion, but an illusion it would be to suppose that what science cannot give us we can get elsewhere," ibid., 60. This goes far beyond the realm of science into "epistemic naturalism" or "scientism." Smith notes on pages 62–63 that not all scientists accept the "epistemological privilege of science," like the French microbiologist Francois Jacob and others. Scientism is not, as some scientists purport it to be, the belief that science will be able to "predict everything," which would make it held by only a few.

definitionally exclude anything but naturalism. "The Darwinian establishment, by definition excludes everything except the material and the natural . . . By defining science as a form of inquiry restricted solely to what can be explained in terms of undirected natural processes, the Darwinian establishment has ruled intelligent design outside of science."[44] It is one thing for science to be the study of empirical data; it is quite another for science to *a priori* limit the realm of possible answers for the arrangement or existence of empirical data to only material answers, regardless if the evidence suggests otherwise.

Concerning this artificially restricted definition of science, Dembski says, "The view that science must be restricted solely to undirected natural processes . . . [is] called *methodological naturalism.*"[45] Alvin Plantinga cogently declares the outcome of such a restriction in science: "If one accepts methodological naturalism then naturalistic evolution is the only game in town."[46]

In other words, seeing science as limited to dealing with material things is not the problem. The problem is seeing science as capable of answering the questions of life in every area—at least the ones that can and should be answered—or allowing only naturalistic answers to have public or educational value. This is expanding science beyond what it is capable of or what is scientifically provable. This indefensible expansion transforms science into a faith or religion called materialism or naturalism. It is important to notice that the acceptance of this unjustifiable expansion of science's domain happens gradually through generational infection, a result of the Trojan horse.

The significance of this epistemological leap from science to methodological naturalism cannot be overstated. Phillip Johnson summarizes the accepted status of science in our society when he says, "Science is the only universally valid form of knowledge within our culture. This is not to say that scientific knowledge is true or infallible. But within our culture, whatever is purportedly the best scientific account of a given phenomenon demands our immediate and unconditional assent."[47] This consigns the possibility of God, or any explanation that includes non-natural intelligent causes, to the distant realm of the possible, but excludes it from the knowable or educationally and culturally meaningful.

---

44. Dembski, *Intelligent Design*, 117.
45. Ibid., 119.
46 As cited in Dembski, *Intelligent Design*, 119.
47. Dembski, *Intelligent Design*, 118.

This unwarranted expansion clearly misdefines and misjudges the proper role of science, which is the study of empirical data that is formulated into a hypothesis, tested by replication and observation (excluding sciences such as Forensic which operate more from plausibility and probability), and then is turned into a theory, which can be challenged and debated within the scientific community. A theory concerning the data should give the most plausible answer for the data regardless if the best answer involves natural, purposeless non-intelligent antecedents or intelligent antecedents. That is if science is truly a search for truth (as most believe it to be) and not merely a seeker for a certain kind of truth—material. The exclusion of any category of possible answers prior to the study of the data or the debate signifies the tyrannizing of science by naturalism, thereby leaving it profoundly biased.

Concerning liberal science, Jonathan Rauch heartily proclaims, "No Final Say and No Personal Authority are not just operational procedures for professional intellectuals. Socially speaking, they are also moral *commandments, ethical ideas*. They are a liberal society's epistemological constitution."[48] (italics added) Of course, if science is the only game in town, and science only allows natural processes, then contrary to Rauch and like-minded individual's espousals otherwise, science becomes the final arbiter of 'truth.' Therefore, if science can explain everything, then everything is necessarily reduced to matter and all other answers are either false or unknowable. If science can give only answers consistent with methodological naturalism, and science is the universal knowledge, then you have what Johnson refers to as "epistemic naturalism," and like scientism, limits epistemology—what we can know— to nature.[49] Based on naturalism, nature is all there is and is sufficient to eventually explain everything; hence, the supernatural world is an illusion—a fairy tale for adults.

Imagine a murder trial where the judge says we will not consider evidence that would suggest that Mr. Davis committed the murder, but only evidence that Mrs. Davis committed the murder. That is not letting the evidence speak for itself, but rather speaking before and for the evidence. This is not the same as excluding kinds of evidence that may not be permissible in science or law, but rather it is the problem of excluding possible answers based on the empirical evidence allowed. It is severely prejudicial.

Huston Smith distinguishes between materialism and naturalism thusly; "Materialism holds that only matter exists. Naturalism grants that subjective experiences—thoughts and feelings—are different from matter and cannot be reduced to it, while insisting that they are totally dependent

---

48. Rauch, *Kindly Inquisitors*, 75–76.
49. Johnson, *The Right Questions*, 82.

on it. No brains, no minds; no organisms, no sentience."⁵⁰ The important thing to note is that in each theory, nature is the genesis and ontology of everything. Remember this is not to say that one cannot believe in God, the afterlife, or the immaterial, but it forthrightly means that the metaphysical has no public value—formulating law, education, health, etc. In a scientific culture, a faith or belief can never mean more than "this is my opinion."

The dilemma for science is this: if science claims, or presents itself, to be a pursuer of truth, following the evidence wherever it may lead, then all plausible answers regarding the questions and observations of the empirical data must be weighed and debated based upon their own merit and ability to explain a particular phenomenon or set of phenomena. For example, if based upon the empirical data, the plausibility of the universe coming into existence by an immaterial cause is either the most plausible answer or even one among several plausible answers for the existence of matter, then it, as well as purely natural cosmogonies, must be evaluated based upon its own merit. An immaterial cause, under this definition of science, cannot be excluded *a priori* from consideration merely because it is an immaterial answer, one held by religion/s, or seems to support the probable existence of God because science is seeking truth by following the empirical evidence regardless where it leads.⁵¹

On the other hand, if science is defined as the study of empirical data, which allows *only* natural or material antecedents, thereby *a priori* excluding any answer involving immaterial or other than natural antecedents, it may theoretically do so. However, it cannot thusly be defined and simultaneously presented as a pursuer of the truth unbiasedly following the evidence wherever it leads because possible answers are *a priori* and definitionally excluded from consideration. This exclusion is unchallengeable regardless of whether immaterial antecedents provide an empirically based plausible answer. Scientists cannot have it both ways, and scientists need to be precise and honest about what science *is* and *is not*. Moreover, the public needs to demand that science do so and operate accordingly, thereby dispelling the illegitimate hegemony of science in pronouncements and areas that it has no real domanial supremacy as well as dispelling the ubiquitous misleading representation and understanding of science as an unbiased pursuer of truth.

---

50. Smith, *Religion Matters*, 83. For simplicity, I use naturalism and materialism interchangeably since they both ultimately say that matter is all or the source of all.

51. Another consideration regarding rejecting an immaterial answer because it happens to be a religious belief is that would cause all material answers to be rejected since some religions believe in the eternality of matter.

Unfortunately, and I think rather deceptively, many scientists intentionally present science as the foremost objective pursuer of the truth. Therefore, science becomes the self-evident best basis for public education and for determining what is and is not suitable knowledge for public policy. This idea is simultaneously and dogmatically combined with defining science to exclude any rival non-natural answers. Of course, these ideas result in religious knowledge being understood as unsuitable for public debate or education because it is automatically classified as innately inferior, albeit artificially so. The two areas, public policy debate and education, necessarily explore and affect every consequential area of human life. If science is the sufficient guide, then by definition life and all knowable and publicly meaningful knowledge is knowable empirically, which *ipso facto* reduces life to nothing more than nature. This is not only naturalism; it is a tyrannical, stealthy, religious naturalism sanctioned by the state masquerading as a truth seeker. It is government's exclusive religion, which must in time banish all rivals.

Tragically, most of the American people and the vast majority of the church seem not to understand this subterfuge, and therefore grant science far too much authority and influence without requiring accountability or an unambiguous clarification of the true nature of science. Unfortunately, most people think if science speaks, it is true because science is the unbiased, noble pursuer of truth, and religious beliefs are just that, beliefs. The truth is that when one pulls back the cloak of objectivity draped around many of the most significant scientific claims, one often finds philosophical and religious commitments rather than unsullied scientific evidence driving scientists to embrace one conclusion over the alternate. For example, Nobel Prize winner Steven Weinberg says that the "steady state theory is philosophically the most attractive theory because it least resembles the account given in Genesis."[52] Here again, the heralded untainted objectivity of scientific enquiry is seen for what it is.

Third, discounting the place of faith in education

Progressives and many scientists overtly reject the place for faith in education. Actually, they merely replace supernatural faith with faith in 'epistemic naturalism' under the guise of science. This faith is apparent each time the scientific community expresses views that are outside the sphere of science proper. For example, the 1995 U.S. National Association of Biology Teachers 'Statement on Teaching Evolution' guide to high-school teachers

---

52. Cited in Barrow, *The World Within*, 226.

demonstrates "the diversity of life on earth is the outcome of evolution: an *unsupervised, impersonal,* unpredictable and natural process of temporal descent with genetic modification that is affected by natural selection, chance, historical contingencies and changing environments."[53] (italics added)

Of course, it is impossible for 'true science' to declare that evolution is *unsupervised* and *impersonal* because it is obviously beyond the pale of empirical inquiry. Science and religious faith are not in conflict nor are they mutually exclusive, but naturalism and supernaturalism are. It is naturalism, not science, that has created an educational milieu that trivializes faith in God, excludes any non-material answers to life's questions, and summarily dismisses 'religious truth' from state education as though there is only one legitimate kind or source of truth suitable for the public. Although some are not so blunt as Richard Dawkins, he expressed the sentiment of naturalism quite candidly when he stated, "It is absolutely safe to say that if you meet somebody who claims not to believe in evolution, that person is ignorant, stupid, or insane (or wicked, but I'd rather not consider that)."[54] In other words, a natural explanation of reality is the only real explanation. The obvious problem with such a pronouncement is that it is a faith statement to conclude that nature is all there is or can be known.[55]

Atheist John Gray, after having met Richard Dawkins said, "There seemed no question in Dawkins's mind that atheism as he understood it fell into the same category as the world's faiths. In this, Dawkins is surely right. To suppose that science can liberate humankind from ignorance requires considerable credulity. We know how science has been used in the past—not only to alleviate the human lot, but equally to serve tyranny and oppression. The notion that things might be fundamentally different in the future is an act of faith."[56]

It is essential to remember that every individual operates by faith on a daily basis. Almost all learning is by faith. Until one has stood at the foot of the Eiffel tower, he accepts its existence by faith, regardless how many pictures he has seen or how many people say it exists. To discount faith is disingenuous at best. Johnson observes that even "the rationalist also has a first premise: the relativity of the autonomous mind and its powers of reasoning,

---

53. Johnson, *Objections Sustained*, 85. Later the words "unsupervised" and "impersonal" were removed after considerable pressure, see pages 85–90.

54. Dawkins, review of *Blueprints* by Johanson and Edey.

55. Dawkins is clearly using evolution to mean more than micro-evolution.

56. Gray, "The Closed Mind of Richard Dawkins," par. 23 and 24. From a critique of Richard Dawkins' autobiography, "An Appetite for Wonder: The Makings of a Scientist" (Ecco Press). John Gray is emeritus professor of European thought at the London School of Economics.

powers that, according to scientific materialism, amount to nothing more than so many neurons firing in the physical brain. I wonder if anyone has ever held on to such a faith in the aftermath of a stroke."[57]

Robert Bork points out that science is a faith endeavor as well. He notes, "A belief that science will ultimately explain everything, however, also requires a leap of faith. Faith in science requires the unproven assumption that all reality is material, that there is nothing beyond or outside the material universe. Perhaps that is right . . . but it cannot be proven and therefore rests on an untested and untestable assumption. That being the case, there is no logical reason why science should be hostile to or displace religion."[58] As Appleyard points out, "Scientists who insist that they are telling us how the world incontrovertibly is are asking for our faith in their subjective certainty of their own objectivity."[59] He also states, "Science's faith in the objective investigation of a real world is a metaphysic like any other."[60]

During my first stay in Oxford, England in 2004, the Oxford Round Table had prepared guided tours of Oxford University. On one of the tours, we came to the museum of natural history. The guide, who had been a professor at Oxford, pointed out the science building. I asked her if that was where Richard Dawkins taught, and she responded, "Yes." She then asked if I knew him, and I responded that I did not, but I was familiar with his writings and views on evolution. She asked what I thought of him. I responded that I thought he went beyond the scope of science in some of his views and that he was quite a fundamentalist in his espousal of naturalism. She said—mind you she had already told us she was a feminist—"He can't prove all that he says, can he?" I responded, "No." She said, "He operates by faith, doesn't he?" I said, "Yes he does." My interaction with this self-proclaimed liberal feminist quite compellingly reminded me that it is not always just conservatives that recognize when a scientist has gone far beyond science to scientism.

The elevation of science as *the* discoverer of truth, knowledge, and help; the final arbitrator of truth; the source of real knowledge and the infallible guide for man because of its (supposed) objectivity and self-correcting nature, places it in a position of supremacy and judge of all other judgments. It makes all judgments that are unable to withstand the test of naturalism mere opinions, and they can never be anything more. Thus, in many respects, science in general, and scientists in particular, are isolated from any

---

57. Johnson, *Right Questions*, 91.
58. Bork, *Slouching Towards Gomorrah*, 281–82.
59. Appleyard, *Understanding the Present*, 51.
60. Ibid., 196.

meaningful critique simply because they are scientists. This is not to say that frauds have not been perpetuated by scientists that are later exposed, or that people do not criticize them. It simply means that science in the role as the final arbiter goes unchallenged in a way that others are correctly not allowed. When the news reports that scientists have discovered . . . that is the end of the debate on a popular level. As Appleyard, in somewhat of a different discussion, warns, "Scientists need to be observed and criticized more than any other members of society. I say this not just because of the horrors that might emerge from their laboratories, but also because of the necessity for making them as morally and philosophically answerable as the rest of us."[61]

Fourth, overestimating the possibility of value-neutral education

State education often purports to be 'value neutral.' However, many are of the opinion that education cannot separate itself from religion because education is itself a religious endeavor. Ronald Nash says, "There is a sense in which education is an activity that is religious at its roots. Any effort to remove religion from education is merely the substitution of one set of ultimate religious commitments for another."[62] Concerning the religious nature of education, David Sant says, "All education is undergirded by presuppositions about the origin of the universe, the origin of man, the purpose of man, ethics of governing relationships between men, and the continuing existence of the universe in an orderly and predictable manner. It is an inescapable fact that all of these basic assumptions are fundamentally religious."[63] Dr. Schmidt argues that multiculturalists are determined to change the educational experience when he notes, "Once the purpose of college/university education was to teach students to examine, think, analyze, and understand the accumulated knowledge of the past and present. Today, education is being redefined by multiculturalists who see themselves as missionaries who have to convert their students to their leftist perspective."[64]

Paul C. Vitz makes the point well when he says, "The actual moral position of values clarification is usually personal relativism: something is good or bad only for a given person. At other times the model seems to assume the still more drastic position that values don't actually exist—there

---

61. Ibid., xv.
62. Nash, "The Myth of a Value-Free Education."
63. Cited by Sampson, *What Your Child Needs to Know*, 19.
64. Schmidt, *The Menace*, 165.

are only things that one likes or dislikes."⁶⁵ He then points out the contradiction that while the theorists do not allow for one value to be better than another, they certainly believe their way of determining values is better than others, "that is, relativity aside, students *should* prize their model of how to clarify values."⁶⁶ They attack teaching traditional values while urging teachers to "inculcate values clarification . . . [but] when values clarification brings up the question of whether children in the classroom should be allowed to choose anything they wish, the answer is 'No.'"⁶⁷

Vitz sums up the seriousness of the issue by saying, "The public schools in recent years have given values clarification much support, and in so doing the schools have given the morality of personal relativism a privileged position. That is, the public schools have used tax money systematically to attack the values of those students and parents who believe that certain values are true, especially those who have a traditional religious position. Such a policy is a serious injustice to those taxpayers who expect that in the public school classroom their values will be treated with respect or a least will be left alone."⁶⁸ He further warns, "Be on your guard against programs that focus on 'deciding,' 'choosing,' 'decision making,' etc. Programs that emphasize the *process* of deciding, and ignore the *content* of what is chosen, are almost always relativistic."⁶⁹

As noted earlier, if science is the determiner of everything, everything must be open-ended including morals. Science can determine what laws might need to be passed in order to protect society from a mass murderer, but it can never determine if mass murder is objectively morally wrong, absolutely wrong, or that someone or anyone for that matter should believe that it is personally wrong. A fortiori, science cannot even say that the morality regarding murder is anything more than an *is* or a human construct. Science does not answer what is moral; it only addresses problems. Thus, if science is the answer, and society applies science to every area of life—including morals and values—then objective morals cease to exist at least as something to be taught and upheld publicly and passed from one generation to the next. Moral problems are replaced with mere problems and

---

65. Vitz, *Psychology*, 72.

66. Ibid.

67. Ibid., 72–73. Vitz notes that they may explain that as not being wrong but intolerable for the teacher. Then he reminds us that is similar to saying it is wrong to rob my grocery store but you may steal in other stores, or "you are not to be a racist—or a rapist—in my class, but elsewhere that is up to you," ibid., 74.

68. Ibid., 74. He says on page 83 that the name "values clarification" is gone but the same self-oriented moral relativism continues.

69. Ibid., 83.

science determines a solution to the problem, but not whether the problem or answer is moral. In fact, in a scientific liberal culture (see definition in Authorial Definitions), morals degrade into personal opinion and nothing more. In a scientific liberal culture, it is not that objective morals are not important, but rather that they simply do not exist; only problems and solutions exist.

Fifth, underestimating the biases in science

It is quite common to hear "they proved it scientifically" or "science deals with facts objectively" and the conclusion once again is that the answer to the problem, question, or debate is science. Children are taught scientific conclusions as though if science says it, it can always be believed. However, science is neither homogeneous nor unbiased.

Science is often presented, or understood to be presented, as being so objective that there is very little if any bias, and if there is any it will soon be found out. The objectivity of science is portrayed as towering above other means of knowing. However, while science, particularly the scientific method, is an excellent method of studying and hypothesizing about empirical data, it is not without biases that can result in breaches of ethics. Alexander Kohn, Professor of Virology at Tel Aviv Medical School points out, "Breaches of ethics as encountered in scientific research cover a whole spectrum ranging from outright fraud and conscious falsification, through plagiarism and concealment of information, to minor infractions such as 'grantsmanship' and negligence."[70]

He further mentions that "many a research project, especially in the field of psychology, is burdened by so-called 'experimenter bias.'"[71] Ruth Hubbard states, "The pretense that science is objective, apolitical and value-neutral is profoundly political."[72] She explains her position thusly, "The scientific method 'rests on a particular definition of objectivity that we feminists must call into question'—a definition very much a culprit in the social exclusion of women, nonwhites, and other minorities."[73] She might have added fundamentalist or evangelical Christians but did not. As a scientist, Kohn acknowledges that studies "would indicate that the prevalence of misconduct in science is greater than the scientific community is willing

---

70. Kohn, *False Prophets*, vii.
71. Ibid., 6.
72. Hubbard, *Politics of Women's Biology*, 32.
73. Rauch, *Kindly Inquisitors*, 12.

to admit."[74] Some fraudulent theories like German biologist Ernst Haeckel's "Ontogeny and Phylogeny" and doctored drawings remain in textbooks for years as illustrative of evolutionary themes or truths even after they are determined to be fraudulent.[75]

Kohn explains what prevented scientists from discovering or correcting the Piltdown hoax sooner, even though the true explanation was available, was "hope, cultural bias and prejudice."[76] In response to creationists' charge that evolutionists are biased, Rauch says, "*Of course* evolutionists . . . are biased."[77] Concerning the reason English paleontologists accepted the Piltdown man so easily, Kohn notes, "Scientists, contrary to lay belief, do not work by collecting only 'hard' facts and fitting together information based on them. Scientific investigation is also motivated by pursuit of recognition and fame, by hope and by prejudice. Dubious evidence is strengthened by strong hope: anomalies are fitted into a coherent picture with the help of cultural bias."[78]

My point is not to bash science nor diminish its rightful place in education and society, but rather to make sure that our view of science is not overly naive or prejudiced. In other words, because science says it does not make it true. This is in addition to the previously mentioned innate limitations of science. If we are unaware of the domanial limits and biases of science, then we permit naturalism, posing as science, to define realities beyond the scope of science proper. Thus, scientism determines what answers are off limits *a priori*—regardless what the evidence may suggest—like the theory of intelligent design; thereby, eliminating all other biases and challenges to what are purportedly scientific answers. The elimination of other biases is a dangerous road to travel. Even Rauch, who argues for liberal democracy, also argues against seeking to eliminate all prejudices because it

---

74. Kohn, *False Prophets*, 8. He does say more research would need to be done and that the studies he refers to should not be used for extrapolation because they do not cover a wide enough range of scientific activities. This book covers several frauds, misrepresentations, cheatings, and biases of scientists and science. Some of these are well-known frauds like the so-called 'Piltdown Man' on page 133; others are generally unknown to people outside the scientific community.

75. Hanegraaff, *The Face*, 93–96. Stephen J. Gould recognizes the fraudulence of the drawings, but then says, "Properly restructured, it stands as a central theme in evolutionary biology." Gould, *Ontogeny and Phylogeny*, 2. This very drawing was in my oldest daughter's college science book at the University of Oklahoma in the 1999 spring semester. When a student mentioned the inauthentic nature of the drawing, the professor said it was still illustrative of the truth.

76. Kohn, *False Prophets*, 140.

77. Rauch, *Kindly Inquisitors*, 67.

78. Kohn, *False Prophets*, 140.

is actually impossible to do so, and even if it were accomplishable, tyranny would result. He says, "For not only is wiping out bias and hate impossible in principle, in practice eliminating prejudice through central authority means eliminating all but one prejudice—that of whoever is most politically powerful."[79] This singular prejudice pervades public education and leaves students believing that science (or worse that scientism under the guise of science) has the final answer because there are no dissenting voices allowed in state education. The teaching of Darwinian evolution is as though it has no insurmountable problems and there are no other plausible answers for life, neither of which is true.

The harsh reality is that we are all biased. Our goal should be to be as objective and unbiased as possible, but if we endeavor to be objective while having failed to see our own lack of objectivity, we are doomed to blinding bias. The easiest path to the acceptance of unbridled biases, as objectively and obviously correct, is to eliminate other biases *a priori*. In order for true public education to take place in state schools, the strengths and weaknesses of religion and science need to be taught. The 1967 *Joint Statement on Rights and Freedoms of Students* adopted by the American Association of University Professors clearly states that the "freedom to teach and freedom to learn' are inseparable."[80] In response to a controversy concerning a course at UC Berkeley in the spring of 2002, UC Chancellor Robert Berdahl said, "It is imperative that our classrooms be free of indoctrination—indoctrination is not education."[81] Regrettably, science as the best or only suitable source of publicly imposable knowledge is still applied to ever-increasing areas of study. This includes areas that are clearly beyond the domain of legitimate science or at least their conclusions are set forth as the best conclusion based upon science (and science is the best or only way to know, i.e., everything else is imaginary).

For example, I listened to a presentation by a cognitive scientist regarding the scientific evidence for the existence of the soul (the immaterial aspect of man that is involved in thinking and acting). He defined the theory as "the best current explanations of facts." Then he asked, "What observable phenomena might the soul be posited to explain?" He concluded that subjective experience could be explained physiologically; therefore, "neural theory is a better explanation for subjectivity, and there is not a scientific explanation of the soul."[82] His presentation made it quite clear that only

---

79. Rauch, *Kindly Inquisitors*, 68.
80. "Joint Statement on Rights and Freedoms of Students," 47.
81. Schevitz, "Cramped speech at UC Berkeley," par. 5.
82. Vick, "Soul as Theory." Vick has a PhD in Neurosciences and Cognitive

material explanations were entertained and if there were one, it would be sufficient to displace the idea of a soul. To wit, if a material explanation exists, it is better than a non-material theory regardless if the non-material offers a better or even an equally plausible explanation for subjectivity. Of course, the clear conclusion that was to be drawn from his presentation was that there is no sound reason to believe in the existence of the soul—or the immaterial world and God for that matter. What he failed to realize is that he presupposed that facts are only material, the best answer could only be natural facts, and that determinism is true. That is to say, everything he was saying and doing was determined by material determinative antecedents. Now his answer (for argument's sake) may be correct, but to talk about the reality of the immaterial and consider only natural explanations, and to suppose that a natural explanation is better or sufficient because it is natural, is biased indeed. As far as the "best current explanations of the facts" one must ask, best according to whom. Materialists, yes but not to scientists or countless others who are not naturalists and are therefore willing to consider all possible answers. True to his naturalism, he would deny the legitimacy of belief in God, spiritual sensitivity of humans, acts of worship, acts that emanate from the spiritual realm according to the actor, libertarian free will (including otherwise choice), etc. Interestingly, at the end of the scientist's presentation, a political scientist from the U.S. Naval Academy asked him why he was at this symposium and presenting what he did. Of course, the answer based upon the presentation was it was determined by material neurons (not allowing a choice not to be at the symposium). Not surprisingly, he did not understand the nature of the question.

Atheist John Gray rightly notes "A rigorously naturalistic account of the human mind entails a much more skeptical view of human knowledge than is commonly acknowledged."[83] If science's applicability remains unqualified in education, culture at large will eventually adopt the same mindset. Much of the denigration of religion, limiting the free exercise of religion, and expanding the phrase *separation of church and state* beyond its historical or logical meaning, is due in part to the continued shift from a religious society, where science is welcomed and appropriately limited in applicability, to a scientific secular society, where religion is compartmentalized and privatized. The church's inability or unwillingness in some cases to recognize the massive shift in public education to a philosophy that precludes religion as suitable for public knowledge or policy will eventuate in the demise of any public expression or influence upon society by the church

---

sciences. Statements are from my notes.

83. Gray, "The Closed Mind of Richard Dawkins," par. 19.

(humanly speaking without limiting God). This eventuality is because she will lose her credibility as "the pillar and ground of truth" (1 Timothy 3:15) to science, and she will lose her ability to speak truth in the secular liberal culture to which she has actually become significantly amalgamated. This shift is already so pervasive that the church often flounders in trying to understand the world today and therefore continues to address merely the consequences of the shift rather than the shift itself. It seems to me that the only way to stem the tide is for pastors to be educated regarding the threat of progressive education to the work of the church and freedom of Christianity, and they in turn educate their churches.

3

What the Church Must Do to Stem the Tide of Progressivism

Countering the Corrosive Influence of State Schools upon Culture and the Church

EARLY IN OUR COUNTRY's history, the church and church leaders were the educators. The education that the public at large received was based on the Bible and was essentially Christian. Virtually everything was taught and studied from a Christian worldview. It is easy to see Christianity's profound historical influence upon our educational systems, which I document later in this chapter and elsewhere in this book.[1] This ever-present influence continued right up to the twentieth century, even though with a somewhat diminished presence in certain areas of the country and a growing absence in some spheres and localities in our country. However, since the beginning of the takeover of public education by the progressives at the turn of the twentieth century, there has been an intentional systematic and systemic agenda to eradicate Christianity from influencing public education and expunging the record of its historical influence.

As a result, the church's influence in public education has been reduced to a remnant of Christian teachers and administrators. Still worse, what influence they have is marginalized either by the ever-pervasive secularist's restraints or by Christians themselves who may have developed their spiritual and moral Christianity but failed to develop a thorough Christian

---

1. See also chapter 4 in my book, *The Death of Man as Man*.

intellect; therefore, they neither understand nor engage the all-out war declared by progressivism and scientism on Christianity. Consequently, they become non-factors in stemming the tide or even unwittingly complicit in progressivism's advancement. The hard truth is if Christianity is not significantly influencing public education, then public education is influencing Christianity. If Christianity is influencing public education, then public education becomes more Christianized. In like manner, if public education is not influenced by Christianity and is therefore influencing Christianity, Christianity becomes more secularized. Recognizing and countering this secularization of the church is at the heart of this book and its companion book, *Somewhere Between Fundamentalism and Fluff*. Before we can seriously stand against the tsunamic tidal wave of secularism and progressivism, we must understand its threat and tactics. The following is intended to offer some help in that respect.

Considering the influence of progressive education, which de-emphasizes the need for all students to learn (more than minimally) American history, deconstructs religion and faith, belittles mental discipline and memorization,[2] emphasizes learning only what is immediately practical to the individual, and teaches multiculturalism's revisionist history along with an entirely different way of learning and thinking, it takes little effort to see how students move into adulthood without any historical context to discuss or evaluate the place that religion in general and Christianity in particular has had and should have in personal and public life.[3] This results in not only accepting the level of secularization of the day as being right but actually and quite unfortunately also results in becoming, albeit unknowingly, a co-agent in the continuation of the secularization of the culture and ultimately the church. Thus, many who profess to love the church are unaware of the antichristian influence of progressivism upon their own thinking and thereby unwittingly undermine the very nature and mission of the church.

C.S. Lewis once commented:

> This very obvious fact—that each generation is taught by an earlier generation—must be kept very firmly in mind . . . None can

---

2. Usually pejoratively referred to as rote memorization, i.e., without any concern for understanding the meaning of what was memorized. While I recognize that some teachers have done this, the normal practice of memorization was not and should not be detached from understanding. The answer to rote memorization is not the present disdain for memorization, but memorization that is connected to meaning. Let one see how far he advances in his medical or legal pursuits without memorization.

3. With regard to learning differently, I have in mind things like overemphasis upon experiential learning as opposed to reading classics or critical thinking without equal emphasis upon the facts about which one is supposed to think critically.

give to another what he does not possess himself. No generation can bequeath to its successor what it has not got. You may frame the syllabus as you please. But when you have planned and reported ad nauseam, if we are sceptical we shall teach only scepticism to our pupils, if fools only folly, if vulgar only vulgarity, if saints sanctity, if heroes heroism. Education is only the most fully conscious of the channels whereby each generation influences the next. It is not a closed system. Nothing which was not in the teachers can flow from them into the pupils. We shall all admit that a man who knows no Greek himself cannot teach Greek to his form; but it is equally certain that a man whose mind was formed in a period of cynicism and disillusion, cannot teach hope or fortitude. A society which is predominantly Christian will propagate Christianity through its schools: one which is not, will not. All the ministries of education in the world cannot alter this law.[4]

I believe the best description of what we call secularists, political liberals or progressives can be encapsulated in what I call "Scientific Liberal" (SL), and our ever progressive culture as a scientific liberal culture (SLC). So let me explain these concepts. This will better summarize the tsunamic philosophy with which we are at war. It is one that expands science beyond its legitimate domain, thereby stealthily transforming it into scientism, i.e., naturalism, where God is not only unwelcome, his existence is denied, and people who think he exists are problematic.

SCIENTIFIC LIBERAL CULTURE, SLC

Science

Science is the systematic study of the physical nature, relationships, and interactions of physical phenomena.[5] Within that limitation, science is supposed to be "impartial fact-finding, the objective and unprejudiced weighing of evidence. Science in that sense relies on careful observations, calculations, and above all, repeatable experiments. That kind of objective science is what makes technology possible, and where it can be employed it is indeed the most reliable way of determining the facts."[6] This definition of science is in contradistinction to some "modernists [who] also identify

---

4. Lewis, "On the Transmission of Christianity," *God in the Dock*, 116–17.

5. This is my definition of science proper, which seeks to express the full breadth of science proper without morphing it into naturalism.

6. Johnson, *The Wedge*, 14.

science with naturalistic philosophy. In that case, science is committed to finding and endorsing naturalistic explanations for every phenomenon—regardless of the facts. That kind of science is not free of prejudice. On the contrary, it is defined by a prejudice. The prejudice is that all phenomena can ultimately be explained in terms of purely natural causes, which is to say unintelligent causes."[7]

The latter understanding is often referred to by terms such as scientism, epistemic naturalism, naturalism, materialism, or metaphysical naturalism in order to distinguish between real science and philosophical or religious beliefs ensconced under the banner of science.[8] Antony Flew pointed out, "When you study the interaction of two physical bodies, for instance, two subatomic particles, you are engaged in science. When you ask how it is that those subatomic particles—or *anything* physical—could exist and why, you are engaged in philosophy. When you draw philosophical conclusions from scientific data, then you are thinking as a philosopher."[9] Therefore, science as defined here refers to legitimate science. However, when it becomes the supreme sovereign governing public life, publicly imposable knowledge, and other issues beyond science proper, it is thereby necessarily transformed into scientism; therefore, having no innately superior status over any other philosophy or religion, because they must all compete at the level of a worldview.

Liberal

By liberal, I mean someone who holds to one or more of the following three tenets from which flow many liberal characteristics, as the term is commonly used in politics and theology. First, a liberal is someone who looks to science as the sufficient or supreme guide for how and what society and government should do, support, teach, or be.[10] Second, a liberal is someone

7. Ibid.

8. While science can demonstrate strong probabilities, it can never produce a final answer, which is both a strength and weakness of the scientific method. It is a strength in that it always leaves the door open for a better solution. It only becomes a weakness when scientists transform science into scientism. Moreover, it most certainly does not *require* that ultimate answers be limited to natural answers or that science is the only or best source of knowledge. However, this is the way that science is often presented today even when one may not actually believe that science is the best or only source of all knowledge, but it is in fact what is believed and promoted by many scientists.

9. Flew, *There is a God*, 89.

10. My definition of liberal is not to be understood as the only definition because I do distinguish between liberal and conservative politics, liberal and conservative

who generally views change as good if there is sufficient science on which to base his decision; if there is enough science in support of change, anything can and perhaps should change.[11] Third, for a liberal, science is either knowingly believed to be the only or supreme publicly imposable guide in all areas of public life, or at least the person generally operates according to such a belief.[12]

Some liberals could be further classified by such appellations as humanist, atheist, or secularist. However, a liberal, as I am defining him, may also claim or be a person of faith in something more than nature. Usually, he views his faith as very personal or even private. The criterion for determining whether a person is a liberal is not based upon whether he is an avowed atheist, secularist, or political or theological liberal. Rather it is determined by whether his thinking processes and determinations are supremely guided or governed by scientific polls, studies, or the purported proof of the most recent experiment. Add to this the idea that his faith is not merely personal but private and therefore may have little obvious influence upon him; therefore, it should not exert influence upon anyone else nor should anyone else's faith exert influence upon him. He recognizes that faith is something, but not much of something beyond a private affection, which may be evidenced by his actions in spite of his feelings, words, or even desires to the contrary.

A liberal may be immoral or moral, lazy or hardworking, married or single, and he may even hold many of the same values that the Bible teaches. However, the distinguishing mark is that these values are predominately so personal that they are considered private or coincidental because what

---

Christians, etc. But this is how I am using it in this book. A person may claim to be a conservative or liberal Christian, secularist, New Ager, etc., but they can be a liberal under this definition if they view science as the sufficient or supreme guide of society. For example, if one is satisfied with the present philosophy of public education, which is progressivism, a purportedly science-based education, then he is a scientific liberal even if he is unaware of it. Because of the transmogrification of public education from classical to progressive, science became the guardian of what is suitable for public education, and is now virtually indistinguishable from naturalism in public education.

11. For an example of this, see Appendix A.

12. For example, studies, polls, and experiments that show homosexuals, singles, and divorced families as equally healthy environments for child-rearing as monogamous marriages would have an influence upon the values of a scientific liberal; whereas, it would not upon a non-liberal because his view would be based on Scripture or something other than the latest scientific finding. One does not have to be a consistent liberal to be a scientific liberal any more than one has to be one hundred percent consistent with the teachings of Christ to be considered a Christian. In practical terms, a liberal treats science as absolute even though it is intrinsically relative. In addition, this is not to say that a non-liberal does not value science and even concur with science, but in contradistinction to a liberal, a non-liberal limits the domain and prestige of science to the empirical and does not limit what is knowable or imposable to the empirical.

actually molds a scientific liberal is science or naturalism. Consequently, a liberal may be considered spiritual in some respects, but his guiding light is science with everything (beyond the private or personal) open-ended. A liberal, in the sense that I have defined, is a relativist, but his relativism is not necessarily a technical nor developed philosophical relativism; it is the fruition of his faith in science to guide culture. Remember that science is open-ended, and therefore, everything is an experiment, i.e., relative. Therefore, he may be very much at peace with what seems to the philosopher to be an inchoate relativism.

I would further argue that post-modernism, rather than being antithetical to the Enlightenment view that science is supreme, is actually the Enlightenment taken to its logical conclusion. If science is the best or only way to know, and all knowledge from science is fragmentary and falsifiable, then everything is merely personal, subjective, or an open-ended experiment. Consequently, one cannot say that she is marrying for life because she does not know what the experiment will bring. Therefore, a liberal in this sense may very well esteem religious faith, but he is truly persuaded that science is the fairest and best guardian of the public mind and determiner of imposable knowledge.[13]

Culture

By culture I concur with the definition given by David Wells: "The set of values, the network of beliefs that are institutionalized in a people's collective life that govern their behavior. It is that collectively assumed scheme of understanding that defines both what is normal and what meanings we should attach to public behavior."[14] Important to remember is that culture, so defined, is changeable given the beliefs and influence of the people who make up the culture under consideration. Wells goes on to say, "Culture, then is the outward discipline in which inherited meanings and morality, beliefs and ways of behaving are preserved. It is what reveals eccentrics for their eccentricity, rebels for their rebellion, no-gooders for not doing good. It is what tells us what owning a Cadillac means, what significance being gay has, how we can measure someone who we learn is a doctor, an engineer, a street artist, or homeless."[15]

---

13. Public mind refers to how culture as a whole thinks, the public square in a sense, and imposable knowledge refers to the genre of knowledge that can be imposed upon a culture. This would include areas such as law, policy, and education.

14. Wells, *No Place for Truth*, 167.

15. Ibid.

Accordingly, My definition of scientific liberal culture is that meaning, truth, morality, the definition and understanding of life, what is normal and what is abnormal, what is good and what is not good, and what is suitable for politics, education, and public policy are ostensibly determined by science, and scientific thinking is the process for objectively knowing. A scientific liberal culture seeks to explain or justify virtually everything that is truly important for society scientifically, which necessarily results in culture operating according to naturalism since true science is limited to the systematic study of the physical nature, relationships and interactions of physical phenomena.[16] While individuals or groups may personally and privately operate according to their faith in the supernatural, that faith has little or no marketplace value. To put it another way, an individual *can at times* be permitted to publicly express his personal faith, or tenets of his faith, but such expressions have no value or place in establishing public policy because it is not imposable knowledge, whereas that which is labeled science is. At other times even the expression of religious faith elicits an invective.[17]

At times, I use secular scientific culture or scientific liberal culture interchangeably.[18] The secular/scientific culture is the fruition of bringing to bear the full orb of Enlightenment thinking.[19] It is readily apparent that our culture has moved far from its historical roots of being guided by the Judeo Christian worldview; for example, its legal banishment from being foundational for state education, the primary means for teaching our culture what and how to think. Almost every discussion that relates to public life must now be seen through a poll, study, experiment, or the recitations of a scientist—regardless if he is trained in the field that he is addressing. Psychologists and sociologists have now replaced religious leaders as the

16. Reductively describing humans as being merely physical is beyond the scope of science and is therefore a philosophical or religious assessment. Even the premise that what can be known about humans physically is what is in fact true about humans is not a scientific statement, but rather a philosophical one.

17. An example might be when a president speaks of his faith or God, or when someone in public debate refers to his own faith.

18. I describe individuals who operate according to the principles of an SLC as scientific liberals (SL) or scientific liberal citizens (slc).

19. The European intellectual movement of the seventeenth and eighteenth centuries elevated the use of the powers of reason to the supreme mechanism for knowledge about the universe, man, God, and improvement. Reason had been long relied upon and extolled in Christianity, but in Christianity it was subordinated to the revealed truths of Christianity, whereas the Enlightenment made everything subject to human reason, best exemplified through the methodologies of the natural sciences. This elevation of reason resulted in religion, faith, the supernatural, etc., either being explained or explained away based upon reason and empirical science and deductions.

public experts regarding the nature and behavior of man, and because both of these disciplines fall under the banner of science, they generally reduce man to merely matter or the epiphenomenal, although some recognize an actual spiritual reality.

A culture dominated by Christianity provides ample room for science, reason, and nature, but one governed *solely* by Enlightenment thinking will ultimately privatize faith by banishing the supernatural—including Christianity—to the realm of myths, fairytales, and legend, or being publicly illegal, although it may recognize some psychological value in man's evolution. That we are inexorably headed in this direction is evidenced by the heretofore-unstoppable removal of God from public education and policy debate, which actually has no historical or constitutional warrant. Consequently, when one refers to his faith or the teaching of Scripture, it is commonly received in the same way as if one were to quote a nursery rhyme. If there are no experiments, studies, or polls, then not only does faith carry little if any weight in the debate, it is nonsensical.

Marx sought to build a scientific culture and failed because scientific secular culture failed to explain man as he really is and sought to replace God with man because God is believed to be both the remotest and most inconsequential of ideas or non-existent in a purely secular society. He used a particular natural theory, economics, to explain the problems and solutions for cultural problems. In scientific liberalism, the idea of change is good as long as it is based upon science, and the change usually results in the expansion of government. Freedom is defined, granted, guarded, and promoted by science and its consequent relativism. Everything is an experiment, and we learn right and wrong from this experiment, but there are no absolutes or morals from God. This in spite of the fact that one can only legitimately derive what works and does not work from science and not what is morally right or wrong. Human life is just a higher form of animal life—the human animal—so we can learn from the animal kingdom many things for humans, like whether monogamy is good or not. This is the nature of the culture in which we live.

Both the church and school are educational by nature. Historically in America, they have maintained complementary roles. Because of the prominence of Christianity in America during the beginning of our country, public schools were basically extensions of the church; consequently, such things as morals, epistemology, and goals that were taught and practiced in school were consistent with what was taught in the church. In the last century, this supportive and collaborative relationship has radically changed; church and community-run schools were properly called public schools whereas now, what is often referred to as public schools are more accurately described as state or government schools.[20] Some contributors to and evidences of this change from public to state schools are: the Department of Education, National Education Association, conflating of the First and Fourteenth Amendments of the Constitution by Hugo Black in the Everson case, and the federal government grants of federal tax dollars to local schools in response to their adherence to federal government-mandated educational guidelines. This transition from community, or truly public schools, to state (government) schools has, but for a few remote places, positioned the government schools and the church in conflict. The reason is that government schools, unlike public schools of the past, are educating students based upon a secular scientific worldview. Imposing community standards of faith or morals in a local school is immediately met with threat of lawsuit from the ACLU and defunding from the federal government.

The reason that I have argued so fervently for understanding what is and has gone on in our state schools should become more apparent as we look at our history, culture, the direction our culture is heading, and the mindset of conservative churches and evangelical Christians. There are four very important reasons for understanding these changes. First, everyone, to varying degrees, has been influenced by the philosophy of progressive education and its foundational building block of naturalism or social Darwinism.[21] Second, in order to change the governmental educational system, we must deal with more than just epiphenomenal objectionable concepts like values clarification or the look-say method of reading.[22] We must deal with the underlying philosophy of naturalism and scientific liberalism. Third, in order to purify and protect the church from the subtle deleterious influence of progressivism, we must grasp this as a significant cause of the contamination that is eroding the very foundation of the church and not just focus upon the symptoms, e.g., people not reading the Bible as much, not believing in absolutes, or devaluing substantive preaching. Fourth, to fulfill the mandate of Scripture to equip believers, we must train them to live and think Christianly in a scientific liberal culture. Simply put, almost all believers—including pastors—have attended government schools, and therefore have been impacted negatively by the philosophy of progressivism. The way to counter this is to understand it, seek to minimize it in government

---

20. By state I mean the federal government, national, rather than individual states.

21. See Spencer, *Education,* for more about the total reliance upon nature, natural laws, and science as the foundation for formulating education and discipline for both intellectual and moral education. His examples of what is natural—183, 185, 160, 197, 203, 223, etc. This influence may be direct or indirect.

22. Also known as the "look-and-say-method," "look-see," or "whole-language" approach and as within psycholinguistics.

schools, and be pro-active in the church. We need to explain how believers have been duped into a dumbed down, spiritually doltish existence and this to the point where, for some, the essentials of the Christian life may even seem foreign and dispensable.

This chapter will focus on some steps that can be taken to influence our government schools and begin to stem the tide of progressivism upon our culture and churches. Later, we will look at the local church in particular. This book is not about addressing public education per se, but rather about addressing its systematically pernicious influence upon the spiritual openness of the lost and the spiritual vitality of Christians and local churches. The trend of marginalizing the significance and influence of supernatural religion in general and Christianity in particular upon the world and specifically America must be exposed and arrested. There are many seeking to do this, but what I am calling for is pastors to work at understanding the nature of this conflict and train their churches to engage appropriately. The following provides reasons for giving prominence to the place of religion and faith in government schools. This is not a plan for another Comparative Religions class, but rather the beginning of reintegrating supernatural religion into the very foundational philosophy of education. Following that, I propose a model for starting this process.

The place to start is by training Christian schoolteachers at both government and Christian schools because many Christian teachers unknowingly adopt the philosophy of progressive education, although they may believe they have countered it or rejected it by incorporating some spiritual aspects into the curriculum. This is not meant to condemn all Christian teachers and schools, for without them the damage would be far more pervasive and systematized than it is. It is to say that most teachers have been taught how to educate others by the very educational philosophy they need to be countering. Consequently, while rejecting the most obvious antichristian ideas, they are still subtly influenced by dangerous and substantive anti-Christian concepts.

Therefore, teachers need to be thoroughly trained in the church about the biblical worldview as well as other major worldviews. Particular emphasis has to be placed on teaching them about the real underlying ideas of progressives so that they are able to detect the philosophy itself in such vital areas like pedagogy, textbooks, and policies, rather than just detecting the symptoms. This needs to happen through special training of teachers, but the primary place that this needs to take place is in the local church. Schooling and seminars can supplement the local church, but it cannot replace its premier position in framing the minds and hearts of believers. While many Christian teachers love God and may believe the Bible, they also often compartmentalize their faith. They may have seen so many methods come and go that they, at least tacitly, believe in methodological neutralism. Not that they think they are all equally effective in educating children, but they think they are spiritually neutral, which they are definitely not.

What are some things pastors can do? First, teach the Bible expositionally. There simply is no more effective counter to progressivism than teaching the Scripture and emphasizing the importance of knowing the warp and woof of God's Word. Second, they must teach some history of the influence of Christianity upon America. Pastors need to give not just a sermon once a year, but offer advanced classes, encourage reading, and preach series that explain these things and call Christian teachers to be the change agents by living out their Christianity not only morally but intellectually as well. Everyone needs to be reminded that Christianity, whether viewed theologically or historically, is transformational and not merely accommodational. This begins when God transforms a person's life through the new birth, this new life is equipped and then lived out in the culture, transforming the culture. This transformational influence can be seen by looking at first century Rome and how it was eventually totally transformed by Christianity, at America and its heritage, or even by contrasting the Western world, where Christianity has had the greatest impact, with the Middle East.

Third, the church must teach Christians how progressivism is eroding (not actually but in the minds of children and citizens) the heavenly distinction of the church and the uniqueness of Christianity. Educators, whether in government or Christian schools, must become the most informed about these issues, and at present it seems that the vast majority are not. They must not just seek a career but a vocation wherein they see themselves as missionaries, an extension of the church to affect the world for the kingdom. They should see their mission of teaching as one of the great undertakings not only for time but also for eternity. They need to know that if they teach, and whether knowingly or unknowingly inculcate children with the modes of learning and thinking that characterize the ideas of progressivism, they become more of an instrument of earthly wisdom than heavenly. The reason is that progressivism erodes openness to Christianity, absolutes, the exclusivity of Christianity, and the place of Christian teaching in the marketplace, as well as expanding the limits and application of science beyond its proper sphere, thereby stealthily transforming science into naturalism without having to acknowledge the change. Christian teachers must recognize that education is never neutral.

Fourth, the church must help teachers become knowledgeable about the laws and the reasons they are changing, learn how to stem the tide, and challenge the status quo historically, morally, legally, and intellectually. I develop this more thoroughly in my book, *The Death of Man as Man: The Rise and Decline of Liberty*. Administrators and teachers must be able to demonstrate the non-neutrality of education and the naturalistic persuasion of modern education, as well as the intellectual, historical, and legal legitimacy of challenging that naturalistic persuasion and fully integrating supernatural religion. This includes being able to present a workable model for reintegrating supernatural religion into education as not only an idea or class but as a bedrock and pervasive worldview from which education is based, as indeed it once was in America.

The difference between modern progressive education and the education model that preceded progressivism is more than a difference in emphasis or subjects that are taught or not taught. It is an essential and foundational difference. Historically education was based upon a worldview that recognized the immaterial, supernatural, or metaphysical, and therefore while the empirical world was real, it was neither exhaustive nor final. Further, education did include science, but educators rejected any notion that education was to be based solely on science or that mere nature and natural laws offered sufficient explanatory power for all of life. Actually, this is the critical irreconcilable dissimilarity in modern—progressive—education and the former system, because progressive education is based exclusively on the idea that knowledge of the natural world, its laws, and empirical reality constitutes a sufficient knowledge and guide to life, and education should be scientific. Supernatural religion has a place, but it is no longer in government, education, or the public square of debatable and imposable knowledge. Of course there are similarities in the two systems, but this does not ameliorate the destructive nature of a naturalistic education system. If anything, the similarities in the systems, or the influence some Christians have on some students, although I am thankful for this, actually obfuscates the profound and essential differences as well as the polarized destinations to which they lead a people or country.

The naturalistic base of progressivism can be seen by its total reliance upon science, the expansion of the domain of science so as to include virtually every area of life like the soft sciences, the devaluing of the non-sciences, e.g., history, the marginalizing and personalizing or total banishment of the Christian faith, its sociologically and psychologically driven pedagogy, and its open hostility to absolutes and spiritual morals or values. Further, religion is restricted to comparative religions or philosophy classes except for the almost unbridled misrepresentation, belittling, and general criticizing of the Christian faith. And finally, the underlying issue of the debate between exclusively teaching the positives of evolution and either eliding or rejecting any opposing ideas like intelligent design demonstrates the problem in the science classroom that exemplifies the problem that pervades the entire educational philosophy of our day.

Francis Schaeffer captures the importance of understanding how modern man thinks (as a result of his education). He says, "You have to preach the simple gospel so that it is simple to the person to whom you are talking, or it is no longer simple. The dilemma of modern man is simple: he does not know why man has any meaning. He is lost. Man remains a zero. This is the damnation of our generation, the heart of modern man's problem."[23] Understanding progressive educational philosophy aids not only in protecting the church, but also in understanding the lost man in order to make the claims of Christ more intelligible to him.

To demonstrate how long this has been going on and how intrinsic it is to the system, let me mention eight significant people who have influenced our modern education. The common denominator that these individuals share is the belief that nature is the best and sufficient teacher, which excludes the need for supernaturalism, revelation, and absolute authority, ultimately now most often referred to as science. Unfortunately, some of their unbiblical notions about humans and how to educate them have found their way into the church, which I seek to demonstrate throughout this book.

The French social reformer Jean Jacques Rousseau (1712–1788) influenced modern progressives like John Dewey. He communicated his pedagogy in his didactic novel *Emile*. "Rousseau considers submission to the natural order not only as a necessity of method, but as implying the very end, the normal accomplishment, of education."[24] "Nature provides for the child's growth in her own fashion, and this should never be thwarted."[25] Rousseau believed that education comes to us "from nature, from men, or from things."[26] We can control the last two, but not the first, nature; therefore all three must work together, according to nature. By nature he means the tendencies or sensitivities that cause us to be naturally drawn to pleasantness and shun non-pleasantness before these tendencies "are more or less warped by our prejudices."[27] He says, "Everything should therefore be brought into harmony with these natural tendencies."[28]

Johann Heinrich Pestalozzi (1746–1827) was a Swiss educational reformer, "and most of his principles have been absorbed into modern

---

23. Schaeffer, *The Complete Works*, vol. 1, 285.
24. Rousseau, *Emile*, viii.
25. Ibid., 50.
26. Ibid., 7.
27. Ibid.
28. Ibid.

elementary education . . . [Pestalozzi's curriculum] was modeled after Jean Jacques Rousseau's plan in *Emile* . . . His ideas flow from the same stream of thought that includes . . . John Dewey, and more recently Jean Piaget."[29] His work, *The Evening Hour of a Hermit*, "outlines his fundamental theory that education must be 'according to Nature.'"[30]

Herbert Spencer, (1820–1903) English philosopher and social Darwinist, exercised profound influence upon American education.[31] As previously noted, "Historian Lawrence A. Cremin described Spencer's book on education as 'probably the most widely read in America.'"[32] Historian Henry Steele Commager observed "it requires an effort of the imagination, now, to appreciate the dominion that Spencer exercised over American thought in the quarter century or so after the Civil War and, in some quarters, down to the eve of the First World War."[33] Spencer asserted that "utility was the measure of all things." He taught that the most worthwhile knowledge was, "knowledge for self-preservation"[34] and whether it resulted in desired consequences—namely pleasure and happiness.[35] Two inseparable components of utilitarianism are practicality and immediacy. Does it have immediate practical value for real life?[36] The most valuable knowledge and method of learning is "Science . . . for direct self-preservation, or the maintenance of life and health, the all-important knowledge is—Science."[37] Therefore, education must be based upon science, the only thing we can really know.[38] Of course by science Spencer means the empirical and experiential knowledge that is drawn from nature.[39] Spencer argues that while Pestalozzi was wrong in his applications, he was right in his fundamental ideas about education being natural. We have seen that Rousseau influenced Pestalozzi, and now we see how Rousseau influenced Spencer, and that all of them believed education should be based upon nature.

29. Encyclopedia Britannica 2005 (DVD), s.v., "Johann Heinrich Pestalozzi."

30. Ibid.

31. He advocated the preeminence of science over religion. As a social Darwinist he believed people were subject to the same processes noted by Darwin in biology.

32. Cremin, *The Transformation*, 91.

33. Commager, *Lester Ward*, xviii.

34. Ravitch, *Left Back*, 27.

35. Spencer, *Education*, 183.

36. Spencer evaluated the relative importance of knowledge by its "practical value," whether it helped in "how to live." To wit, would it be useful now or in later life excluding knowledge for "after life." Spencer, *Education*, 7–8, 16–17.

37. Ibid., 89–90.

38. Ibid., 88, 120.

39. Ibid., 140, 144, 203.

Two of the most influential men in the spread of naturalism and the establishment of a systematized and rational explanation of life based upon naturalism were Charles Darwin (1809–1882) and Sigmund Freud (1856–1939). Darwin provided a plausible natural explanation of the origin of biological life including animal, plant, and human life as well as material things; Freud provided a naturalistic explanation for human behavior and thought, including religious beliefs. These have since been refined, modified, and applied to every area of life. It would be difficult if not impossible to overstate their significance in the burgeoning of naturalism.

It should be noted that Spencer coined the phrase "survival of the fittest," and as a social Darwinist he believed "that persons, groups, and races are subject to the same laws of natural selection."[40] This is why Spencer's book on education relies on the guide of nature rather than authority or anything remotely supernatural. Despite the insights that Darwin and Freud provided, and that some of their ideas like microevolution are obviously correct, their theories provide the empirical and intellectual basis for scientism. Spencer and the progressives wanted to make education scientific, which meant elimination or marginalization of mental and moral philosophy, and eradication of the need for an ultimate or secondary immaterial cause or influence upon life and behavior. They accomplished this by a restrictive definition of science that included not only natural studies, but also naturalistic answers regardless if they were the best answer to describe the data. Then they, as well as their successors, expanded the domain of science to include the area called soft sciences like social studies, psychology, and sociology. Thus, the spiritual and immaterial were excluded from being anything but epiphenomenal (emanating from matter or the empirical) by definition.[41]

The important thing to note is that science studies only the material world, and if science can be applied to everything, then everything must be merely material or epiphenomenal. To state this positively, if everything is material, as Rousseau, Spencer, and the progressives believed, then science can give us the answer to such great questions regarding human origin, development, behavior, thinking, value, and morals. In addition, if everything is the result of natural processes, some things are more beneficial than others are, but there is no real right or wrong. Moreover, if everything is knowable by science, and science by its very nature is always falsifiable, then there can be no moral absolutes. I pray as church leaders we see the deleterious effect this philosophy has had on the spiritual sensibilities of America's

---

40. Encyclopedia Britannica 2005 (DVD), s.v., "Social Darwinism."
41. The product of material or natural causes.

citizens and the American mind, but even more so its crippling effect upon the church.

Edward L. Thorndike (1874–1949) was an American psychologist and educator. Thorndike earned "his doctorate in psychology in 1898 for studies of animal behavior, and he went on to become a founder of the field of educational psychology and a leading figure in the progressive education movement . . . His behaviorism led him to conclude that school studies were effective only for specific, particular purposes, not for general improvement."[42] He taught at Columbia Teachers College for a number of years. His work on animal behavior and the learning process led to the theory of connectionism, which he applied to human education. He influenced two major areas of educational psychology, and their contemporary significance is due in large part to his influence.

First, from his animal studies: "He first proposed his two behavioral laws, the law of effect and the law of exercise, in his doctoral dissertation, written 1898–1901 and published in 1911 as Animal Intelligence.[43] He regarded adaptive changes in animal behavior *as analogous to human learning* and suggested that behavioral associations (connections) could be predicted by application of the two laws."[44] (italics added) He later modified the law of effect, which has profoundly influenced the educational distaste for discipline. His modification changed the "law of effect to state that rewards for appropriate behavior always substantially strengthened associations, while punishments for inappropriate responses only slightly weakened the association between the stimulus and the wrong response."[45] Note of course, this is based fundamentally on naturalism. Scientific experiments dealing with the nature of animals are applied to the so-called human animal. According to naturalism, this makes sense because man is only different from animals in degree rather than in kind. To wit, man is merely matter and the soul is (as is salvation, sin, and God) an illusion.

Second is his influence in moving education away from a common core academic curriculum to a more vocational or immediately relevant subject matter, all determined by science, e.g., mental testing and rejecting

---

42. Ravitch, *Left Back*, 64.

43. Encyclopedia Britannica 2005 (DVD), s.v., Edward L. Thorndike. "The law of effect stated that those behavioral responses that were most closely followed by a satisfactory result were most likely to become established patterns and to occur again in response to the same stimulus. The law of exercise stated that behavior is more strongly established when the connection of stimulus and response has been more frequently made," ibid.

44. Ibid.

45. Ibid.

the concept of mental discipline. "While still a graduate student at Columbia, Thorndike began an association with Robert S. Woodworth, with whom he studied transference of learning. In a paper published in 1901, Thorndike and Woodworth found that learning in one area does not facilitate learning in other areas; where specific training in one task seemed to cause improvement in learning another, the improvement could be attributed to common elements in the two exercises, not to overall enhancement of the subject's learning abilities. *This finding supported proponents of school curricula that emphasized practical, relevant subject matter and activities.*"[46] (italics added) He was a professor of educational psychology at Columbia from 1904 to 1940, and consequently he influenced several generations of teachers.

G. Stanley Hall (1844–1924) was an American educator. "Frequently regarded as the founder of child psychology and educational psychology, he also did much to direct into the psychological currents of his time the ideas of Charles Darwin, Sigmund Freud, and others."[47] He was the first American to earn a doctorate in psychology from Harvard, and he received a professorship at Johns Hopkins University in psychology and pedagogics. In 1878 Hall gave special lectures on education at Harvard, and he utilized questionnaires from a study of the Boston schools to write two significant papers; one dealt with children's lies (1882) and the other with the contents of children's minds (1883).

Through a lectureship in philosophy (1883) and a professorship in psychology and pedagogics (1884) at Johns Hopkins University, Hall became a major force in shaping experimental psychology into a science. He believed that mental growth proceeds by evolutionary stages. As a leading spirit in the founding of the American Psychological Association, he was its first president (1892).[48] While teaching at Johns Hopkins, Hall had a student named John Dewey. Dewey is acclaimed to be the father of progressive education in America and is the founder of the American Journal of Psychology, the first such American journal and the second of any significance outside Germany. "By 1893 he had awarded 11 of the 14 doctorates in psychology granted in the United States. The first journal in the fields of child and educational psychology, the Pedagogical Seminar, later the Journal of Genetic Psychology, was founded by Hall in 1893."[49]

> He was an enthusiastic herald of Darwinian Theory and zealously attempted to apply evolutionary biology to studies of the

---

46. Ibid.
47. Encyclopedia Britannica 2005 (DVD), s.v., "G. Stanley Hall."
48. Ibid.
49. Ibid.

mind. An enthusiastic exponent of 'natural education,' Hall blended the romanticism of Jean-Jacques Rousseau's *Emile* with his own interpretations of evolutionary science and genetic psychology. His main contribution to American education was his leadership of the child study movement, which—like Thorndike's experiments—was used by critics to diminish the status of the academic curriculum and provide an intellectual rationale for the child-centered school . . . He counseled . . . that education should be based on a child's own nature and needs, not on subjects that existed outside the child's immediate experience."[50]

Consequently, he furthered the quest to make all education—at least the main core—based on science and naturalism.

John Dewey (1859-1952) was an American philosopher, educator, and one of the most influential leaders in establishing progressive education in America. Dewey was a philosophical pragmatist and signer of the Humanist Manifesto I. His definition of the primary purpose of progressive education "was to make the schools an instrument of social reform . . . He also maintained that the advance of education depended on the application of the social sciences, particularly psychology to education."[51] His writings encouraged those who wanted to base education upon science and the needs of the child.[52] He along with Thorndike, Hall, and progressives incessantly and vehemently attacked academic education. Dewey argued that education should focus on problems and processes rather than academic subjects.[53] He was a huge proponent of the child-centered model. Like other progressives, he was familiar with and affirming of Rousseau's *Emile*. He commented that Rousseau "was almost the first to see that learning is a matter of necessity . . . If we want, then, to find out how education takes place most successfully, let us go to the experiences of children."[54]

Each of these men, who provided the reasoning for the switch to progressive education, agreed on such ideas that education should be based on naturalism as opposed to supernaturalism, that science—matter—trumps metaphysics, authority is in the experiment not derived from an absolute, and animal knowledge is applicable to humans. This is what we have today,

50. Ravitch, *Left Back*, 70.
51. Ibid., 57.
52. Ibid., 59.
53. Ibid., 58.
54. Dewey and Dewey, *Schools of To-Morrow*, 2–3. Ravitch argues that Dewey did disagree with Rousseau's lack of any fixed program, 171, but still agreed that education is to be child centered, natural, and experiential; both Spencer and Rousseau rejected state supported education, 27 and 170 respectively. Ravitch, *Left Back*, 170.

and it is not only changing *what* children—soon to be adults leading our churches and country—think, but also *how* they think. The reality that children become or grow into relativists, resist any authority outside of themselves, and base their opinions upon the most current poll, study, and scientific data is not surprising when progressive education is exposed for what it is.

People not only have learned to think differently about matters than they once did, but they have also learned how to think differently. For example, people are taught *decision-making* (also known as critical thinking skills) in a way that marginalizes or excludes what used to be considered essential facts for making such decisions. In addition, as Christians we must disabuse ourselves of thinking shortsightedly—which is just how we have learned to think based on progressivism. In order to stem the erosive and corrosive impact this is having upon the church, we must educate Americans, particularly Christian schoolteachers, how to reintroduce religion into the underlying substructure of education as opposed to merely offering an elective religion course. This includes educating teachers in Christian schools so that they do not unwittingly become purveyors of what they actually abhor—progressivism.

The following provides information for initial training and familiarizing teachers with the kind of arguments that can be legitimately made in educational and academic debates. It is to help them move beyond merely arguing against using a particular book or the look-say method, which is important and must be done, to dealing with education in history and demonstrating the flaws of the system upon which progressive education is built. Dealing with the consequences of naturalistic education will never produce the change that needs to take place, which is a rejection of scientism as the basis for truth, knowledge, and learning. Moreover, one must not merely deconstruct an idea, but do the hard work of offering a superior alternative.

Pastors or teachers who view this as merely dealing with public education are failing to see the ramifications it is having upon the church, evangelism, Christians who live in America, and missions. For example, if the path of secularization continues, one can see a day where the tax-exempt status of religion becomes politically unacceptable—this is already a view held by many. If the tax-exempt status is revoked from churches and faith-based organizations that will hurt our ability to finance missions at home and abroad. The influence of progressivism upon pastors is already having an eternally devastating impact upon preaching, teaching, and church life.[55] It

---

55. See my book *The Equipping Church* for more specifics and the biblical paradigm for countering such.

is important to remember that the restriction on 501(c)(3) entities—such as churches, pastors—speaking out on political issues with the same freedom as every other American is not due to a restriction in the Constitution but rather was inserted into the federal tax code by then Senator Lyndon B. Johnson ca. 1953. This has now raised the ire of many when we speak out against homosexuality or anything that bears the politically correct stamp of approval.

THE HISTORICAL BASIS FOR TEACHING RELIGION

In consideration of the history of the United States, teaching religion in government schools seems to be both constitutionally compatible and ethically demanded. Historically, teaching religion, connecting religion to education, or emphasizing its essential relationship to America and Americans was not viewed as violating the Constitution or First Amendment. In fact, the Founding Fathers of the United States believed that morality was essential for a republic form of government, and religion was essential for morality; therefore, education necessarily involved teaching both morals and religion.

It is constitutionally compatible

President George Washington in his farewell address wrote, "Of all the dispositions and habits which lead to political prosperity, religion and morality are indispensable supports . . . And let us with caution indulge the supposition that morality can be maintained without religion . . . Reason and experience both forbid us to expect that national morality can prevail to the exclusion of religious principle."[56] Concerning government he says, "It is substantially true that virtue or morality is a necessary spring of popular government."[57]

Based on their belief that religion was an integral part of the Great Experiment, the Founders wrote and adopted documents like The Northwest Ordinance of 1787.[58] Dr. Cleon Skousen says, "The very year the Con-

---

56. Adler et al., *The Annals*, 612.
57. Ibid.
58. This related to land west of states like Virginia, Connecticut, North and South Carolina, and others that they claimed as their land, which led to a delay in the ratification of the Articles of Confederation. Eventually, the land was freed up for redistribution. The Ordinance of 1785 provided that the area north of the Ohio River would be called the Northwest Territory. This land would be divided up and eventually become states with all the rights of the original thirteen states. Anticipating this, a land law

stitution was written by the Convention and approved by Congress, that same body of Congress passed the famous Northwest Ordinance."[59] Article 3 dealt specifically with state education and religion and says, "Religion, morality, and knowledge being necessary to good government and the happiness of mankind, schools, and the means of education shall forever be encouraged."[60] It is important to note that this was a governing document designed to assimilate the new states with the original states, which said that good government necessitated that religion, morality, and knowledge would be taught in schools.

Concerning the need for virtue, morals, and truth to be a part of education, Thomas Jefferson said, "[A] people [can become] so demoralized and depraved as to be incapable of exercising a wholesome control . . . Their minds [are] to be informed by education what is right and what is wrong, to be encouraged in habits of virtue . . . in all cases, to follow truth as the only safe guide . . . These are the inculcations necessary to render the people a sure basis for the structure of order and good government."[61] In addition, we know that he held the moral teachings of Jesus Christ in the highest esteem. He said, "A more beautiful or precious morsel of ethics I have never seen; it is a document in proof that I am a *real Christian*, that is to say, a disciple of the doctrines of Jesus."[62]

The Founders took great precautions to preclude Congress from establishing a Church of America where membership, offerings, and beliefs were required by law like the Church of England. They were all too familiar with the suffering that would inevitably result when a government made tyrannical demands for religious support in violation of any citizen's conscience. However, they did not desire to separate government from the influence of religion or religious people. Nor did they desire to separate religion from public life and education. On the contrary, they actually sought to accommodate and foster religion in public life and education.

---

based on Thomas Jefferson's earlier proposal was adopted, Graff, *America*, 162–165. This Northwest Ordinance "established for the Northwest Territory a plan of government that would, in time, be applied to all the land included in the national domain," ibid., 165. This ordinance was a "compact between the original States and the people in the said territory," ibid., 166.

59. Skousen, *Making of America*, 676.
60. Graff, *America*, 166.
61. Ford, *The Writings of Thomas Jefferson*, 10:152.
62. In a letter to Charles Thomson in 1816, referring to *The Jefferson Bible*, http://www.let.rug.nl/usa/presidents/thomas-jefferson/letters-of-thomas-jefferson/jefl239.ph, par. 1. This is not to say that Jefferson was not also fond of the classical Greek and Roman moral philosophers. Furthermore, this is not intended to define Jefferson as a Christian, which by every accurate appraisal he was not.

To ensure the teaching of religion and morals drawn from religion in public schools, the Founders emphasized the commonalities they believed all religions and denominations believed. For example, Jefferson wrote a bill for Virginia schools that emphasized this point, which read, "No religious reading, instruction or exercise shall be prescribed or practiced inconsistent with the tenets of any religious sect or denomination."[63] Samuel Adams referred to these unifying tenets of religion as "the religion of America [which is] the religion of all mankind."[64] John Adams called these tenets the "general principles" on which the American civilization had been founded.[65] Jefferson identified them as the principles "in which God has united us all."[66] These were what Benjamin Franklin considered the "fundamental points in all sound religion. He summarized them in a letter to Ezra Stiles, president of Yale University."[67]

1. Recognition and worship of a Creator who made all things.
2. That the Creator has revealed a moral code of behavior for happy living which distinguishes right from wrong.
3. That the Creator holds mankind responsible for the way they treat each other.
4. That all mankind live beyond this life.
5. That in the next life individuals are judged for their conduct in this one.[68]

According to Dr. Skousen, "These are the beliefs which the Founders sometimes referred to as the 'religion of America,' and they felt these fundamentals were so important in providing 'good government and the happiness of mankind' that they wanted them taught in the public schools along with morality and knowledge."[69] Further evidence of the prominence of religion in education in the U.S. is seen in the use of the Bible as a textbook. In addition, the McGuffey's Readers, which were overtly religious and moralistic texts from a Christian worldview, were widely used for over eighty years.[70]

63. Randolph, *Early History of the University of Virginia*, 96–97.
64. Wells, *Samuel Adams*, 3:23.
65. Bergh, *The Writings of Jefferson*, 13:290–294.
66. Ibid., 14:198.
67. Smyth, *The Writings of Benjamin Franklin*, 10:84.
68. Skousen, *Making of America*, 677.
69. Ibid.
70. "This series of schoolbooks teaching reading and moral precepts, originally

Whether one agrees with the Founders and the history of America mixing religion, morals, and public education, it does seem that the Founders and populace saw it as essential to good education and good government. They simply did not entertain the idea of teaching or advancing an atheistic or naturalistic view of life. Therefore, historically, the Founders and citizens up to the latter half of the twentieth century interpreted the Constitution to endorse teaching religion in the public domain.[71]

It is ethically demanded

Because the Founders deemed religion to be so important to education and government, and because religion played such an important part in the history of America, and indeed in the world, it is essential that the role of religion in the development of man, cultures, behaviors, and progress be taught. To ignore religion or mention it disproportionately is to revise rather than teach history. Following are a few facts that can demonstrate the profound and pervasive influence of religion in general, and specifically in this case, Christianity.

We have all heard of the Pilgrims, but many fail to grasp who they actually were. They were Puritans who eventually separated from the Anglican Church and became known as Separatists. Henry Graff says, "Some Puritans feared that the Anglican Church could never be 'purified.' Among them were a band of humble folk from Nottinghamshire, in central England,

---

prepared by William Holmes McGuffey in 1836, had a profound influence on public education in the United States. McGuffey was a professor at Miami University in Oxford, Ohio, and a Presbyterian minister . . . As a young schoolmaster, McGuffey had used the eighteenth-century Puritans' *New England Primer*, Noah Webster's *American Spelling Book*, and the Bible. His *Eclectic First Reader* and *Eclectic Second Reader* were published in 1836, the *Third* and *Fourth* in 1837. They contained stories of widely varied subject matter appealing to youngsters and taught religious, moral, and ethical principles that reflected both McGuffey's personality and society at the time . . . The books passed through a series of seven owners while their content evolved during almost a hundred years of publication . . . The revised texts issued in 1857. . .moved away from the Calvinist values of salvation, righteousness, and piety and reflected the morality and cultural values of a broader American society that had incorporated religion within the civil structure. The 1879 editions taught morality and good character to the emerging middle class and provided children with a common knowledge and worldview . . . By 1879 more than 60 million had been sold, and by 1920 over 122 million. In 1978 they were still in use in some school systems." https://mcguffeyreaders.ipower.com/history.htm, accessed 2/13/17.

71. This is not to say that one cannot find individuals who wanted total separation, but rather I mean that it was the common sentiment and practice to blend them together.

who called for a total break with the Anglicans. For that reason they were called Separatists."[72] Puritans believed that the Church of England was corrupt, but she could be purified; however, Separatists believed that she had strayed too far from the Scripture to be purified and the only way for them to remain faithful to the Scripture was to separate from her. The Pilgrims took their name from the Bible, in 1 Pet 2:11, because they were sojourners, "wanderers in search of a new homeland."[73]

In 1606 they organized themselves into a secret Separatist church in England. As soon as they organized themselves as a local congregation of believers set on following the teaching of Christ as they understood the Scripture, opposition arose.

"They were persecuted by the Church and civil authorities. They had to hide and move from place to place; their homes were watched; they were thrown into jail. Robinson and his followers finally decided there was nothing else for them to do but leave England if they were to worship according to the Word of God. They planned to cross the sea to Holland and religious liberty . . . They arranged for an English captain to take them there, but when they got into the longboats to go out to the ship, he betrayed them. They were robbed of their money and possessions, brought back to the magistrates, and thrown into prison. They were finally released, and after facing many other difficulties, they finally arranged with a Dutch captain to sail to Amsterdam."[74]

The Pilgrims were humble farmers and tradespeople who left everything in search of religious freedom. In 1609 they moved to Leyden, Holland where they established the first congregational church.[75] After eleven years, they decided to leave Holland primarily because they believed that there was too much impiety and ungodliness among the Dutch, and this was corrupting their children. They became afraid of losing their church and the freedom to worship and live according to the Scripture; so they decided to head for the new world.[76]

"After a fearful journey of sixty-six days, never coming up on the deck of the *Mayflower* because of the great gales and storms," they landed in New England.[77] Because they landed outside of the jurisdiction of the Virginia Company, before disembarking, forty-one of the forty-four men

---

72. Graff, *America*, 72.
73. Ibid., 73.
74. Kennedy and Newcombe, *What If the Bible*, 82.
75. Schutz and Kirkendall, *American Republic*, 28.
76. Kennedy and Newcombe, *What If the Bible*, 82–83.
77. Ibid., 83.

aboard signed an agreement known as the Mayflower Compact. It was the first governing document for the new settlers in America, and the only one the Pilgrims would have. Therefore, it was their constitution—covenant as they called it. It says in part, "We, whose names are underwritten ... having undertaken for the glory of God, and advancement of the Christian faith, and the honor of our King and country, a voyage to plant the first colony in the northern parts of Virginia; do by these presents, solemnly and mutually in the presence of God ... covenant and combine ourselves together into a civil body politic."[78] This was a small group, insignificant in number, but all Americans are beneficiaries of their religious conviction and bravery. How can one understand the nature of our founding without understanding the Christian faith of the founders, without which there simply would have been no Pilgrims and no Americans.

Dr. M.E. Bradford demonstrates that the vast majority of those who signed the Constitution of the United States were professing Christians and were associated with orthodox churches. He identifies 28 as Episcopalians, 8 Presbyterians, 7 Congregationalists, 2 Lutherans, 2 Dutch Reformed, 2 Methodists, 2 Roman Catholics, and one whose religious affiliation is unknown today. He concludes that James Wilson of Pennsylvania, Hugh Williamson of North Carolina, and Benjamin Franklin were deists although he acknowledges Williamson's deism is open to question.[79] Furthermore the constituency of the United States in 1776 was by and large Christian, and scholars like Isaac Kramnick and R. Laurence Moore, who dispute claims that the vast majority of Americans at the time claimed to be Christian, make several mistakes in their formulas for calculating how many Christians there were. For example, their mistakes include equating church membership with the number of Christians, not understanding how different denominations calculate members versus how many attend, and other such errors. The full scope of their error is addressed in Appendix C. "By the time of the American Revolution, the religious composition of the nation was 98.4 percent Protestant, 1.4 percent Roman Catholic, and 0.15 percent Jewish."[80]

The writings of the time also demonstrate the influence of Christianity and the Bible upon the Founders' thinking. In a detailed study of the political writings of prominent Americans between 1760 and 1805 consisting of some 15,000 items, researchers identified "3,154 quotations therein. The most widely quoted source of all was the Bible, accounting for 34% of

---

78. Graff, *America*, 73.
79. Bradford, *A Worthy Company*, v–vi.
80. Hart, "The Wall That Protestantism Built," 44.

all quotations . . . The contemporary writers most commonly quoted were Baron Montesquieu of France and Sir William Blackstone of England, both orthodox Christians; third was John Locke, a Christian although not entirely orthodox."[81] My aim is not to prove that everyone in America at this time professed Christianity, that every Founding Father was a devoted born-again Christian, or that there were no deists, secularists, or unchurched, but rather to demonstrate that the influence of Christianity upon the forging of the United States of America was so profound that it is unethical to omit or marginalize its role. Therefore a respectable place and an accurate understanding of religion must be incorporated into state education.

Whether or not one agrees with the Christian worldview of the Pilgrims, Puritans, Founders, or populace of the past generations should not be a factor in determining what is taught as history. State education has an ethical duty to teach about religion when religion is a part of the worldview of the men and women involved, the event being taught, or the genesis of the event. When religion is omitted, or presented disproportionately to its historical significance, then history is not taught and students are not educated. State education has a moral responsibility to present events as they were and as they are regardless if this requires mentioning a specific religion disproportionately to the mention of other religions. Cultural equivalence or social engineering should not determine educational content; rather facts germane to the subject, in context, should determine curriculum. Therefore, it appears that the only way education can take place is to teach the religious nature of our history even if no one agrees with the religious ideas of history. Mentioning that people are religious is helpful, but real understanding of how their religion influenced events or how their faith influenced their decisions requires exploration beyond merely acknowledging their faith.

In spite of the awe-inspiring, world changing contributions of religion in American history, religion is systematically expunged from state textbooks. Contrary to the reality of history, the importance of religion in the world, and the significant role of Christianity in particular upon the founding and framing of America, religion and Christianity are often marginalized or ignored. Consequently, students are not taught history as it was, and the appreciation for the enormous contributions of religion to mankind is all but lost.

William J. Bennett, former U.S. Secretary of Education, states the current practice succinctly and poignantly: "In too many places in American public education, religion has been ignored, banned, or shunned in ways that serve neither knowledge, nor the Constitution, nor sound public policy.

---

81. Lutz, "The Relative Influence of European Writers," 78:189–197.

There is no good curricular or constitutional reason for textbooks to ignore, as many do, the role of religion in the founding of this country or its prominent place in the lives of many of its citizens. We should acknowledge that religion—from the Pilgrims to the civil rights struggle—is an important part of our history, civics, literature, art, music, poetry, and politics, and we should insist that our schools tell the truth about it."[82]

The intentional omission of religion and the religious nature of the history of the United States, whether because of political correctness, multiculturalism, or lack of interest or knowledge, seems to be a well-recognized fact.[83] Ravitch argues the result of biased guidelines used by various publishers is that "reading passages must not contain even an 'incidental reference' to anyone's religion."[84] The extent of censorship of religion in state textbooks is borne out clearly by Dr. Paul Vitz, an educational psychologist, whose original research on this question is quoted extensively in books and articles on the subject. Dr. K. Alan Snyder summarizes his findings.

> Dr. Vitz completed a study for the National Institute of Education to determine if public school textbooks were biased or censored. The answer to both is yes. And the nature of the bias is clear: Religion, traditional family values, and conservative political and economic positions have been reliably excluded from children's textbooks.
>
> In his study of 40 social studies texts for grades one through four, Vitz found that religion was usually treated as old-fashioned and unimportant to modern life. There was almost a total blackout on Christianity in America beyond the colonial period. He found it disturbing "that not one of the 40 books totaling 10,000 pages had one text reference to a primary religious activity occurring in representative contemporary American life.
>
> A significant instance of bias against religion was a text that had 30 pages on the Pilgrims, but not one word that even mentioned their religion . . . The situation did not improve with fifth and sixth grade texts. Not one of the fifth grade books on American history mentioned the Great Awakening of the 18th century, the great revivals of the 19th century, or the Holiness and Pentecostal movements. Treatments of the 20th century showed profound neglect of anything religious.
>
> The sixth grade world civilization texts were even worse. Mohammed's life gets considerably more coverage than the life

---

82. Bennett, *The De-Valuing of America*, 205.
83. Ravitch, *Language Police*, 99.
84. Ibid., 22.

of Jesus. Two texts talk about Mohammed, but never mention Jesus at all. In another, "The rise of Islam, Islamic culture, and Mohammed himself gets an 11-page section, plus other scattered coverage. The rise of Christianity gets almost nothing (a few lines on p. 116). In these books, then, it is not that great religious figures are totally avoided—it is that Jesus is avoided."[85]

This is indeed a long way from the moral and religious content of the New England Primer or the McGuffey Readers used well into the twentieth century to educate millions of children. For politicians to demagogue revisionist history is shameful, but to find revisionist history in state education is intolerable.

FOUR SUGGESTED GUIDELINES FOR TEACHING RELIGION IN STATE SCHOOLS

Because educational neutrality is theoretically possible but not actually achievable, and the nature of education makes teaching about religion ethically demanding, I suggest the following four guidelines for public education. These should be used at least until such time that education is de-secularized and de-nationalized, thereby returning it to the way it was historically. Then, when education is locally and state controlled, as it should be, it can be more reflective of the community faith and values while still maintaining a comprehensive educational philosophy.

One: The emphasis should be to teach the facts of religion not faith in religion

The following is desired language to be used in related literature to emphasize the appropriate teaching of religion: academic, not devotional; awareness of, not acceptance of; expose, not impose; educates, does not promote or denigrate religion; inform, not conform.[86] In order for state education to be complete, it has to teach students about the role of religion in the past and present because "omitting study about religions gives students the impression that religions have not been and are not now part of the human experience."[87] This leads to not only erroneous ideas about religion but also about people and the world.

---

85. Snyder, "Who is Censoring," portions of par. 6, 7, 8, 11, and 12.
86. Haynes et al., *First Amendment in Schools*, 52.
87. Cited in Haynes, *Finding Common Ground*, 7.1.

There seems to be widespread agreement on the need to teach adequately about religion in state schools. A joint statement by a diverse group including the National Education Association (NEA), the Christian Coalition, and 22 other education associations and religious groups stated, "Public schools may not inculcate nor inhibit religion . . . They must be places where religion and religious conviction are treated with fairness and respect. Public schools uphold the First Amendment when they protect the religious liberty rights of students of all faiths or none. Schools demonstrate fairness when they ensure that the curriculum includes study about religion, where appropriate, as an important part of a complete education."[88] Religion must be taught accurately in order not to misrepresent it. This is stated by NEA Resolution E-7, which says, "The National Education Association believes that educational materials should accurately portray the influence of religion in our nation and throughout the world."[89] Furthermore, religion must be dealt with as substantively as possible in order not to trivialize what is for many the essence of existence.

In addition, while all religions do have shared traits, and it is quite appropriate to teach about these, they also have substantial differences. It is a disservice to the student and democracy to teach only about the similarities. This will handicap students when life confronts them with a host of significant and diverse beliefs in their culture and the larger world. The importance of these differences is communicated by dealing with the reality of those diverse beliefs. The National Council for the Social Studies Curriculum Standards declares: "Knowledge about religions is not only a characteristic of an educated person but is absolutely necessary for understanding and living in a world of diversity. Knowledge of religious *differences* and the role of religion in the contemporary world can help promote understanding and alleviate prejudice."[90] (italics added)

In order for teachers to teach religion accurately, legally, and substantively, they will need to be trained in the subject matter of religion, and they must be taught how to teach it in a constitutionally compatible manner—if education had not been nationalized and the First Amendment had not been conflated with the Fourteenth Amendment this would be unnecessary. California is one state that is making an attempt to prepare teachers. The Modesto, California, public school district has offered workshops on the First Amendment in order to equip teachers to teach religion in class.[91]

88. Kafer, "How To Teach Religion," par. 5.
89. Ibid., par. 9.
90. Ibid.
91. Ibid., par. 10.

"The California County Superintendents Educational Services Association and the First Amendment Center sponsor a statewide program called the California 3Rs Project, which conducts seminars, forums, and workshops on teaching about religions and student religious liberties. The project supports constitutional and educationally beneficial practices and promotes the 'three Rs': rights, responsibilities, and respect in California's diverse school environments."[92] *The Bible & Public Schools: A First Amendment Guide* has also been widely endorsed by diverse groups for teaching about the Bible in public schools.[93] The legality of teaching about religion, the Bible, or other sacred Scriptures is well established as long as the teaching is "presented objectively as part of a secular program of education."[94]

To teach the facts of different religions, textbooks, and teachers will be well served by utilizing scholarly information that makes appropriate distinctions between different religions, including diversity within particular religions. I do not believe this can be accomplished unless the sources for such information come from within the different religions and subgroups within particular religions. For example, when teaching on the differences of Islam and Christianity, material should come from scholars of the Islamic faith and scholars of the Christian faith.

In addition, when religions are compared, or a particular religion is studied, the teachings of the major groups within the religion need to be represented. In Islam this would include at least Sunni, Shiite, and maybe Sufi. In Christianity this would include Catholic/Orthodox, Evangelical/Conservative, and Neo-orthodox/Liberal. If a major religion is defined by scholars of another religion, or by a particular group within the major divisions of the religion, the explanation becomes so reductionistic or skewed it may inadvertently misrepresent a significant diversity of beliefs or distort the true beliefs, which is already a dreadfully pervasive practice. In order to portray religious beliefs substantively and accurately, educators must be sure to source groups appropriately. The difficulty of this task is not to serve as an excuse to continue the present practice of misrepresentation, and is in fact, an argument for local control of education.

---

92. Ibid.

93. *The Bible & Public Schools*, second page. Some of the groups are American Association of School Administrators, American Federation of Teachers, Anti-Defamation League, Christian Educators Association International, Council on Islamic Education, National Association of Evangelicals, National Education Association, etc. See article for a full list of endorsers.

94. Cited in *The Bible & Public Schools*, 6, from the School District of Abington Twp v. Schempp, 374 U.S. 203, 225 (1963) ruling.

Two: The amount of teaching on religion should be based on proportionality not equality

This guideline means that the coverage of religions and subgroups should be proportionate to the significance of their role in the event or in the lives of people under consideration, the need for the specific subject being taught, and the grade level of the students.

The present model based on multiculturalism and political correctness places more emphasis on equal portrayal rather than factual proportionality.[95] This tends toward distorting the beliefs and proportionate contributions of religions by denigrating or minimizing the significance of the dominant religion, and magnifying the contributions of minority religions—regardless of their historical significance. This is particularly true with regard to downplaying the significance of Christianity's positive influence upon the western world—as demonstrated earlier in this book. Moreover, most teachers, who may be well aware of the actual facts concerning religion's role in cultural shaping, elide explaining a particular religion's influence upon cultural changes for fear of leaving out a minor contribution of another religion and thereby being accused of promoting a particular religion. Therefore they ignore the proportional contributions of a religion or religion's contribution all together.

The practice of seeking cultural equivalence is pervasive. Ravitch says concerning this trend, "The textbooks published in the late 1990s do, however, contain a coherent narrative. It is a story of cultural equivalence."[96] This leaves students with a distorted idea that religion played a very minor or no role, or that many religions played an equal role in events and cultural developments. Thus, the end result is a distortion of the facts, marginalizing

---

95. I am not using the term multiculturalism to mean multicultural education which evaluates and highlights the practices and contributions of different cultures in a factual way, but rather I use it to refer to the ideology that sees all cultures, their mores and institutions, as essentially equal. Of course this usually excludes Euro-American cultures with Judeo-Christian underpinnings, which are often condemned. In addition, they seek to highlight and maintain cultural differences and therefore destroy our shared story and unity. I also mean the multicultural methods that emphasize the sins of Euro-Americans and magnify any contribution from minority groups, see Schmidt, *The Menace*, 3, 11, and 57. See also the *Multicultural Guidelines* published by Scott Foresman-Addison Wesley cited in Ravitch, *Language Police*, 34–49. Ethnocentrism includes avoiding contributions by Judeo Christian culture to art or literature, and cultural equivalence, Ravitch, *Language Police*, 141. Ravitch also talks about multiculturalism being ethnocentric or particularistic—focusing on accomplishments of one's own ethnic group, which Ravitch says is actually "inverted racism," Ravitch, *Left Back*, 421.

96. Ravitch, *Language Police*, 140, says the result of this equivalence is "the once traditional emphasis . . . on the growth of democratic institutions has nearly vanished."

of religion, and trivializing the religious genesis of the ideas behind many cultural phenomena.[97]

This equality model based on cultural equivalence actually impedes one culture learning from another. For if all religions or cultures are the same, then why spend any time learning about others, for to learn about your own culture or religion is to know about all cultures. It is our differences and proportionate influences in different parts of the world that enhance learning, resulting in true education. Therefore, rather than equalizing all religions to the lowest common denominator based on the equality model, educators should teach about religion based on proportionality. The following approach can assist in applying the principle of proportionality.

First, "The academic requirements of the course should determine which religions to study. . . . In a U.S. history course, for example, some faith communities may be given more time than others simply because of their predominant influence on the development of the nation. In world history, a variety of faiths must be studied, based on the regions of the world, in order to understand the various civilizations and cultures that have shaped history and society. Fair and balanced study about religion on the secondary level includes critical thinking about historical events involving religious traditions. . . . Overall, the curriculum should include all major voices, and many minor ones, in an effort to provide the best possible education."[98]

The same principle would be true in studying a contemporary event. If the United States' population is 80–90 percent Christian (at least as reported), and that percentage holds true in influencing a poll, vote, or chosen direction, Christianity's influence or significance can be legitimately referred to more than Buddhism's influence; although, Buddhism's influence can also be taught in a way proportionate to the situation, without fear of hurting any group's self-image or self-esteem. The proportionality principle teaches the facts based on reality rather than a desired outcome.

This very format is followed in other lessons: for example, if one were talking about one person's invention, one need not feel compelled to

---

97. Consider these examples: two-thirds of the abolition movement in the United States were Christian ministers, not counting all of the lay-Christians involved, Kennedy and Newcombe, *What If Jesus,* 22; the influence of Christianity in eliminating slavery from the ancient world, ibid., 18–22; men like John Newton who became Christians and turned from slave trading in order to help slaves, ibid., 193–94, or William Wilberforce's Christianity which caused him to lead the battle for 45 years in England to abolish slavery and free all slaves, Kennedy and Newcombe, *What If the Bible,* 72–77. The Civil Rights Movement was spawned out of religious faith. It is true that religious people were on both sides of each issue; however, that in no way minimizes the Christian influence upon the changing culture.

98. Haynes et al., *The First Amendment in Schools,* 53–54.

mention every other inventor. However, the inventor's faith may very well be germane to his success, and if he so attributes it, it should be mentioned. If one were studying Saudi Arabia, it would be quite ludicrous to mention Christianity or Buddhism each time the influence of Islam upon the culture of Saudi Arabia was mentioned. This neither ignores, minimizes, nor promotes some religions, but rather portrays their presence and influence proportionately, enabling educators to teach without trivializing religion. Moreover, this does not mean that minor religions or their contributions are not mentioned, but rather they are mentioned in proportion to their influence on the subject being studied.

Second, instruction about religion can be taught proportionately in a developmentally appropriate manner. This can be "Elementary students are introduced to the basic ideas and practices of the world's major religions by focusing on the generally agreed-upon meanings of religious faiths—the core beliefs and symbols as well as important figures and events."[99] At the secondary level, social studies and history provide great opportunities for teaching about religion. "The full historical record, and various interpretations of it, should be available for analysis and discussion. . . . Teachers will need scholarly supplemental resources that enable them to cover the required material within the allotted time, while enriching the discussion with study of religion. In fact, some schools now offer electives in religious studies to provide additional opportunities for students to study about the major faith communities in greater depth."[100]

Therefore, whenever the subject of religion, or a particular religion, naturally arises, it should be explained in a substantive, proportional, and age-appropriate manner, whether it is in history, philosophy, science, or contemporary society, in order to better understand the views of the person(s) being discussed or their contributions. For example, a study of the First Amendment necessitates understanding the religious milieu of the people prior to and during the drafting of the Constitution. In addition, even when some operate on the extremes of a religion, whether they are David Koresh and Christianity or Osama Bin Laden and Islam, the prominence that religion plays in their lives must not be trivialized, obscured, or dismissed by the baffled look of the secularist.[101] To refer to Osama Bin

---

99. Ibid., 53.

100. Ibid., 54.

101. This is not to say that these extremists represent the truths of these religions. That must be determined by looking at the life of the founder and the primary documents of the specific faith that the adherent claims. That is what determines if the person is truly reflecting the faith. When anyone operating from a faith in God is handled as though that faith is merely a mental construct or delusion, it actually exacerbates the

Laden as irrational as is often done by the secularist, demonstrates a dangerously narrow view of human behavior.

Three: The context for teaching religion should be one of accommodation not separation

As has been demonstrated, there is simply no historical, legal, or educational reason to seek to separate religion from state education. As a matter of fact, separating religion from teaching is equivalent to turning state education into state propaganda—although I do not believe that most teachers desire that end. The question of teaching about religion is no longer "Should I teach about religion" but rather "How do I teach about religion?"

Unfortunately for students, since *Everson vs. Board of Education*, the trend has been to separate religion from education. My proposal, along with others I have cited, seeks to replace the tendency toward separation with a conscious desire to accommodate the teaching of religion in public education. One need not fear that accommodation will result in promotion of religion, for these are two very different ideas. This can be illustrated by asking how many churches, synagogues, or mosques would be content to merely seek to accommodate their respective faiths instead of promoting them. By accommodating, state schools provide appropriate places for teaching about religion without promoting a particular religion. If students are going to value the Constitution, the First Amendment, our cultural differences, and the ebb and flow of history, they must study the history and importance of religion. This is essential to democracy and the United States.

Four: The approach should be one of constructiveness not destructiveness

This does not mean teaching only the positive aspects or contributions of religion and glossing over troublesome aspects or influence, but it does mean putting things into proper perspective. For example, to point out how many wars have been fought in history because of religion intentionally distorts the good of religion, because almost everyone in the history of man has believed in some kind of religion, and therefore all wars were religious because basically all people were religious. In other words, that is like pointing out

---

anger of the followers and obscures a valuable approach to dealing with the problem, which is taking their religious beliefs seriously and seeking to communicate with them from that premise.

that in antiquity men killed other men with swords rather than machine guns. The reason history is not peppered with wars of atheistic nations is because the history of man is religious.

However, the twentieth century, with the rise of atheism, along with communism and Nazism, has been the bloodiest century in the history of man. Auschwitz survivor Hugo Gryn says, "It was a denial of God. It was a denial of man."[102] The mammoth consequences were the result of a relatively small number of atheists. In addition, if one is required to teach the positive features of religions—beliefs, values, contributions, and believability—without promoting faith in the religion, one should also be able to teach the negative without promoting antipathy or indifference toward religion.

Examples of destructive teaching about religion would include teaching or suggesting that religion is a cultural or psychological construct that originates in man; viewing all faith events reductively; describing faith as a delusion, illusion, or weakness; and portraying religion as something that is antiquated, becoming irrelevant to modern man, or invalidated by science. These destructive ideas are naturally biased; they misrepresent rather than represent faith. Moreover, to use scientific naturalism to determine the validity of religion is like determining the reality of music based on the color of the notes, or like supernaturalism rejecting the value of nature because it can be seen.[103]

Another example of deconstructive teaching is role-playing.

> The California 3Rs project cautioned educators that "role-playing religious practices runs the risk of trivializing and caricaturing the religion that is being studied. It's more respectful and educationally sound to view a video of real Muslims practicing their faith than having a group of seventh-graders pretend to be Muslims ... Role playing runs the risk of putting students in the position of participating in activities that may violate their (or their parents') consciences. Such an issue doesn't arise when teachers teach about religion by assigning research, viewing videos, and through class instruction rather than organizing activities that may be easily perceived, rightly or wrongly, as promoting students' participation in a religious practice."[104]

---

102. Cited in Roth, *Holocaust Chronicle*, back cover.

103. This is called a categorical fallacy in logic.

104. Kafer, "How to Teach Religion," par. 15. "In January, Excelsior School in the Byron Union School District near Oakland, California, drew criticism for its three-week course on Islam. Seventh-graders adopted Muslim names, read verses from the Qur'an, learned to write Islamic proverbs in Arabic, and organized a pretend hajj, or journey to Mecca. The course handout read, "From the beginning, you and your

The current hostility in U.S. public education toward religion in general, and Christianity in particular, along with a disproportionate emphasis on pedagogy vs. facts exacerbates the present problem, and is, in large measure, fueling the drive for more private schools, vouchers, or tax credits.[105] The concern is both religious and academic, and these cannot be totally separated for most religious people. The significant degree of dissatisfaction is illustrated by resolutions at the Southern Baptist Convention over the past few years and one that was proposed for the 2004 Convention, which actually calls for people to remove their children from state schools. This was the most serious proposal concerning the state of public education proposed for consideration by the convention, which is the largest non-Catholic Christian denomination in the world.[106] My experience over the past thirty years of working with Christian students, families, public school teachers, and administrators would confirm this dissatisfaction. The considerable level of dissatisfaction with the present system will become glaringly apparent if parents are given financial freedom to choose the kind of education they want for their children. However, if state education moves back toward education and away from social engineering, epistemic naturalism, and undermining faith, the present frustration may measurably subside over time.

Using the constructive approach would mean that the supernatural aspects of religion would be portrayed in a manner that is respectful to the beliefs of its adherents. This would involve including reasons that the followers give for their major beliefs, even noting empirical evidence—if there is any—for their belief and then letting the students decide for themselves.[107] I do not believe religions are troubled by people not believing in their tenets as long as they are described in a constructive manner. The answer to the concern about so many different religions in the marketplace is, do not be concerned. Teach and honor the free exercise of all of them. The answer is not to banish them from education and keep only naturalism.

The constructive model shows appreciation for what its supporters believe their religion to be. This does not mean that weaknesses or abuses are not considered, but rather that they are assayed in a manner befitting of education without being used to reduce religion to a man-made or antiquated belief superseded by scientific naturalism. In addition, the problems

---

classmates will become Muslims," ibid.

105. Pedagogy used in reference to the methods of teaching (how to) in contrast to actual teaching or content being taught (what to teach).

106. For more on this, see Appendix B.

107. This might include empirical evidence concerning truth claims, historicity of primary documents, etc.

associated with a religion are evaluated proportionately to the history of the religion and in light of their primary documents.

For example, using the constructive model, if a teacher was considering Christianity in light of the Crusades, or Islam in light of modern Islamic terrorism, the teaching should be proportionate and consider whether or not it is a true representation of the religion by evaluating their teachings and actions in light of their primary documents—the New Testament and the Quran and Hadith, respectively. Religious issues should be taught and dealt with substantively; to do otherwise is to trivialize them. In handling them substantively, one will surely find areas of disagreement, and these areas should be given the same degree of respect afforded other disciplines where disagreement occurs.

Additionally, these events should be placed in context by considering valor, truth, the view of human life, and religion as vital and pervasive aspects of human thinking and existence. To marginalize the role of religion actually undermines state education and precludes it from fulfilling its lofty potential. Illustrative of this point, sociologist David Dressler notes the significance of Protestantism's teachings. "The humanitarianism of the 19th century stemmed from Protestant teachings in England and the United States. These teachings fostered attitudes that led to the abolition of slavery, better treatment of the indigent, prison reform, the introduction of probation and parole, factory legislation, the growth of the charities movement and other programs for human welfare."[108]

In education and school life, students must be allowed maximum freedom to express their views. In 2000, the U.S. Department of Education sent out a series of religious-liberty guidelines to every public school in the nation. These guidelines state: "Students may express their beliefs about religion in the form of homework, art-work and other written and oral assignments free of discrimination based on the religious content of their submissions. Such home and classroom work should be judged by ordinary academic standards of substance and relevance and against other legitimate pedagogical concerns identified by the school."[109]

There is not only widespread consensus concerning the need to incorporate more religion, there are also some significant resources available. *Religion in American Life* is a seventeen volume series written for young readers by leading scholars, the first work of this nature and magnitude for young readers. Published by Oxford University Press, "The six books that are already available cover such topics as the church and state, Jews,

---

108. Hobbs and Blank, *Sociology and the Human Experience*, 320.
109. Kickbush, "Religious Expression," par. 8.

Mormons, Orthodox Christians, Native American and African American religions. Titles to follow include 'Women and American Religion,' 'Alternative Religious Traditions' and 'Immigration and Religion.' Three books — on religion in Colonial America and in the 19th and 20th centuries — are grouped by chronology. Catholics, Muslims and Protestants are treated in three separate volumes. Three different authors are writing the one volume devoted to Buddhists, Hindus and Sikhs. The last of the 17 volumes will be an index and study guide."[110] Local school boards working with parents and citizens can adopt policies based on some of the resources available.

Therefore unless the state takes seriously its professional and ethical obligation to teach about religion in state schools, it will fail to provide the citizens an objective, first-class education and thereby forfeit the lofty potential of state education. Christians must seize whatever opportunities remain to bring the concept of faith, the supernatural, and absolutes back into the mainstream of education. Maybe we will never see a return to where it once was, but for the sake of the children and the cause of truth, we should seek to stem the tide of scientism in state education and society.

---

110. "Yale Professors Edit Textbook Series," par. 4.

4

Progressivism's Attack upon Faith through Sociology, Psychology, and Law

Protecting the Church from Culture in Order for the Church to Penetrate Culture

CONTEMPORARY AMERICAN SOCIETY IS unintelligible apart from recognizing past and present influences of Christianity. If one seeks to speak of the greatness of America, its uniqueness, liberty, or prosperity, apart from the influence of supernatural religion in general and Christianity in particular, that not only obfuscates the real reason for such greatness, it necessitates that other reasons be substituted like diversity, rugged individualism, human ingenuity, system of government, etc. However, such substitutions are untrue, as well as absolutely destructive to the importance of religion and will ultimately undermine religious freedom and thereby undermine the greatness of America.

This deemphasizing of Christianity's monumental role in America and the western world should greatly concern every pastor and Christian. For this burden is our stewardship responsibility of not taking for granted, nor losing through laziness or naiveté, the freedoms that have been graciously bestowed upon us by the grace of God and the great sacrifice of others. Even more importantly, we should not take lightly how that freedom directly relates to evangelism, missions, and making disciples, and how the erosion of that freedom will negatively affect our ability to carry out the Great Commission.

One would think the significant role of religious faith in contemporary life would be overwhelmingly obvious, and it would be if there were not an *a priori* commitment by the progressives to the belief that the metaphysical either does not exist or at least is not real knowledge like science and nature. Consequently, their faith in science as being the best provider of knowledge in all areas limits their studies and conclusions to that which is empirical, which means that even when they study humans, they explain humanness in only natural terms. Therefore, the reality of something more than nature, truly transcendent, is discounted, marginalized, distorted, and explained away. By real knowledge I mean that transcendent reality is knowable (albeit differently than empirical knowledge), and has marketplace, educational, and political value as demonstrated in the Declaration of Independence.

Faith in God is explained naturally as though there is the idea of faith but there is no real object of that faith. A scientific liberal granting some benefit to religious faith is merely pragmatic and offers only a semblance of granting reality to the faith that goes beyond a subjective existence. Quite often, the benefits are primarily viewed psychologically. When children have experienced the subtle and not so subtle undermining of faith throughout their education, which is based on scientism with all of its naturalistic corollaries, it becomes obvious why people, even Christians, think more in concert with modernism, postmodernism, or a personal blend of the two rather than biblically. The disquieting reality is that an occasional Christian teacher or fact cannot counter the impact of a system hostile to religious faith being anything beyond a Darwinian adaptive reality.

Therefore, it is essential to teach about faith as a reality, not merely a construct, and consider its influence in the past and its significance and influence upon contemporary life in order for students to understand present-day society and the contributions that emanate from religion and Christianity. However, as with history, the significance of religion in people's lives, national and world events, and its prevalence in culture is regularly ignored or marginalized, and religious phenomena are often explained reductively by social scientists. It is important to remember that these ideas must be substantively communicated from the pulpit to the pew or they merely become quips and quotes that will have no effect on curbing the present destructive course of modern education and its quest for the total privatization of religious faith. If the knowledge of what is happening and how to counter it does not become second nature to those on the front line, regardless of the plethora of sermons attacking progressivism, the evanescence of religious freedom will continue unabated.

The previous chapter focused on state schools and the historical and ethical basis for countering the current trend of rejecting religious teaching and minimizing the importance of religious faith. The present chapter will focus on the contemporary attack upon faith and most importantly, the freedom of religion and the importance of Christianity in today's society. I will then offer answers to the progressive and naturalist arguments. This contemporary attack is interwoven into sociology, psychology, and the legal opinion of the day, which results in unwarranted hostility from culture. Consider the following.

SOCIOLOGICAL DECONSTRUCTION OF RELIGIOUS FAITH

Robert Bellah, a social scientist, spells out the predilection of social scientists toward a worldview that affords no real place for religion in the equation of cultural events. He delineates and explains the underlying assumptions of mainstream social sciences.

> [By] positivism, reductionism, relativism, and determinism . . . I mean to refer only to, in the descriptive sense, their prejudices, their pre-judgments about the nature of reality. By positivism I mean no more than the assumption that the methods of natural science are the only approach to valid knowledge, and the corollary that social science differs from natural science only in maturity and that the two will become ever more alike. By reductionism I mean the tendency to explain the complex in terms of the simple and to find behind complex cultural forms biological, psychological or sociological drives, needs and interests. By relativism I mean the assumption that matters of morality and religion, being explicable by particular constellations of psychological and sociological conditions, cannot be judged true or false, valid or invalid, but simply vary with persons, cultures and societies. By determinism I do not mean any sophisticated philosophical view, but only the tendency to think that human actions are explained in terms of "variables" that will account for them.
>
> Religion, being unscientific, could have no reality claim in any case, though as a private belief or practice it may by some be admitted to be psychologically helpful for certain people . . . There is, of course no God . . . the social scientist says a lot about the 'self,' he has nothing to say about the soul. The very notion of soul entails a divine or cosmological context that is missing in modern thought . . . The traditional religious view found the world intrinsically meaningful . . . the modern view finds the

world intrinsically meaningless, endowed with meaning only by individual actors, and the societies they construct, for their own ends.[1]

Of course these ideas flow from naturalism, which is undergirded by Darwinian evolution. Many Christians are oblivious to the slide toward naturalism; much less do they realize their unwitting cooperation or at least their lack of offering a viable challenge. For example, it is common to hear Christians use descriptive terms used by social scientists to explain human behavior and either not realize or not care that they are replacing a biblical term with a naturalistic term, thereby changing, at least descriptively, the nature of humans and their behavior. Many Christians assume that sociologists use the term self as a synonym for soul, or it is at least inclusive of the immaterial aspect of man, when in fact the sociological use of the term has no provision for the immaterial.

Patrick McNamara, professor of sociology at the University of New Mexico, offers an insight into the reason social scientists give so little attention to religion. "Sociologists tend to see concern for personal challenge— e.g., to get one's own moral life in order—as somehow secondary to social challenge or the effort to identify and criticize those socioeconomic structures that inhibit the individual's own group from attaining a fuller human existence . . . In [the] typical social science analysis, the demands of the inner life are neglected and personal agency and autonomy exercised in the choice to examine one's own life and put it in order according to an internalized ethic of repentance . . . is not acknowledged."[2]

These ideas, that man is merely matter and all behavior is material in nature or epiphenomenal, derived from matter, can be understood only when one realizes the connection to biological evolution. This is why *some* scientists feel justified to study animal behavior and then apply all of their findings to human behavior because in reality, humans are human animals, which make them different in degree but not kind. Unfortunately, Christians use the term human animal all the time without realizing what it means to those in science. As mentioned in the last chapter, Edward L. Thorndike, a founder in educational psychology, derived his two behavioral laws that have profoundly influenced modern education from his study of animal behavior, believing that there was a strong enough connection between animals and humans that what one learned from animals could be applied

---

1. Smith, *Religion Matters*, 84–86.
2. McNamara, "The New Rights View," 449–458.

to humans.[3] Of course this type of thinking is at the heart of Darwinism. Darwin's assumed connection of such continues unabated.

Edward O. Wilson, Pulitzer prize-winning world authority on ants, sums up the naturalistic view well. "Religion itself is subject to the explanations of the natural sciences . . . The final decisive edge enjoyed by scientific naturalism will come from its capacity to explain traditional religion, its chief competitor, as a wholly material phenomenon."[4] The attempt of the naturalistic scientist is not merely to show connections between human behavior and the material aspects of man, but rather to demonstrate a causal or necessary relationship, ultimately reducing man to merely matter, instinctual with no real otherwise choice, and therefore making God created in the image of man rather than man created in the image of God. That is one of the reasons I have argued that the relativism of our day is not technically philosophical, but rather a by-product of the acceptance of science as the determiner of truth in every area, which requires open-endedness to every conclusion.

As Christians, we have no qualms about there being a connection between biology and behavior any more than we have difficulty with belief having an effect upon biology. While man is made up of the material and the immaterial, he is, by that composite, a human being and not two of something living together. In addition, to agree that genetics predisposes a person to certain diseases is not equivalent to concluding the same regarding behavior because man has a choice in morals, which he is often not afforded in physical infirmities. For example, when one is born without an arm there is no choice in the matter, whereas the command "obey your parents" in Ephesians 6:1 does provide the individual a choice. Moreover, Christians believe that man has been corrupted by the fall both materially and immaterially. Therefore, that we get diseases, etc., because of our faulty biology should not surprise anyone. However, that an alcoholic has a gene that is different or malfunctioning, which results in him being more likely, or biologically influenced, to become an alcoholic must be distinguished from being *efficiently* caused to become an alcoholic.

---

3. Encyclopedia Britannica 2005 (DVD), s.v., Edward L. Thorndike, "The law of effect stated that those behavioral responses that were most closely followed by a satisfactory result were most likely to become established patterns and to occur again in response to the same stimulus. The law of exercise stated that behaviour is more strongly established when the connection of stimulus and response has been more frequently made." See chapter 3 of this book for more information on Thorndike, his two laws, and his connection with other educational evolutionists.

4. Wilson, *On Human Nature*, 192.

Homosexuality provides another example. Even if it were discovered that homosexuals have a different gene than heterosexuals that would not demonstrate that homosexuality is desirable or normal. First, no such gene has been discovered even though there have been serious attempts at such discovery by those who advocate such. Second, if such a gene were found, it is highly improbable, if not virtually impossible, for one gene to be responsible for such since behavior is more complex than any one gene can account for, not to mention that such a view would entail an unprovable and excessively reductionistic view of man. Third, the discovery of a different gene would not tell us whether the effect of the gene is moral or immoral, normal or abnormal. We find biological peculiarities that predispose one to all kinds of things like cancer, heart disease, etc., which we do not deem to be good. Consequently, the mere presence of a different gene does not tell us whether the effect is good or bad.

When Christians fail to maintain the distinction between a biological connection and biological causality (Darwinian necessity) as it relates to human behavior, they are actually ridiculing their own faith based upon nothing more than the speculations of Darwinists. The Bible calls drunkenness a sin, which people need to avoid, turn from, repent of and be forgiven in order to avoid judgement, and many have already done so, 1 Corinthians 6:9–11. Now, if this is merely a biological issue, or is *caused* biologically like cancer or the flu, then it is a true sickness, for which one cannot—nor should one have to—seek forgiveness. It is simply a biological issue. Thus, what God calls on men to turn from, they cannot; they did not choose it. If they cannot choose to turn from it, God is either too cruel to be worthy of worship or simply an illusion.

Because of these biases, social scientists, naturalists, and those they influence often view religion as nothing more than a human construct. Therefore, they do not give due consideration to the truthfulness or reality of religious beliefs and the importance of them in the human experience. They seek to explain shifts in society from merely or primarily natural determinants. According to *Sociology and the Human Experience*, "Sociology is the scientific study of social interaction among human beings."[5] However, in its study, sociology seems unwilling to allow for the validity of the immaterial world, the religious genesis of much of the material or social phenomena, and all of the empirical evidence that might suggest the probability of the supernatural.

---

5. Hobbs and Blank, *Sociology*, 6–7.

PSYCHOLOGICAL MISDIAGNOSIS OF RELIGIOUS FAITH

Not only is this antipathy toward faith found in sociology, but in the medical field as well. First let me say that I do not mean everyone in the medical field has antipathy toward faith. Some in the medical field do have a strong personal faith, which they believe is more than a human construct. Rather, I mean the quest of much of modern medical science is to ultimately explain away any immaterial reality beyond what science can deal with. When science gives an answer or explanation for observed behavior, it is a scientific opinion that has varying degrees of probability, but it is not the final or even oftentimes a good answer. For example, sociologists may explain marriage as a necessary derivative arising from the need of society to manage itself. Psychologists may explain it as a psychological need to thwart loneliness by providing security and companionship similar to the needs of squirrels, dogs, and such. Nevertheless, that in no way means it is the best or right answer. A far better answer is that God created humans in his own likeness, and he is by nature relational, which is satisfied in the Trinity; consequently, commanding man and woman to marry and inscribing it into their spiritual and physical DNA.

Professor David Larson of Duke University Medical School draws attention to biases in mental health professions, similar to those found in sociology. He says, "Consider *The Diagnostic and Statistical Manual*, the standard reference manual for the classification of mental illnesses, which essentially defines the practice of psychiatrists, clinical psychology, and clinical social work and is central to the practice, research, and financing of these professions. In the third edition, *religious examples were used only as illustrations in discussions of mental illness, such as delusions, incoherence, and illogical thinking*. The latest edition has corrected this bias."[6] (italics added) The fourth edition was right to correct this misrepresentation, but it did not correct the bias of the community that placed it there and allowed it to stand for so many years.[7]

Allen J. Frances, MD, was chair of the DSM-4 Task Force and is professor emeritus of the department of psychiatry at Duke University School of Medicine. He wrote an article in *Psychology Today* which, although it does not seem to have been his intention, highlights the continued devaluing of religious faith in the DSM-5. Regarding the flawed developmental process of the DSM-5 he wrote, "This is no way to prepare or to approve a diagnostic

---

6. Larson and Larson, "The Forgotten Factor."
7. The DSM-5 was released May 2015.

system . . . [The] APA has proven itself incapable of producing a safe, sound, and widely accepted manual."[8] This level of dissatisfaction by such a qualified analyst should, at least, garner a healthy level of skepticism regarding the diagnosis and treatment of mental health issues that would otherwise be seen as issues of normalcy, religion, and choice. He poignantly notes the seriousness of adding new diagnoses, "New diagnoses in psychiatry are more dangerous than new drugs . . . Before their introduction, new diagnoses deserve the same level of attention to safety that we devote to new drugs. APA is not competent to do this."[9]

He gives his list of the DSM-5's ten most potentially harmful changes. Several of which, either by diagnosis or medicalized treatment, effectively undermine or are inherently dismissive of the *actual reality and importance* of religion. For example, Frances notes, "Normal grief will become Major Depressive Disorder, thus medicalizing and trivializing our expectable and necessary emotional reactions to the loss of a loved one and substituting pills and superficial medical rituals for the deep consolations of family, friends, [and] religion."[10] Consequently, faith (trusting God's love and presence) is no longer a viable and sufficient response to sadness, and the same can be said for many so-called disorders. Disorders do not require a savior or faith, but only a psychologist and a prescription. He says, "Excessive eating . . . is no longer . . . gluttony . . . DSM 5 has instead turned it into a psychiatric illness called Binge Eating Disorder."[11] With this, the DSM erases the sin of gluttony (as it has a long history of medicalizing sin) and the need for repentance.

Regarding normal responses or other behavioral problems he states, "DSM 5 has created a slippery slope by introducing the concept of Behavioral Addictions that eventually can spread to make a mental disorder of everything we like to do a lot. Watch out for careless overdiagnosis of internet and sex addiction and the development of lucrative treatment programs to exploit these new markets . . . Painful experience with previous DSM's teaches that if anything in the diagnostic system can be misused and turned into a fad, it will be. Many millions of people with normal grief, gluttony, distractibility, worries, reactions to stress, the temper tantrums of childhood, the forgetting of old age, and 'behavioral addictions' will soon be mislabeled as psychiatrically sick and given inappropriate treatment."[12] An-

---

8. Frances, "DSM 5 Is Guide Not Bible," par. 8.
9. Ibid., par. 9.
10. Ibid., par. 12.
11. Ibid., par. 15.
12. Ibid., par. 18.

other example is the *Minnesota Multiphasic Personality Inventory (MMPI)*, "one of the most widely used of all psychological tests . . . All the positive religion-connected traits—self-discipline, altruism, humility, obedience to authority, conventional morality—are weighted negatively . . . Conversely, several traits that religious people would regard as diminishing themselves, at least in some situations—self-assertion, self-expression, and a high opinion of oneself—are weighted positively."[13]

Albert Ellis, Executive Director of the Institute for Rational-Emotive Therapy (RET), says concerning "devout or pious religionists, or devotees of religiosity . . . It is my contention that both pietistic theists and dogmatic secular religionists—like virtually all people imbued with intense religiosity and fanaticism—tend to be emotionally disturbed."[14] Ellis teaches that the concepts such as "certain people are evil, wicked and villainous, and should be punished" and "you need something other or stronger or greater than yourself to rely on" are irrational beliefs. This conclusion makes anyone irrational who takes his faith seriously because these kinds of beliefs are essential to orthodox Christianity and many other supernatural religions. In addition, if a person with strong religious beliefs takes the RET Beliefs Inventory, the test results will indicate that the believer has some irrational beliefs, which in RET is a problem to be corrected.[15]

Add to this the profound role that psychology plays in developing the curriculum and pedagogy of state education; that it is also ostensibly based on science, and that knowledge of God is subjective, lacking any objective evidence, or knowable in any real way by the population at large, and you begin to get an idea of how destructive secular psychology can be and pervasively is. Remember Freud and his successors, psychoanalysts, psychologists, and even counselors like Carl Rogers, Ellis, etc., have basically atheistic (or humanistic) theories.

Psychology and psychiatry have been and presently are on a path of ever-expanding their domain. This is done by developing new syndromes to explain certain behaviors or constellations of behaviors. Psychiatrist and philosopher Irwin Savodnik of UCLA wrote an article for the *LA Times* entitled, "Psychiatry's sick compulsion: turning weaknesses into diseases." He highlights the American Psychiatric Association's ever expanding list of "illnesses."

---

13. Fagan, *Why Religion Matters*, 22.
14. Ellis and Blau, *The Albert Ellis Reader*, 251.
15. This is based on the RET *Beliefs Inventory* I have from Henderson State University, where I attended graduate school to obtain an MS in Counseling.

> IT'S JAN. 1. Past time to get your inoculation against seasonal affective disorder, or SAD—at least according to the American Psychiatric Assn. As Americans rush to return Christmas junk, bumping into each other in Macy's and Best Buy, the psychiatric association ponders its latest iteration of feeling bad for the holidays. And what is the association selling? Mental illness. With its panoply of major depression, dysthymic disorder, bi-polar disorder and generalized anxiety disorder, the association is waving its . . . flag to remind everyone that amid all the celebration, all the festivities, all the exuberance, many people will "come down with" or "contract" or "develop" some variation of depressive illness.[16]

This may seem somewhat humorous, and that is the way it is perceived by many, including many in the Christian community, at least at first. Actually, it is another move to bring human behavior under the ever-expanding domain of science. If all of the troubles associated with mere human weaknesses or problems in behavior or thinking are treated as a mental illness or disorder, then that falls under the domain of science, and science affords only natural explanations and cures; therefore, the rampant secularizing of every *truly* spiritual issue results in the perceived absence of sin, something that can only be addressed spiritually. The spiritual truth is, if people are sad after Christmas, it may be that their sadness is because of a spiritual need, loss of love, guilt about sin, etc., which can only be thoroughly addressed by Christ.

Savodnik then shows how the Association has capitalized on turning normal human weaknesses, some of which we might label as sin, into medical diseases.

> The association specializes in turning ordinary human frailty into disease. In the last year, ads have been appearing in psychiatric journals about possible treatments for shyness, a "syndrome" not yet officially recognized as a disease. You can bet it will be in the next edition of the Diagnostic and Statistical Manual of Mental Disorders, or DSM-IV, published by the association. As it turns out, the association has been inventing mental illnesses for the last 50 years or so. The original diagnostic manual appeared in 1952 and contained 107 diagnoses and 132 pages, by my count. The second edition burst forth in 1968 with 180 diagnoses and 119 pages. In 1980, the association produced a 494-page tome with 226 conditions. Then, in 1994, the manual

---

16. Savodnik "Psychiatry's sick compulsion."

exploded to 886 pages and 365 conditions, representing a 340% increase in the number of diseases over 42 years.[17]

The DSM-5 has expanded to 947 pages.[18] The number of conditions does not seem to have increased even though new ones have been added. Robin S. Rosenberg explains, "One way to add new diagnoses . . . but not increase the total is to make a disorder in a previous edition into a "subtype" of another disorder in the new edition, thereby keeping two diagnostic entities, but with one subsumed under another."[19] The Citizens Commission on Human Rights (CCHR) is a mental health watchdog. The following quotes from CCHR regarding the lack of objective criteria for diagnosing mental illness serve as a reminder that while there certainly is a place for psychiatry, its ever-expanding presence is more philosophical than scientific.

> Despite more than two hundred years of intensive research, no commonly diagnosed psychiatric disorders have proven to be either genetic or biological in origin, including schizophrenia, major depression, manic-depressive disorder, the various anxiety disorders, and childhood disorders such as attention-deficit hyperactivity. At present there are no known biochemical imbalances in the brain of typical psychiatric patients—until they are given psychiatric drugs — Peter Breggin, psychiatrist.
>
> [While] there has been no shortage of alleged biochemical explanations for psychiatric conditions . . . not one has been proven. Quite the contrary. In every instance where such an imbalance was thought to have been found, it was later proven false — Dr. Joseph Glenmullen, Harvard Medical School psychiatrist.
>
> The theories are held on to not only because there is nothing else to take their place, but also because they are useful in promoting drug treatment — Dr. Elliott Valenstein, PhD, author of *Blaming the Brain*.
>
> No claim for a gene for a psychiatric condition has stood the test of time, in spite of popular misinformation — Dr. Joseph Glenmullen, Harvard Medical School psychiatrist.[20]

Expanding the definitions of disorders or mental illnesses results in what was normal becoming abnormal, and, therefore, more and more

17. Savodnik "Psychiatry's sick compulsion."

18. Begley, "Psychiatrists' 'Bible' Finally Unveiled." This article also includes the lack of biological science behind the diagnosis and other problems.

19. Rosenberg, "Abnormal Is the New Normal."

20. CCHR International, "The difference between a medical diagnosis and a psychiatric diagnosis."

people are classified as needing psychological treatment and prescriptions. The most alarming thing about this trend is that Christians seem to be largely unaware of the pervasiveness and consequences of such changes in culture, their perspective, receptivity to the gospel, and the church.

Regrettably, I am quite aware that many if not most pastors are equally unaware, or at least uninterested in countering it, because many of them have incorporated the terminology into their sermons or counseling, or have simply ignored the issue except for occasional jabs or quotes. They have unfortunately underestimated the constant erosion of the believability of the gospel and God, or even a context to consider God's relevance. The disastrous effect of shifting from the moral model to the medical model as the cause and treatment of behavioral problems emanates from expanding science beyond its legitimate domanial authority, the supposed adequacy of science to know what needs to be known or can be known, and Darwinian descent as an all-encompassing paradigm for life. As a result, it leads us further down the road of practical determinism, shunning responsibility, and curing behavioral problems pharmacologically. For example, today in many circles, the answer of choice for troublesome, overactive little boys is not discipline, but rather medication-induced docility.

This excessive application of the medical model goes hand in hand with sociology's reductionistic view that every norm, moral, or spiritual concept is merely a social or human construct, is based on man as an animal, and is, consequently, merely matter generated and instinctual. This view has a profound impact on education, politics, law, and the place for religious faith and answers. I am not arguing against the diseasing of sin out of a fear of Christianity losing its place in culture; rather I am arguing against it because it is wrong and because the eternal impact of not dealing with sin, regardless of popular opinion, is of immeasurable consequence. State education since Spencer, Thorndike, Hall, and Dewey has been ostensibly based on science—though more truthfully it has been based on scientism—and the natural order of things, and we are simply seeing that basis become the basis of everything through the primary impact of progressive education.

This redefinition of both the problem and the cures changes the conscience of a nation because it changes the conscience of individual human beings. It seems that the conscience is not an absolute, but rather it is developed by the standards and knowledge that are deposited into it. If one is taught the Scripture and God's love and law, the conscience convicts (although inconsistently because of the fall) based on that standard. If the conscience is built upon other standards of right and wrong, good and bad, or defining behavior, it will respond to that input. The eventuation of which is not merely that people do not *feel* that stealing or divorce is wrong but that they don't *believe* it is and therefore, they experience little or no guilt from such behavior. Without the bad news of sin, the good news of the gospel is unintelligible.

It seems obvious that *many* state educators conceive of religion as archaic or inconsequential. Sociologists presume religion to be the result of human choices and societal variables, while psychology deems its value at best therapeutic for some, and at worst leading to irrational beliefs or illustrative of disorders. Moreover, it appears that these opinions are, at least in large part, a consequence of state education's unconditional acceptance of naturalism as the determiner of real knowledge. This acceptance cultivated an environment that is conducive to normalizing the obfuscation of the positive role and traits of religion while concomitantly magnifying the negative; thus, leaving in its wake a privatized religion, having no public, educational, cultural, or legal value as a source of answers, knowledge, or morals, thereby banished from the public and legal mind. Moreover, rather than the First Amendment being seen as it was designed to be, a protector of the free exercise of religion including evangelism and proselytizing in the public square, it is changed into the super guardian for separating the church from influencing anything to do with the state. It transforms a religiously vibrant public square into a religiously sterile public square—a religious guillotine of sorts.

The members of my immediate family have attended a total of seven state colleges and universities in four states. We have found the denigration of religion to be, with the exception of a few professors, universal. My wife graduated in December 2004 from a state university with a degree in primary education. Additionally, we have a pretty sizable group of college students in our church every semester who attend a state university, and with the exception of a few professors, regardless of the subject—history, sociology, psychology, religion, geology, biology, etc., the students' faith is undermined and marginalized.

On August 23, 1984, President Reagan addressed an Ecumenical Prayer Breakfast in Dallas, Texas.

> I believe that faith and religion play a critical role in the political life of our nation—and always has . . . And this has worked to our benefit as a nation . . . Those who are attacking religion claim they are doing it in the name of tolerance, freedom, and open-mindedness. Question: Isn't the real truth that they are intolerant of religion? They refuse to tolerate its importance in our lives. If all the children of our country studied together all of the many religions in our country, wouldn't they learn greater tolerance of each other's beliefs? . . . We establish no religion in

this country, nor will we ever. We command no worship. We mandate no belief. But we poison our society when we remove its theological underpinnings. We court corruption when we leave it bereft of belief. All are free to believe or not believe; all are free to practice a faith or not. But those who believe must be free to speak of and act on their belief, to apply moral teaching to public questions.[21]

LEGAL CURTAILMENTS OF RELIGIOUS EXPRESSION

Over the last sixty-seven years there have been some significant legal decisions that have had a devastating impact upon the freedom of Americans to practice, voice, and express their Christian faith in the marketplace of ideas, particularly upon government or public property, including but not limited to, state schools. While this has been argued from the First Amendment and the Constitution, it is actually eroding the First Amendment. This section is not intended to present an exhaustive look at all the different legal cases of the twentieth century that have resulted in removing religious influence from where it once flourished, but rather simply to give the following as one of the most, if not the most, significant Supreme Court cases as an example. This will also provide an understanding of the historical and constitutional understanding of religious expression and the First Amendment, and the contemporary distortion of the same.

In the 1947 Everson v. Board of Education case (1947—330 U.S.1), the Supreme Court applied the establishment clause to the states for the first time. It also imbued this guarantee with a firm separationist reading. Justice Hugo Black's words for the *Everson* majority have served as a benchmark for deciding establishment cases: "The establishment of religion clause [of the First Amendment] means at least this: Neither *a state* nor the federal government may set up a church. Neither can pass laws that aid one religion, *aid all religions*, or prefer one religion over another.... In the words of Jefferson, the clause against establishment of religion by law was intended to erect 'a wall of separation between church and state.'"[22] (italics added)

---

21. Reagan, "Remarks at an Ecumenical Prayer Breakfast."

22. "Establishment clause overview." par. 4. Black also used the words "high and impregnable" (see *Everson*, 330 U.S. at 18), which Jefferson did not use, Dreisbach, *Thomas Jefferson*, 125. Fences were a common sight in New England, but they were not "high and impregnable." Black's wall has been called an iron curtain, when it should have been seen as a line or a wall between neighbors, ibid., 92. The Supreme Court has de-historicized the phrase and thereby made it merely mechanical rather than organic, ibid., 123.

This was the first time Jefferson's phrase "wall of separation" was applied to states and expanded by the wording of a legal decision.[23] Justice Hugo Black elevated Jefferson's wall of separation "to [an] authoritative gloss on the First Amendment religion provisions."[24] This ruling opened the door for a host of lawsuits against states and provided legal recourse for excessively delimiting the theretofore freedom and influence of religion in our culture.

Although Black relied on Jefferson's wall, he actually modified Jefferson's wall, which, as related to the First Amendment, prohibited the federal government from restricting freedom of conscience in religion by prohibiting the Congress from making any laws that established a national church, or in any way limited free exercise of religious opinions or infringed upon the state's right to determine such matters. Black's modification encroaches upon states' rights and limits free exercise. The difference between Black's and Jefferson's wall is clear when one compares Black's words to Jefferson's second inaugural address March 4, 1805, and the fact that as governor of Virginia he gave a proclamation appointing a day of "publick and solemn thanksgiving and prayer" in November 1779.[25]

Law professor Daniel L. Dreisbach explains:

> By incorporating the First Amendment nonestablishment provision into the due process clause of the Fourteenth Amendment, Black's wall separates religion and civil government at all levels—federal, state, and local. Thus, a barrier originally designed, as a matter of federalism, to separate the national and state governments, and thereby to preserve state jurisdiction in matters pertaining to religion, was transformed into an instrument of the federal judiciary to invalidate policies and programs of state and local authorities. By extending its prohibitions to state and local jurisdictions, Black turned the First Amendment, as ratified in 1791, on its head."[26]

The First Amendment clearly restricted government, because it explicitly forbids making laws—"congress shall make no law"—which only

---

23. The first time Jefferson was quoted in a Supreme Court case was in the 1878 case of *Reynolds v. United States*, stating that Jefferson's term "wall of separation between church and state" "may be accepted almost as an authoritative declaration of the scope and effect of the [First] Amendment." Cited in Dreisbach, *Thomas Jefferson*, 1. However, 1947 was the first time it was applied to states and expanded by the wording of the decision.

24. Dreisbach, *Thomas Jefferson*, 4.

25. Ibid., 137, Appendix 4.

26. Ibid., 125–26.

government, and in this case federal government, can do. The wall metaphor restricts both religion and government, which is not what the First Amendment was intended to do.[27]

Even the use of Jefferson's wall is inherently flawed for several reasons. First, one may rightly ask why use Jefferson as the sole interpreter of the First Amendment? His wall metaphor was not used until ten years after the adoption of the First Amendment; consequently, Jefferson's wall was not even considered in making or ratifying the First Amendment. Secondly, why should any one citizen's opinion or words replace the opinion and words adopted by all of the people, and why focus on the words of someone who was not at the Constitutional Convention or in the country when the First Amendment was adopted? Third, why allow a metaphor to displace the powerful wording of the First Amendment, especially when the metaphor is inadequate to capture the full breadth of the First Amendment? And since Black's use of the phrase, we can offer a fourth and fifth reason why it should not be used. Fourth, Black de-historicized the phrase, both in its imagery—fences were neither high nor impregnable in New England at the time that Jefferson used the phrase—and its conceptual context, as it was a phrase used in correspondence with Baptists, and thereby distorted its original meaning. Fifth, while he relied upon Jefferson's metaphor, he expanded the applicability of it and the First Amendment beyond what Jefferson or the Founders intended, and thereby reconceptualized the First Amendment. As ratified by the people, the First Amendment was to protect individuals and states' rights against the intrusion of the federal government, and that is why the First Amendment reads, "Congress shall make no law."

Therefore, it is crucial when discussing the First Amendment to use First Amendment wording rather than a flawed metaphor. Further, it is important to recognize that the phrase a wall of separation does not appear in the Declaration of Independence or the Constitution, but as quoted by Justice Black, came from a letter that Thomas Jefferson had written to a group of Baptists in Danbury, Connecticut.[28] The imagery of a wall of separation was actually in use prior to Jefferson and so it is wise to find out how it had been used in the context of religious freedom in America, and this is particularly important in light of the fact that Jefferson used it while corresponding to Baptists, who had felt the brunt of government persecution in America. The phrase had a theological genesis as opposed to the modern supposed deistic, constitutional, or secular genesis.

---

27. Ibid., 92.
28. Kennedy and Newcombe, *What If Jesus*, 75.

Roger Williams, a clergyman, staunch advocate of religious freedom, and "founder of Rhode Island" used the phrase before Jefferson.[29] Therefore, before looking at Jefferson's use of the phrase, one needs to be familiar with how Williams used it. In order to understand the metaphor, one has to understand the man and the times. Williams was a Puritan who eventually separated from the Church of England, became a Baptist in 1639 for a short time, and later became a seeker.[30] Unlike his Puritan brothers in Massachusetts, Williams adamantly rejected the idea that the civil authorities had any jurisdiction over the church or spiritual matters. "Therefore he declared that the state should not undertake to punish such purely religious offenses as idolatry, blasphemy, heresy, or Sabbath-breaking. No attempt should be made to maintain religious conformity by law; nor should civil penalties be imposed on sinful persons. The entire religious realm should be removed from the sphere of competence of the state."[31] These views kept him in constant conflict with the Puritan leaders, and Williams was banished in 1635 from the jurisdiction of the Bay colony.[32]

The theological basis for a wall of separation grew out of Williams' understanding of the church being based on the New Testament model instead of the Old Testament with theocratic Israel as the model. "Drawing upon the analogy of Eden, he spoke of the church or community of the faithful as a garden. Beyond its bounds lay the wilderness of the sinful world from which the garden was preserved by a *wall of separation*. Should the *wall be breached, weeds from the wilderness would invade the garden and choke off its flowers.*"[33] (italics added) Notice that a breach in the wall allowed the wilderness—government—into the garden—church, and not the other way around, which is the same idea expressed in the First Amendment by the words, "Congress shall make no law respecting an establishment of religion, or prohibiting the free exercise thereof; or abridging the freedom of speech, or of the press; or the right of the people peaceably to assemble, and to petition the Government for a redress of grievances."

Williams' basis for this grew out of his belief in the corruption of man. He did not believe in government coercion of the unregenerate in order to cause them to believe in the teachings of Christ, the declaration of an official state church, taxation of citizens to pay ministers, or use of civil power to assure religious conformity or preserve the church from doctrinal error.

---

29. Persons, *American Minds*, 53.
30. Ibid.
31. Ibid., 52.
32. Ibid.
33. Ibid., 54.

Williams said, "So far as the natural man was corrupt and sinful, the power of the magistrate must be the power of Satan. How could the protection of the church safely be entrusted to such a power?"[34] Therefore, the wall of separation was a separation of institutions so that the government or world, "wilderness," would not corrupt the church, "garden."

Stow Persons sums up Williams' influence.

> In later times, when it became the fashion to extol Williams for his principles of liberty of conscience and the separation of church and state, his fame was celebrated by liberals who would break the remaining shackles of official religious power over the state. But it was *precisely the opposite situation* that had concerned Williams. *It was the release of religion from the incubus of state control for which he contended.* Why? Because the state was the instrument of natural men. It was the wilderness, evil, and the domain of the devil. It tended, therefore, in the nature of things to be corrupt. It was the corruption of the church by the world that stood out in Williams' mind as the great fact of modern history"[35] (italics added)

Therefore, in Williams' original figurative expression, the wall was not to protect the wilderness—government and world—from the garden—church—but the very opposite. A cursory reading of his books on the subject evidences this.

In Williams' book, *The Bloudy [Bloody] Tenent of Persecution for Cause of Conscience,* he gives twelve theses that are developed in the book as he engages the Puritan John Cotton concerning the freedom of conscience. To summarize them, numbers one through four are against people being persecuted by the government because of their religious faith, or as he puts it, "persecution for conscience sake . . . is not required nor accepted by Jesus Christ the Prince of Peace." Numbers five and eight through eleven specifically address the role of states, which is civil not spiritual, and in Williams' words, over "bodies and goods, not souls and spirits." Numbers eight through ten use the phrase "enforced uniformity of religion" to argue against the civil state forcing people to embrace a certain religion that "is the greatest occasion of . . . ravishing of conscience . . . and destruction of millions of souls." Number eleven argues that freedom of conscience to worship contrary to the state results in the good of the civil state through "uniformity of civil obedience." Numbers six and seven give the theological basis for his position, which is that the Old Testament state of Israel is not

---

34. Ibid., 57.
35. Ibid., 59.

the pattern to be followed since the coming of Jesus Christ. The pattern is "permission of the most paganish, Jewish, Turkish, or anti-Christian consciences and worships be granted to all . . . and they are only to be fought against with . . . the sword of God's Spirit, the Word of God." Number twelve declares, "True civility and Christianity may both flourish in a state or kingdom, notwithstanding the permission of divers and contrary consciences, either of Jew or Gentile."[36]

In summary, Williams said that laws "concerning only the bodies and goods of such and such religious persons, I confess are merely civil."[37] Whereas, state laws concerning religion that required obedience in areas such as worship, belief, church governance, etc., are "far from reason."[38] Sometimes he referred to the domain of the church as the first tablet, and the government as the second tablet—referring to the first four and the last six, respectively, of the Ten Commandments.

The real issue today concerning the wall of separation is obscured when it is forgotten that Williams argued against the government passing laws that required obedience in areas covered by the first tablet. It was not merely the government doing something like allowing prayers at school games, but rather that they would require everyone to pray or suffer due penalty. The loss of historical context is seen clearly in the words that are used. Today, when religious symbols or words are used in public forums, people claim a violation of church and state because someone: is embarrassed, does not agree, is potentially influenced, feels peer pressure, is uncomfortable, inconvenienced, asked or called upon. In contrast, Williams used words like persecution, forced, violated, constrained, bloody act of violence, rape, commandeer, violent, imprisonment, banishment, compel, molest, kill, and devour.[39] Note the words in the title of his book, *Bloudy* [Bloody] and *Persecution*, and he wrote another book, *The Bloudy Tenent Yet More Bloudy*.

He and the Baptists fought so that everyone could practice their religion according to the dictates of their own conscience without being prosecuted by the government for violation of the law. They were not fighting to remove every vestige of religion from government or public life, regardless

---

36. Williams, *Bloudy Tenent*, 3–4.
37. Ibid., 156.
38. Ibid., 156–57.
39. Ibid. The use of the words mentioned can be seen in context on the following pages: persecution, 11; forced, 146; violated, 6; constrained, 6; bloody act of violence, 7; rape, 7; commandeer, 14; violent, 14; imprisonment, 15; banishment, 15; compel, 15; molest, 14; kill, 17; devour, 17.

how inconvenient it is for citizens. They fought for freedom of conscience, not freedom of comfort.

This fact is further demonstrated by Williams' service as the president of Rhode Island for three years beginning in 1654,[40] along with his public ridicule of the Quakers' beliefs and practices, finding them unfit for certain public offices because of their religious beliefs like pacifism, which would, in his estimation, make them poor governors.[41] Despite Williams' adamant disagreement with the Quakers' teaching and his conviction that their beliefs made them unfit for certain public offices, consistent with his wall of separation he would not allow government to punish them for their beliefs. They were free to worship according to their conscience. "Williams himself linked religion to morals, and he expected magistrates in Rhode Island to enforce the second table of the Ten Commandments," because Williams believed that the second table of the Ten Commandments, Exodus 20:12–17, was appropriate for civil law, but the first table, Exodus 20:1–11, was not.[42] He clearly understood that the second table, the last six of the Ten Commandments, dealt with human relationships and interactions whereas the first four were personal. Even the first four could be expressed, valued, in public but not forced.

Williams referred to the second table as "the doctrine of the civil state" and the first table as "the spiritual doctrine of Christianity."[43] Therefore, the commandments dealing with men's bodies, relationships, and things, e.g., adultery, lying, or stealing could become civil laws, but the first four commandments dealing with a person's relationship and choice to worship God or not worship God or worship a different God than everyone else could not become civil law that citizens were required to obey or be punished. This distinction between the first and second tablet was a belief that was shared by others like John Leland, a Baptist preacher, who "emerged a leader among the Commonwealth's Baptists. He was instrumental in allying the Baptists with Jefferson and Madison in the bitter Virginia struggle to disestablish the Anglican Church and to secure *freedom for religious dissenters.*"[44] (italics added) According to L.H. Butterfield, Leland "was as courageous and resourceful a champion of the rights of *conscience* as America has produced."[45] (italics added) Leland, who allied with the Baptists, supported

40. Kramnick and Moore, *Godless Constitution,* 53.
41. Ibid., 58.
42. Ibid., 60.
43. Williams, *Bloudy Tenent,* 146
44. Dreisbach, *Thomas Jefferson,* 13
45. Butterfield, "Elder John Leland,"157.

Jefferson because of his commitment to "the rights of *conscience.*"[46] (italics added)

The distinction between the two tables or rights of conscience did not refer to separating religious beliefs from politics, but rather allowed one to be able to believe according to one's own conscience without governmental interference. Leland celebrated Jefferson's election from his pulpit. He preached in a congressional church service January 3, 1802, and Jefferson attended.[47] By conscience, Leland and others referred to the first tablet of the Ten Commandments as Williams did. Conscience refers to 'opinions' referred to by Jefferson and the Danbury Baptists in their correspondence. Jefferson said, "The legitimate powers of government reach actions only and not opinions." The Baptists said, "The legitimate power of civil government extends no further than to punish the man who works ill to his neighbor."[48] These refer to the same things as Williams did when he referred to the second tablet.

Jefferson said, "The legitimate powers of government extend to such acts only as are injurious to others . . . the opinions of men are not the object of civil government nor under its jurisdiction."[49] Tablet one dealt with worship and opinions, and the second with relations toward other men, which was appropriate for civil law as distinguished by Williams. Leland said, "Government has no more to do with the religious opinions of men, than it has with the principles of mathematics. Let every man speak freely without fear, maintain the principles that he believes, worship according to this own faith, either one God, three Gods, no God or twenty Gods; and let government protect him in so doing, i.e., see that he meets with no personal abuse, or loss of property, for his religious opinions."[50]

More evidence that Williams did not intend to create a secular public square is that: "in pursuit of his political aims, Williams spent much of his time lobbying members of Parliament."[51] Roger Williams' religious views formed his political views and actions, like establishing Rhode Island "with the famous guarantee of religious liberty."[52] Williams named the place where he purchased the land from the Indians, Providence, "in a sense of

---

46. Morais, "Life and Words," 44–50.
47. Dreisbach, *Thomas Jefferson*, 10.
48. See the full text of these letters in Appendixes D and E.
49. Dreisbach, 133–35, 182.
50. Leland, *The Writings*, 184.
51. Groves, Preface, *Bloudy Tenent*, vii.
52. Torbet, *A History of the Baptists*, 202.

God's merciful Providence to me in my distress."[53] He said of oaths, "An oath may be spiritual though taken about earthly business."[54] "Civil government is an ordinance of God, to conserve the civil peace of people so far as concerns their bodies and goods . . . and foundation of civil power lies in the people."[55] Therefore, one cannot legitimately use the argument of separation of church and state to exclude or limit religious involvement in public life because the argument is based on a religious argument from Roger Williams, as demonstrated by Williams' responses to John Cotton in the *Bloudy Tenent*.

Liberal scholars like Kramnick and Moore in the *Godless Constitution* express confusion by what they believe are Williams' inconsistencies. They seem unable to reconcile Williams, the great protector of religious freedom, bringing his religious views into public life. Of course Kramnick and Moore's confusion actually arises out of trying to read a modern day secularized use of Jefferson's phrase back into history. They erroneously conclude that Williams gave a "prescription for a godless politics."[56] This is a misreading of Williams. He did not seek to create a secular square where religious input, morals, ideas, and accommodation were not welcome. To their credit, Kramnick and Moore do acknowledge that when people take religion seriously "religion can never be private, in the sense of irrelevant to public issues."[57]

Williams clearly did bring his religious views into the public square. There is a categorical difference between having the government establish official required religious obedience and the government being influenced by the views of the people, whether religious or non-religious. There are some beliefs held by religious people that they believe are good for all of society; therefore, they should vote and encourage others to vote accordingly, e.g., marriage between a man and a woman, and that murder and stealing are wrong. This is not promoting religion, but rather recognizing the right to allow religious people the same public rights as non-religious people. Even if a person will only vote for a person of a certain religious or non-religious persuasion, that has no bearing on violating the principle of the church and the state being separate. Free exercise of religion must include the freedom for a Christian to pray in public, and an atheist the freedom not to pray, a Christian official to speak about his faith and an atheist

---

53. Gaustad, Historical Introduction, *Bloudy Tenent*, xxiii.
54. Williams, *Bloudy Tenent*, 157.
55. Ibid., 154.
56. Kramnick and Moore, *Godless Constitution*, 61.
57. Ibid., 60.

the freedom to speak about his atheism. It is not freedom of religion when the public square is silent about religion, for then the voice of the secularist mutes the First Amendment.

It seems that William's message could be summarized as: the wall of separation would be breached if the church and state were to become so intertwined that the state passes laws regarding the first tablet, which required observance or punishment by the state. For Williams, this would be the bloody persecution of conscience. This reminds us that just because a belief is religious, or emanates from faith, does not mean that it has no place in the public square. Some, like William G. McLoughlin, have argued that Williams' work and view on the wall of separation had no influence upon the Founders. Others, like Loren P. Beth, have argued that while Jefferson may not have been directly familiar with Williams' writings, one cannot therefore conclude that the Founders did not know his doctrines. Men like Jefferson were quite familiar with Baptist views on religious liberty; some argue that Williams had an indirect influence upon men like John Locke and Isaac Backus.[58]

In addition, Williams was the first on American soil to argue for total freedom of conscience; he founded Rhode Island on this basis. Jefferson was well aware of the Baptist's same belief in freedom of conscience. They fought with him for the disestablishment of the church of Virginia and supported his religious freedom views, without which he may well not have been elected. Often we are influenced by people's views indirectly and only learn later who that person was. Moreover, if one takes into consideration the Christian milieu of the time, it makes perfect sense that Jefferson was aware of Baptist teachings in this area.

Of course many seek to marginalize the influence of Christianity upon our founding, in spite of the evidence. Even those arguing for A Godless Constitution say, "Those who crafted American national government as a secular institution called upon two traditions. They use the strong vision of separate spiritual and worldly realms found in the American religious

---

58. Dreisbach, in *Thomas Jefferson*, quoting others in pages 208–209 demonstrates in footnote 44 that many like Perry Miller and William G. McLoughlin have concluded that Williams's works had no influence upon the Founders. However, Loren P. Beth said, "It is probably true that Madison and Jefferson were not familiar with the writings of Roger Williams, yet it does not follow that they did not know his doctrines. They were exceedingly familiar with Baptist views on religious liberty which had been expressed in hundreds of petitions and memorials presented to the state legislature. It is perfectly possible that some of their ideas stemmed thus indirectly from Williams." Beth, *American Theory*, 65. David Little argues "Williams indirectly influenced the American struggle for religious liberty in the founding era through John Locke and Isaac Backus." Little, "Roger Williams and the Separation," 7–16.

thought of Roger Williams and the Baptists of the founding era."[59] In laying out their case for a godless constitution, they refer to Williams' influence upon the Constitution when they refer to Roger Williams, John Locke, and Thomas Jefferson as "proponents" who arose out of "religious and secular sources." In addition they point to the influence of American Baptists in like manner.[60] As stated earlier, I adamantly disagree with their understanding of this influence, but what is being argued here is the significance of the influence.

Williams never believed that a Christian left his morals or Christianity in the garden when he went into the wilderness. He knew the church had to go into the world in order to follow Christ, Matthew 5:13–16; 28:18–20. Those who seek to exclude religious views from public debate assert that religion is exclusively private; however, while religion in general and Christianity in particular is very personal, it is not merely private. In fact, it is actually very public. The New Testament calls on Christians to follow Christ in private and public, Matthew 10:16. Williams' chief priority was the purity of the church, and his concern for government was a derivative of that priority. However, when he did concern himself with the government, he did so as a Christian.

Now concerning Jefferson's use of the phrase, the wall of separation, Dreisbach comments that one cannot begin to understand the phrase "apart from the extraordinary political milieu in which Jefferson wrote it."[61] At the time of the elections, "religion . . . was an important element in the political strife."[62] The phrase appears in Jefferson's response to a congratulatory letter he received from the Danbury Baptists.[63] He used the occasion of the missive "first, to broadcast a 'condemnation of the alliance between church and state, under the authority of the Constitution' and, second, to explain why he declined to follow his presidential predecessors in issuing proclamations for public fastings and thanksgivings."[64] Additionally, it is often

59. Kramnick and Moore, *Godless Constitution,* 24.
60. Ibid.
61. Dreisbach, *Thomas Jefferson*, 42.
62. Parton, *Life of Thomas Jefferson*, 570.
63. See the congratulatory letter in Appendix D, Jefferson's response in Appendix E, and a comparison of Four Texts relative to the phrase *the Wall of Separation between Church and State* in Appendix F.
64. Dreisbach, *Thomas Jefferson*, 43. The Congregationalists and Federalists had been railing Jefferson as an atheist because he did not proclaim days of fasting as his predecessors had. Even though this was part of the reason Jefferson responded, he eventually omitted the words that dealt specifically with this based on counsel from Attorney General Levi Lincoln. Actually Lincoln recommended modifying it, but Jefferson deleted the words, possibly fearing it would offend some of his Republican

erroneously stated that the Baptists had asked him to proclaim such things as fast days, but actually they did not. Jefferson says to Attorney General Levi Lincoln concerning the letter from the Danbury Baptists, "It furnishes an occasion . . . of saying why I do not proclaim fastings and thanksgivings . . . the address to be sure does not point at this, and it's [sic] introduction is awkward. But I foresee no opportunity of doing it more pertinently."[65]

Generally, Baptists, dissenters, and Republicans were supporters of Jeffersonian Republicanism because of his emphasis on religious freedom, and the New England Congregationalists, establishment clergy, and Federalists were not Jeffersonian supporters because of their belief in a stronger relationship between state and church. In the letter to the Danbury Baptists Jefferson said, "Believing with you that religion is a matter which lies *solely* between man and his God, *that he owes account to none other for his faith or worship,* that the legislative powers of government reach actions only and not opinions, I contemplate with sovereign reverence that act of the whole American people which declared that their legislature should make no law respecting an establishment of religion, or prohibiting the free exercise thereof; thus building a wall of separation between church and state."[66] (italics added) Note that the wall protected the reality that a person's faith and worship was between God and him alone. The wall protected man from having to give account for his faith to the government. Baptists had fought alongside Jefferson for the disestablishment of the established church in Virginia. The First Amendment phrase Congress shall make no law respecting an establishment of religion was in that historical context.[67]

One cannot understand the phrase wall of separation unless one understands, along with Roger Williams, the Baptists and their insistence on "the voluntary principle in religion," which means "that for faith to be valid,

---

supporters in New England, Dreisbach, *Thomas Jefferson*, 46; or Jefferson may have abandoned it as one of his purposes in the letter as suggested by Randall, *The Life of Thomas Jefferson*, 3.2. That this was one of Jefferson's objectives can be seen in his letter to Lincoln, Dreisbach, *Thomas Jefferson*, 43. Further, Dreisbach says some scholars understand the desire he stated to Lincoln about using this occasion "of sowing useful truths & principles among the people" as an admission that the strong Separationist ideas in the missive were not widely held, ibid., 44. In this same book in chapter 3, Dreisbach gives a full discussion and has photocopies of the original drafts of Jefferson's missive.

65. Ibid., 43.
66. See Appendix E.
67. Dreisbach, *Thomas Jefferson*, 51–53. New England Baptists did not support Jefferson's use of wall of separation or his deism. No New England Baptists ever used the phrase.

it must be free."⁶⁸ They suffered and fought for the freedom to worship according to the dictates of one's own conscience. They suffered abroad and in New England because they refused to baptize babies. They "insisted upon their right to worship in their own way and in their own churches" and were "haled before the Salem Court."⁶⁹ "Henry Dunster, first president of Harvard College, was compelled to resign his office in 1654, after twelve years of service, because he had accepted Baptist views and refused to remain silent on the subject of baptism . . . Dr. John Clarke, the founder of the Baptist church at Newport, was fined; and Obadiah Holmes . . . was imprisoned and whipped in Boston for having preached against infant baptism."⁷⁰ The Massachusetts Bay Colony in 1691 had religious toleration and not freedom, consequently, Baptists were not exempted from support of state churches with their taxes, and they thought this unconscionable, and fought it for years, experiencing both victories and setbacks.⁷¹ Beginning in 1768 in Virginia, until the outbreak of the Revolution, initiated by irate clergymen of the established church, some "thirty-four ministers were imprisoned, some on several occasions."⁷² "There is one case at least where a sheriff whipped a minister, John Waller, so severely that he carried the scars to his grave; but there is no proof that he was carrying out an order of the court."⁷³

Dreisbach summarizes the situation for Baptists in Connecticut, which sheds light upon their letter to Jefferson and his response as well.

> The established Congregational ministry . . . continued to dominate the institutions of politics and public policy in Connecticut at the start of the nineteenth century. The Baptists . . . reported . . . their 'religious privileges' were not recognized as 'inalienable rights.' They bitterly resented policies that required them to petition the established powers for modest religious privileges extended to them . . . The Congregationalists and 'the Federalists' . . . were so closely allied that the party of the government and the party of the [ecclesiastical] Establishment were familiarly and collectively known as 'the Standing Order'. Congregationalists enjoyed many privileges, and dissenters suffered many disabilities, both social and legal, under this regime . . . All citizens, Congregationalists and dissenters alike, had to pay taxes for the support of the established church, civil authorities

68. Shurden, Foreword, *Bloudy Tenent*, xiii–xiv.
69. Torbet, *History*, 203.
70. Ibid., 203–4
71. Ibid., 234–35.
72. Gewehr, *The Great Awakening*, 122.
73. Little, *Imprisoned Preachers*, 229.

imposed penalties for failure to attend church on Sunday or to observe public fasts and thanksgivings, and positions of influence in public life were reserved for Congregationalists.

Dissenters were often denied access to meetinghouses, their clergy were not authorized to perform marriages, and dissenting itinerant preachers faced numerous restrictions and harassment by public officials. In the 1770s . . . the legislature had begun to dismantle elements of the standing order. This development signaled . . . a growing spirit of toleration. Dissenters were permitted to worship in congregations of their own choosing, tax exemption was extended to the estates of clergymen from all denominations, and the Toleration Act of 1784 exempted dissenters from the tax for the Congregational Church upon certification that they were active members of another religious body. These modest concessions did not fully satisfy the Baptists . . . who were agitating for disestablishment and religious liberty. By the turn of the century, the standing order was beginning to unravel, although the Congregational Church was not formally disestablished until 1818. When they wrote to Jefferson in 1801, the Danbury Baptists understood that, as a matter of federalism, the national government had little authority to 'destroy' the odious 'Laws of each State.'

Nevertheless, they hoped the new president's liberal sentiments on religious liberty would 'shine & prevail through all these States . . . till Hierarchy and tyranny be destroyed' . . . The issue . . . to the Baptists was whether 'religious privileges' (and the rights of conscience) are rightly regarded as 'inalienable rights' or merely 'favors granted' and subject to withdrawal by the civil state. The Baptists, of course, believed that religious liberty was an inalienable right, and they were deeply offended that the religious privileges of dissenters in Connecticut were treated as favors that could be granted or denied by the political authorities . . . The Baptists described religion as an essentially private matter between an individual and his God. No citizen, they reasoned, ought to suffer civil disability on account of his religious opinions. The legitimate powers of civil government reach actions, but not opinions. These were principles Jefferson embraced, and he reaffirmed them in his reply to the Baptists.[74]

These experiences provide the context for the words used by Jefferson in his letter to the Danbury Baptists and demonstrate that Black's usage is without warrant. Jefferson's emphasis is even clearer in his second

---

74. Selected text from Dreisbach, *Thomas Jefferson*, 32–34.

inaugural address when he said, "In matters of religion I have considered that its free exercise is placed by the Constitution *independent* of the power of the *General Government*. I have therefore *undertaken on no occasion to prescribe the religious exercises* suited to it, but have left them, as the Constitution found them, *under the direction and discipline of the church or state authorities acknowledged by the several religious societies.*"[75] (italics added) Constitutional law authority Edward S. Corwin comments, "In short, the principal importance of the amendment lay in separation which it effected between the jurisdiction of state and nation regarding religion, rather than on its bearing on the question of the separation of church and state."[76] "Jefferson's 'wall,' strictly speaking, was a metaphoric construction of the First Amendment, which governed relations between religion and the *national* government. His 'wall,' therefore, did not specifically address relations between religion and *state* authorities."[77]

Dreisbach, commenting on this, says clearly, "Jefferson's 'wall,' like the First Amendment, affirmed the policy of federalism. This policy emphasized that all governmental authority over religious matters was allocated to the states. The metaphor's principal function was to delineate the legitimate jurisdictions of state and nation on religious issues. Insofar as Jefferson's 'wall,' like the First Amendment, was primarily jurisdictional (or structural) in nature, it offered little in the way of a substantive right or universal principle of religious liberty."[78] Therefore, the phrase, along with the First Amendment, actually has for its purpose providing for the freedom *of* religion not freedom *from* religion.

Further confirming that this was his understanding, Jefferson sent a letter to the Danbury Baptists on January 1, 1802, the same day that Baptist Pastor John Leland brought him the Cheshire cheese as a betokening of celebration of his election as president.[79] Leland accepted an invitation to preach in the House of Representatives on January 3, 1802, which Jefferson attended, just two days after Jefferson used wall of separation in his letter.[80] Jefferson asked for prayer in his second inaugural address.[81] In addition, "so far as the extant evidence indicates, he never again used the

---

75. Plymouth Rock Foundation, *Biblical Principles*, 226.
76. Ibid., 227.
77. Dreisbach, *Thomas Jefferson*, 50.
78. Ibid., 69
79. Ibid., 17.
80. Ibid., 21.
81. Ibid., 174, note 11.

'wall' metaphor."[82] Jefferson concludes the Danbury letter with prayer as an official presidential act.[83]

As president, he used religious content in his official communication that was comparable to his predecessors. In his first inaugural address he said, "Acknowledging and adoring an overruling Providence, which by all its dispensations proves that it delights in the happiness of man here and his greater happiness hereafter . . . And may that Infinite Power which rules the destinies of the universe lead our councils to what is best, and give them a favorable issue for your peace and prosperity."[84]

In his first annual message to Congress he said, "While we devoutly return thanks to the beneficent Being who has been pleased to breathe into them the spirit of conciliation and forgiveness, we are bound with peculiar gratitude to be thankful to him that our own peace has been preserved through so perilous a season, and ourselves permitted quietly to cultivate the earth and to practice and improve those arts which tend to increase our comforts."[85]

Second annual message to Congress, "When we assemble together . . . our just attentions are first drawn to those pleasing circumstances which mark the goodness of that Being from whose favor they flow and the large measure of thankfulness we owe for His bounty. . . . These, fellow-citizens, are the circumstances under which we meet, and we remark with special satisfaction those which under the smiles of Providence."[86]

Second inaugural address, Jefferson concluded by asking the people for their continued indulgence from his own human errors, and then offers these words of prayer and recognition of his need for God, as well as asking the people to join him in prayer, "I shall need, too, the favor of that Being in whose hands we are, who led our forefathers, as Israel of old . . . who has covered our infancy with his providence, and our riper years with his wisdom and power; and to whose goodness I ask you to join with me in supplications, that he will so enlighten the minds of your servants, guide their councils, and prosper their measures."[87]

As a member of the House of Burgesses, on May 24, 1774, he participated in drafting and enacting a resolution designating a "Day of Fasting,

---

82. Ibid., 54.
83. See Appendix E.
84. Jefferson "First Inaugural Address," par. 3 and 6.
85. Jefferson, "First Annual Message to Congress," par. 1.
86. Jefferson, "Second Annual Message to Congress," par. 1.
87. Jefferson "Second Inaugural Address," par. 15.

Humiliation, and Prayer."[88] In 1779, when Jefferson was governor of Virginia, he issued a proclamation appointing a day of public and solemn thanksgiving and prayer to Almighty God. It says in part, "Whereas it becomes us humbly to approach the throne of Almighty God, with gratitude and praise, for the wonders which his goodness has wrought in conducting our forefathers to this western world . . . And above all, that he hath diffused the glorious light of the gospel, whereby, through the merits of our gracious Redeemer, we may become the heirs of his eternal glory."[89]

"In the late 1770s, as chair of the Virginia Committee of Revisors, he was the chief architect of a revised code that included a measure entitled, 'A Bill for Appointing Days of Public Fasting and Thanksgiving' . . . The bill authorized 'the Governor, or Chief Magistrate [of the Commonwealth], with the advice of the Council,' to designate days for thanksgiving and fasting and to notify the public by proclamation."[90] This included directing ministers of the gospel to preach sermons and conduct services according to the prescribed occasion, with a fine of fifty pounds for failure to comply.[91]

In light of these events, and that Jefferson did not draft the First Amendment, the wall phrase should not be given the final word on the First Amendment. He was minister to France and was out of the country when the Bill of Rights was adopted. He neither participated in the Constitutional Convention nor the First Federal Congress, which in the summer of 1789 debated the content of a provision that came to be known as the First Amendment that was later approved in September.[92] In addition, "it is obviously incorrect to substitute this private opinion for the First Amendment."[93]

Therefore, in light of Jefferson's practice as governor, his communication with the Baptists, and his first and second inaugural addresses as president, his first and second annual messages to congress as president, it is clear that he emphasized a jurisdictional understanding of the First Amendment based on federalism and freedom of conscience. Thus, whether one looks at the First Amendment in light of Williams, the Baptists, or Jefferson, the theist is free to follow God both privately and publicly, and the atheist is

---

88. Dreisbach, *Thomas Jefferson*, 58.

89. Jefferson, "Proclamation Appointing a Day of Thanksgiving and Prayer," par. 2. This proclamation was issued on November 11, 1779, which is after the bill Jefferson drafted for establishing religious freedom was signed into law on January 19, 1776.

90. Dreisbach, *Thomas Jefferson*, 59.

91. Ibid., 59. The bill was never actually enacted, but it is important that Jefferson supported the bill

92. Ibid., 98.

93. Brady, *Confusion Twice Confounded*, 74.

free not to. Even the Supreme Court has noted the enormous influence of Christianity upon America.

In the Trinity Decision of 1892, the Supreme Court examined literally thousands of documents that had anything to do with the founding of this country—every state constitution, all of the compacts that led up to 1776, all of the various decisions of the courts. Their verdict was, "This is a religious people. This is historically true. From the discovery of this continent to the present hour, there is a single voice making this affirmation . . . These are not individual sayings, declarations of private persons; they are organic utterances; they speak the voice of the entire people . . . These and many others which might be noticed, add a volume of unofficial declarations to the mass of organic utterances that this is a Christian nation."[94]

Similar affirmations of Christianity's influence on America can be found in speeches and writings of Supreme Court Justices like Earl Warren, Joseph Story,[95] and John Marshall as well as other significant historical persons.[96] Maybe this is why Congress declared in 1982, "The Bible, the Word of God, has made a unique contribution in shaping the United States as a distinctive and blessed nation . . . deeply held religious convictions springing from the Holy Scriptures led to the early settlement of our Nation . . . Biblical teachings inspired concepts of civil government that are contained in our Declaration of Independence and the Constitution of the United States."[97]

Jim Allison seeks to minimize the influence of religion or Christianity upon the founding of the United States by noting the paucity of references to God, religion, or Christianity in our founding documents.[98] However, he makes several unfortunate mistakes. *First, he fails to understand the nature of the time.* It was their belief in God that led them to say what they said and omit what they did; thereby leaving religion to the domain of conscience and the individual states. *Second, he supposes that Christianity would have to be specifically mentioned, and that religion and God would have to be mentioned more for them to be significant.*

---

94. *Church of the Holy Trinity v. U.S.*; 143 U.S. 457, 465, 470–471 (1892) cited in Kennedy and Newcombe in *What if Jesus*, 73–74. "In 1931, US Supreme Court Justice George Sutherland reviews the 1892 decision and reiterates that Americans are a 'Christian people.'" Plymouth Rock Foundation, *Biblical Principles*, 365.

95. Kennedy and Newcombe, *What if Jesus*, 57–58 and 75 respectively.

96. Kennedy and Newcombe, *What if the Bible*, 99; also Plymouth Rock Foundation, *Biblical Principles*, 353–68.

97. Public Law 97–280 Joint Resolution approved 4 October 1982.

98. Allison, "A Big Fuss."

Concerning God and religion, although he notes their mention, he quickly minimizes their significance based on the number of times they are mentioned. One wonders how many times one has to mention God or religion before it becomes important. He deduces that the absence of the word Christianity proves this was not a Christian nation. In response, no one ever said the term Christian appeared in the Constitution, but rather the milieu of that day was religious and most prominently Christian, which is a fact of history.

Only by de-historicizing the Constitution can one conclude that a nation, where the predominant worldview was Christian, would adopt a governing document contrary to that. In addition, to imply that because Christianity was not mentioned in the Constitution, it was not important to them, is an argument from silence. For example, the Southern Baptist Convention (SBC) did not incorporate Article III (1), which precludes membership to churches "which act to affirm, approve, or endorse homosexual behavior" (wording from Southern Baptist Convention Constitution) in their constitution until 2000. However, to interpret its absence from the SBC Constitution as a prior endorsement of homosexuality would be a grave error indeed. Its absence was because historically there was no need to mention churches that act to affirm, approve, or endorse homosexual behavior because there was no such thing in SBC life. Moreover, that a church which condoned homosexuality would not be accepted—if it did exist—was a given.

Lastly, his opinion that the overriding determiner that God, religion, and/or Christianity were insignificant to the time or the design of the founding documents because of the paucity of times they appear is misguided. The significance of concepts or words in documents is better determined by weighing how they were used rather than by how many times they were used. By his method of counting, one must conclude that neither independence nor a declaration about independence is significant in the Declaration of Independence because the word declaration only appears once in the body and the word independence is absent. Furthermore, the Constitution would not have anything to do with liberty because it only appears once in the entire Constitution. The five most important founding documents of America are The Declaration of Independence, Articles of Confederation, the Northwest Ordinance, the Constitution, and the Bill of Rights. All of them include phrases referring to God or the prominence or importance of religion.[99]

---

99. See Appendix G.

CULTURAL HOSTILITY IS UNWARRANTED

Society

Apart from the progressives' success with expanding science beyond its proper domain, it is difficult to understand why open hostility by many leaders is allowed when the empirical evidence attests to the importance of religion in people's lives today. Gallup polls indicate that more than 8 in 10 Americans identify themselves as Christian, 2 percent as Jewish and only 10 percent say "they have no specific religious preference."[100] This makes the religious viewpoint in general and Christianity in particular the dominant worldview of the United States. The poll says, "Roughly 6 in 10 Americans say that religion is very important in their personal lives."[101] Patrick F. Fagan notes, "The overall impact of religious practice is illustrated dramatically in the three most comprehensive systematic reviews of the field. Some 81 percent of the studies showed the positive benefit of religious practice, 15 percent showed neutral effects, and only 4 percent showed harm."[102]

Even the harm can be explained in part by what many Christians have known for a long time. Faith that is not serious or directed at knowing and following God is of no spiritual value (James 2:18) and has limited social value. Now social scientists are distinguishing between "intrinsic" and "extrinsic" religion. "Intrinsic practice is God-oriented and based on beliefs that transcend the person's own existence. Research shows this form of religious practice to be beneficial. Extrinsic practice is self-oriented and characterized by outward observance, not internalized as a guide to behavior or attitudes. The evidence suggests this form of religious practice is actually more harmful than no religion."[103]

Some of the positive psychological effects of intrinsic religion are characteristics like a greater sense of responsibility, self-motivation, better performance in their studies, greater sensitivity to others; in contrast to extrinsic practice where people are more likely to be dogmatic, authoritarian,

---

100. Carroll, "American Public Opinion About Religion," par. 2.

101. Ibid., par. 4. "An additional 24% say that religion is fairly important, and 15% say it is not very important. The importance of religion to Americans has remained quite stable over the past decade, with a low of 57% saying religion was very important in 1996 and a high of 61% saying it was very important in 1998," ibid. The younger the population, the less important religion is to their lives, which I would attribute much to the influence of secular education.

102. Fagan, *Why Religion Matters*, 2–3.

103. Ibid., 20.

less responsible, inferior in their studies, more self-indulgent, indolent, less dependable, and more prejudiced.[104]

Religion has positive results in the areas of happiness, sense of well-being, lowering stress, better personal relationships, greater sexual satisfaction for women, lower risk of cardiovascular diseases, longer life for the poor; it affects blood pressure and different cancers; it decreases illegitimacy, crime, delinquency, welfare dependency, alcohol and drug abuse, depression, and suicide; it enhances general overall mental, physical and social well-being.[105]

"The American Medical Association says the growth in health-care expenses today can be traced largely to 'lifestyle factors and social problems.' Some studies indicate that up to 70 percent of all diseases result from lifestyle choices."[106] Harvard professor Herbert Benson, "though not a professing Christian himself, admits that humans are 'engineered for religious faith.' We are 'wired for God . . . Our genetic blueprint has made believing in an Infinite Absolute part of our nature.'"[107] The field of psychiatry, strongly influenced by Freud, has been predisposed until recently to ignore the spiritual dimension of a person, or to view it reductively, and dismiss all faith as neurotically determined, an illusion, a projection of childhood wishes, or a hallucinatory psychosis, etc.[108]

According to Armand M. Nicholi, Jr., associate clinical professor of psychiatry at Harvard Medical School, things are changing. "During the past several years, however, physicians increasingly recognize the importance of understanding the spiritual dimension of their patients. At the Annual Meeting of the American Psychiatric Association held in May of 2000, no less than thirteen of the proceedings focused on spiritual issues, the highest number of such events in the history of the organization."[109] He tells of research he conducted with Harvard University students who experienced religious conversions while undergrads and experienced positive changes in lifestyle including the immediate cessation of the use of drugs, alcohol, and cigarettes along with academic improvement and enhanced self-image.[110]

---

104. From articles by Wiebe and Fleck, "Personality Correlates," 111–117 and Donahue, "Intrinsic and Extrinsic Religiousness," 400–419.

105. Fagan, *Why Religion Matters*, 5–20. Fagan sources numerous studies that corroborate the benefit of religion in a person's life. Some of them deal specifically with the positive impact on areas of life from church attendance.

106. Cited in Colson and Pearcey, *How Now*, 309.

107. Ibid., 314.

108. Nicholi, *The Question*, 80.

109. Ibid.

110. Ibid.

In light of the prevalence of religious beliefs, its demonstrable contributions to personal and cultural health, and the goals of education, it is socially irresponsible not to give religion its proportionate place in state education. However, care must be exercised so that social scientists do not reduce it to merely a product of human choice. Statements by social scientists like "above all, people are social beings," need to be balanced with the non-secular view that "above all, people are religious beings."[111] There seems to be plenty of empirical evidence to at least present this view as a plausible alternative or rival to the previous statement. Many religions maintain that man is a spiritual being, and he will worship someone or something, be it God, ancestors, nature, science, or self.

Atheist John Gray even remarks that "there is no necessary connection between atheism and hostility to religion, as some of the great Victorian unbelievers understood. More intelligent than their latter-day disciple, the positivists tried to found a new religion of humanity—especially August Comte (1798–1857), who established a secular church in Paris that for a time found converts in many other parts of the world. The new religion was an absurdity, with rituals being practiced that were based on the pseudo-science of phrenology—but at least the positivists understood that atheism cannot banish human needs that only faith can meet."[112]

Science

It is odd indeed that modern science, which was originated by men, many of whom were Christians like Isaac Newton, Michael Faraday, Johannes Kepler, Galileo, Blaise Pascal, and Copernicus, now sees Christianity as an enemy of science.[113] Even men like J. Robert Oppenheimer—one of the physicists responsible for splitting the atom and developing nuclear power—points this out with regard to the origins of the scientific revolution. "It took something that was not present in Chinese civilization, that was wholly absent in Indian civilization, and absent from Greco-Roman civilization. It needed an idea of progress, not limited to better understanding for this idea the Greeks had. It took an idea of progress which has more to do with the human condition, which is well expressed by the second half of the famous Christian dichotomy—faith and works."[114]

---

111. Hobbs and Blank, *Sociology and the Human Experience*, preface.

112. Gray, "The Closed Mind of Richard Dawkins," par. 21.

113. Kennedy and Newcombe, *What If the Bible*, 102–18.

114. Oppenheimer, *Uncommon Service*, 127; Francois Jacob makes a similar observation in his book, *Of Flies, Mice and Men*, 128–29.

Francis Bacon, the father of the scientific method, once put it this way, "There are two books laid before us to study, to prevent our falling into error; first, the volume of the Scriptures which reveal the will of God; then, the volume of the Creatures, which express His Power."[115] This does not mean that a scientist has to be a Christian or even believe in God, but it does demonstrate the weakness of the claim by naturalists that belief in God stifles scientific inquiry.

Now the very possibility of design is banished from scientific inquiry in areas such as biology and geology. Scientists like Richard Dawkins and Francis Crick remind themselves and their readers that the appearance of design in things must be ignored.[116] Dembski says, "By dogmatically excluding design from science, scientists are themselves stifling scientific inquiry."[117] In addition, he says, the fear that allowing design as a possible answer will stifle scientific inquiry or result in natural effects being attributed to intelligence is unwarranted.[118] He defines intelligent design as "a theory of biological origins and development. Its fundamental claim is that intelligent causes are necessary to explain the complex, information-rich structures of biology and that these causes are *empirically* detectable . . . It is the *empirical detectability* of intelligent causes that renders intelligent design a fully scientific theory."[119] (italics added) For scientists to *a priori* preclude the possibility that the empirical evidence might be best explained by intelligence is naturalism, not science.[120]

When one considers the influence of Christianity and the Bible upon the founding of America, as well as her founding documents, laws, system of government, science, systems of education, contemporary culture, medicine and health, art, music, morality, society, and everyday things, it seems that the evidence supports the contention that it is good social and legal

115. Cited in Morris, *Men of Science*, 35.

116. Dembski, *Intelligent Design*, 125.

117. Ibid.

118. Ibid., 106. This refers to Kepler's mistake of wrongly inferring design of craters on the moon; inferring design leaves open the question of the designer, the purpose, and the how or moral character of the designer, ibid., 106–7. I would add that it also leaves open the possibility of displacing the design theory with a non-design theory.

119. Ibid., 106–7.

120. Francois Jacob argues that we cannot stop the quest for knowledge or pursue only what will turn out as good science when he said, "We have nothing to fear from the truth, whether it comes from genetics or elsewhere. What we have to fear is misrepresentation of findings and the distorted meaning that people give them." Jacob, *Of Flies*, 150. This is not to say that he believes in Intelligent Design, but rather I give this as an example of true science, which, followed to its logical conclusion, will go wherever the empirical evidence leads, whether it is from non-intelligence or elsewhere—intelligence.

policy to foster religion.[121] This is not a violation of the First Amendment, which guarantees freedom to practice one's religion and therefore forbids Congress from establishing a national religion. History is clear that religion has not only been tolerated but also fostered in the public domain. "Federal policies encourage many other institutions: the marketplace, education, medicine, science, and the arts. Even religion itself is explicitly encouraged by the tax treatment of contributions to religious institutions. It makes no sense, therefore, not to encourage the resource that most powerfully addresses the major social problems confronting the nation."[122]

To fail to present religion, both its positive and negative contributions, does not prepare students for life. Further, it misrepresents many events and de-contextualizes many ideas, statements, and values. Moreover, it creates an environment that is far more difficult to reach with the good news of Jesus Christ since it is seen as either unnecessary or unintelligible.

121. See Kennedy and Newcombe's books, *What If the Bible Had Never Been Written?* and *What If Jesus Had Never Been Born?*
122. Fagan, *Why Religion Matters*, 25.

5

Scientism, the New De Facto Public Religion

How Naturalism Is Replacing Christianity in America

IN ORDER TO TRAIN Christians to live out their faith and effectively engage their world with the truth in love, they must have an adequate grasp of the world of ideas that they are going to encounter and with which they will be challenged. This involves more than just a superficial acquaintance with some of the terminology. They must comprehend some of the ideas that drive and permeate their world, as well as the consequences from these philosophies. Thus far, we have focused on state education, which is driven by the naturalistic philosophy of the progressives. This includes the idea that many leaders today believe, by in large, that science is able to provide either the answer, or at least the best answer to any observable phenomena, whether that is the movement of mice through a maze or a person praying to God. Any belief in immaterial reality is explained reductively or merely epiphenomenally.

This chapter is intended to draw attention to some obvious and some not so apparent issues. The less palpable issues are rarely appreciated for the changes they have undergone, are undergoing, or have facilitated. In addition, other matters will be addressed in order to afford further clarification and affirmation of certain truths and realities in order to help Christians effectively engage their culture for the cause of Christ rather than being so utterly assimilated that they lose any value as an ambassador for Christ beyond clichés and eschewing some moral taboos. One reality that Christians have to concede before we can really embark on engaging our culture at every level is that Christians as well as non-Christians have been unduly influenced by scientism and her bridesmaid progressive education. Further, this harmful influence upon the church must be acknowledged, explained, and countered before the church can truly be the pure church in our day.

With regard to the influence of education, it is crucial to keep in mind that education itself is a religious endeavor. Consequently, when progressives claim that progressive education is religiously neutral, they are either naive or disingenuous. To wit, progressive education is not supplementary to religious education; it is a replacement. I think it would be helpful to demonstrate the religiousness of education itself. When I say that state schools, built upon scientism, reject religion, I am referring specifically to supernatural religion because education is in fact a religious endeavor. Even science becomes a religion—naturalism—when embraced as the supreme source of truth in every area.

Let me clarify and elaborate on this point. The task of deciding what should be the government's policy toward teaching religion in state schools is a difficult one. Charles C. Haynes, Freedom Forum Senior Fellow, says, "Unfortunately, when religion in the schools is at issue, extremes often dominate the debate. On one end of the spectrum are those who advocate promotion of religion (usually their own) in school practices and policies. On the other end are those who view public schools as religion-free zones. Many educators (and textbook publishers) have tried to quell controversy by avoiding religion altogether. This strategy hasn't worked. Ignoring religion only increases tension, builds distrust, and frequently culminates in lawsuits."[1]

I will be using the term education to mean "the act or process of imparting or acquiring general knowledge, developing the powers of reasoning and judgment, and generally of preparing oneself or others intellectually for mature life."[2] Additionally, I will use the term religion defined as "a set of beliefs concerning the cause, nature, and purpose of the universe . . . and often containing a moral code governing the conduct of human affairs . . . something one believes in and follows devotedly; a point or matter of ethics or conscience."[3] Generally, when I refer to religion, I will be referring to what is known as supernatural religion. This is particularly true regarding

---

1. Haynes, *Teaching about Religion*, 7–8.
2. *Random House Webster Unabridged Dictionary* (CD-ROM, ver. 3.0), s.v. "education."
3. *Ibid.*, s.v. "religion."

the religion that is markedly absent from public education; however, the definition for religion fits non-supernatural religion as well, such as humanism, naturalism, secularism, or atheism.[4]

Former professor of Philosophy of Religion and Ethics, J. Clayton Feaver says, "Note that religion and philosophy serve the same psychological functions or purposes in human nature—they satisfy these two common needs of mankind. A religion gives a world view and a way of life, and a philosophy does the same."[5] Defining religion is critical for considering the subject of religion, education, and the role of government because a clear understanding of what education is and what religion is elucidates how it is actually impossible to completely separate religion from comprehensive education. Feaver points out, "While the word 'religion' is a single term, the various phenomena it supposedly describes are numerous and complex."[6]

Even secular humanism is best defined as a religion and religious. The Humanist Manifesto I describes the adherents as "religious humanists," and it argues a great need "to establish such a religion" referring to the tenets of naturalism spelled out in the manifesto.[7] The manifesto claims, "Religion consists of those actions, purposes, and experiences which are humanly significant. Nothing human is alien to the religious. It includes labor, art,

---

4. Humanism comes in many forms, but what they have in common is a dependence upon man, and nature is all there is. The following is a quote of a spiritual humanist. A secular humanist will be considered in the next paragraph. "As Spiritual Humanists we believe that every person has innate right (sic) to make a spiritual connection to the rest of the cosmos. Our premise is simple: *We can solve the problems of society using a religion based on reason,*" http://www.spiritualhumanism.org/, par. 2 and 3.

In 1961, the U.S. Supreme Court acknowledged that Secular Humanism was a religion. For arguments why the mention in footnote 11 [of the Supreme Court decision] is considered by some more than just dicta, see the following information and corresponding website.

"Justice Scalia wrote: In *Torcaso v. Watkins*, 367 U.S. 488, 495, n. 11 (1961), we did indeed refer to "SECULAR HUMANISM" as a "religio[n]." *Edwards v. Aguillard*, 482 U.S. 578 (1987) note 6. Justice Harlan summed it all up: [Footnote 8] [of the Supreme Court decision] This Court has taken notice of the fact that recognized 'religions' exist that 'do not teach what would generally be considered a belief in the existence of God,' *Torcaso v. Watkins*, 367 U.S. 488, 495 n. 11, *e. g.,* 'Buddhism, Taoism, Ethical Culture, SECULAR HUMANISM and others." *Ibid.* See also *Washington Ethical Society v. District of Columbia,* 101 U.S. App. D.C. 371, 249 F.2d 127 (1957); 2 *Encyclopaedia of the Social Sciences* 293; J. Archer, *Faiths Men Live By* 120–138, 254–313 (2d ed. revised by Purinton 1958); Stokes & Pfeffer, *supra,* n. 3, at 560. *Welsh v. United States* 398 U.S. 333 (1970) note 8. . . . Secular Humanism is a religion is a religion 'for Free Exercise Clause purposes.' . . . [and] Secular Humanism is Not a religion 'for Establishment Clause purposes.'" "Is 'Secular Humanism' a 'Religion'?".

5. Feaver and Horosz, *Religion in Perspective,* 341.

6. Ibid., 338.

7. "Humanist Manifesto I," first affirmation and introduction.

science, philosophy, love, friendship, recreation—all that is in its degree expressive of intelligently satisfying human living. The distinction between the sacred and the secular can no longer be maintained."[8] This religious view of naturalism is also expressed in the Humanist Manifesto II and III.[9]

John Dewey, a signer of the Humanist Manifesto I, sought to mediate between supernatural religions and harsh atheism—between "religion, *a* religion and the religious."[10] The religious idea that he believed accomplished this was "the religious aspect of experience."[11] He says, "It is this *active* relation between ideal and actual to which I would give the name 'God.'"[12] Additionally he says, "Whatever introduces genuine perspective is religious, not that religion is something that introduces it."[13] His *common faith* of man is religious faith in man, or man's common experience without supernaturalism or dogma, but it is still religious.

Julian Huxley says, "I disbelieve in a personal God in any sense in which that phrase is ordinarily used."[14] However, this does not mean that he was irreligious. Huxley says, "I believe that it is necessary to believe something. Complete skepticism does not work."[15] He defined the way to determine what to believe as "the method, which has proved effective, as a matter of actual fact, in providing a firm foundation for belief . . . usually called the

---

8. Ibid., seventh affirmation.

9. The first affirmation of Humanist Manifesto II states, "In the best sense, religion may inspire dedication to the highest ethical ideals. The cultivation of moral devotion and creative imagination is an expression of genuine 'spiritual' experience and aspiration." "Humanist Manifesto II."
While the Humanist Manifesto III does not use the word religion to describe itself, it does extol the virtues of scientific naturalism to a place of peerless supremacy over all other worldviews. Scientific naturalism is seen to hold the key to advancing such things as, values, happiness and freedom, which is precisely what religion claims to do. "Humanist Manifesto III."

10. Dewey, *A Common Faith*, 3.

11. Ibid., 2.

12. Ibid., 51.

13. Ibid., 24.

14. Huxley, *Religion*, 17–18. A *LIFE* magazine article said, "Julian Huxley is an atheist. . . . the materialist, denying the need for religion or God," "The Huxley Brothers," *LIFE* magazine, 53.

15. Huxley, *Religion*, 13. Dr. Charles Frances Potter, Founder of the First Humanist Society of New York, writes a letter to the editor of *LIFE* magazine contesting their article's assertion that Julian Huxley denied the need for religion. Potter quotes Huxley's book *Man Stands Alone*, which says, "Religion, to continue as an element of first-rate importance in the life of the community, must drop the idea of God." Potter, "Letters to the Editor," *LIFE* magazine, 26.

scientific method."[16] Of course this means of knowing expanded to include all of life transforms science into scientism or epistemic naturalism.

Jonathan Rauch, a widely published author who personally has no place for the supernatural,[17] responds to the complaint "that the liberal scientific order ('secular humanism') is itself a form of faith" with the reply that "belief in liberal science is a faith."[18] Albert Einstein once proposed that, "Science itself could serve as the religion of the devoted scientist."[19]

The religious features of psychology are readily apparent. This is significant because psychological and counseling theories have such an enormous influence upon our educational system today. For example, Carl Jung says, "Patients force the psychotherapist into the role of priest, and expect and demand that he shall free them from distress. That is why we psychotherapists must occupy ourselves with problems which strictly speaking belong to the Theologian."[20]

Abraham Maslow, speaking of the essential quality of self-actualization, says, "A few centuries ago these would all have been described as men who walk in the path of God or as godly men . . . if religion is defined only in social–behavioral terms, then these are all religious people, the atheist included. But if more conservatively we use the term religion so as to include and stress the supernatural element and institutional orthodoxy . . . then our answer must be quite different."[21]

Carl Rogers, "deeply believes that humans are innately good, trustworthy, and rational."[22] This is why "the goal of client–centered counseling is a reorganization of the self."[23] It should be clear that both of these ideas are philosophical or religious in nature because one must have a very clear idea of what that reorganization is to look like and act like. Prior to Rogers' training at Columbia University under John Dewey, he had been heavily

---

16. Huxley, *Religion*, 15.

17. Rauch, *Kindly Inquisitors,* 80. He says, "Some of us — I am one — are so constituted as not to mind very much if the supernatural and the subjective are banished from our public knowledge base."

18. Rauch, *Kindly Inquisitors,* 77. His faith in liberal science is so strong that he claims Jesus' words to Thomas "blessed are they that have not seen, and yet have believed" (John 20:27) have been "roundly repudiated" by liberal science, ibid., 79. This is indeed a faith statement.

19. Cited in Reiser and Davies *Planetary Democracy,* 118. Einstein also said, "I maintain that the cosmic religious feeling is the strongest and noblest motive for scientific research," http://www.endlesssearch.co.uk/science_cosmicreligion.htm.

20. Jung, *Modern Man*, 278.

21. Cited in Vitz, *Psychology*, 10.

22. Shilling, *Perspectives*, 170.

23. Ibid., 177.

influenced by his Protestant upbringing, involvement in religious groups at the University of Wisconsin, and two years at Union Theological Seminary, where he would have been exposed to liberal Christianity.[24] Though he rejected the essence of Christianity, the liberal Christian ideas are still very present.[25] He even expanded the goal of his psychotherapy beyond a specialized activity to encompass all of life. When he spoke of becoming more of a person he said, "I believe this statement holds whether I am speaking of my relationship with a client, with a group of students or staff members, with my family or children. It seems to me that we have here a general hypothesis which offers exciting possibilities for the development of creative, adaptive, autonomous persons."[26]

The religiousness is unmistakable in Ellis's rational emotive therapy when he says, "*Humans are only human*, and are neither angels, nor devils, nor 'dumb' animals . . . As far as is now known, all humans are mortal—we all die—and *there is no evidence* of immortality or life after death."[27] (italics added) He gives a disclaimer that he is not speaking as an atheist, but his religion of atheism is evident in his absolute declaration "Humans are only human" and "there is no evidence," for many would beg to differ with those conclusions.[28] Ellis deems what he calls "absolutizing" or "musterbation" as irrational as well as the idea that "one should be dependent on others and needs someone stronger than oneself on whom to rely."[29] Of course this virtually eliminates all supernatural religious beliefs because they are generally or necessarily absolute.[30] Interestingly, Ellis seems religiously absolute in his anti-religious animus.

Many others hold similar views, but these are sufficient to demonstrate that our endeavors, regardless how secular, are still in some measure religious. This is important with regard to state schools, because it seems

---

24. Ibid., 166–67.

25. This would include concepts like humans being innately good, what it means to become more of a person, etc., although this is a characteristic of humanism as well.

26. Rogers, *On Becoming a Person*, 37–38

27. Cited in Shilling, *Perspectives*, 95.

28. See books like Josh McDowell's *The New Evidence that Demands a Verdict* and Richard L. Wessler, "A Bridge Too Far: Incompatibilities of Rational Emotive Therapy and Pastoral Counseling." Ellis is in fact concluding there is no evidence, meaning there is no physical evidence. First, there is objective, empirical evidence for the claims of Christ. Second, regarding the spirit this is a categorical fallacy since supernatural religions do not speak of the spirit as having a physical nature. Therefore, it is like concluding that there is no physical evidence of non-physical reality, which is absurd.

29. Ellis, "Reason and Emotion," 81. See also Wessler, "A Bridge Too Far," 264.

30. For more on the religious nature of modern psychological theories see Paul C. Vitz, *Psychology as Religion, The Cult of Self-Worship*.

inevitable that religion and religious ideas will be taught. In fact, the very endeavor of education is endowed with religiousness. David Sant notes, "All education is undergirded by presuppositions about the origin of the universe, the origin of man, the purpose of man, ethics of governing relationships between men, and the continuing existence of the universe in an orderly and predictable manner. It is an inescapable fact that all of these basic assumptions are fundamentally religious."[31] Thus, the real question is not will state schools teach religion, but rather will they teach about religion accurately, including supernatural religion, because what seems to be lacking from state education is not religion, but more precisely supernatural religion.

Of course other driving forces behind any culture are money, power, and various and sundry sins or a rejection of the reality of sin. Obviously, the multimedia environment we live in affects us, including the volume of information and the vivid and seductive images. My emphasis is not to minimize or ignore their undue influence upon our culture and the church, but rather to highlight what drives them, what created the value system that accepts them, what has unleashed the moral downward spiral in America that rivals the rapidity and breadth of the advances of the technological revolution.

As I have maintained throughout the book, I believe that not only has *what* we think changed over the last one hundred years, but I also believe that the *way* we think has fundamentally changed. This basic change is due largely, not to movies, modern media, etc., but to the influence of progressive education, which is premised upon Darwinian naturalism. Let me state again, science is a good thing when it used within its proper domain and viewed as a source of truth in certain areas. But when it becomes the source of truth or the most reliable source of truth or the only knowledge worthy of the public domain of debate and policy and seeks to describe the essence or reality of things like religion, faith, the totality of humanness, or human actions like faith, love, hate, violence, heroics, it metamorphoses into scientism or naturalism.

Moreover, when science becomes the only basis of modern education—all educable or knowable truth and knowledge based on only empirical data, the observable—and the knowledge that trumps all other knowledge in education, it is both natural and inevitable that it will become the accepted arbiter of truth in the public domain, and religion and faith will be marginalized and privatized. And if science is the final arbitrator in all matters of education and public life, why should we not marginalize

---

31. Cited by Sampson, *What Your Child Needs to Know*, 19.

religious faith because it is merely a product of material antecedents and no more real than a fairy tale. This is not to say that matters of faith cannot be spoken of in public, although even this is becoming more and more taboo, but it simply cannot be relied upon for public policy such as we find so prominently in the Declaration of Independence. This results in the situation that we have today where virtually any recent study that seems to support secularism repeatedly trumps the faith of the majority of Americans as well as the founding documents of America. Actually, science proper is not able to be the purveyor of everything just mentioned (all imposable knowledge, educational philosophy, religion, morals etc.). Thus, the subtle but necessary transformation of science into scientism, and ipso facto, and without fanfare, naturalism is the new state religion.

Francis Schaeffer describes the change this way, "The early scientists believed in the uniformity of natural causes. What they did not believe in was the uniformity of natural causes *in a closed system*. That little phrase makes all the difference in the world. It makes the difference between natural science and a science that is rooted in naturalistic philosophy. It makes all the difference between what I would call modern science and what I would call modern modern science. It is important to notice that this is not a failing of science as science, but rather that the uniformity of natural causes in a closed system has become *the dominant philosophy* among scientists."[32]

He elaborates further regarding this definitional shift. "Under the influence of the presupposition of the uniformity of natural causes in a closed system, the machine does not merely embrace the sphere of physics; it now encompasses everything . . . The modern modern scientists insist on a total unity of the downstairs . . . and the upstairs disappears. Neither God nor freedom are there anymore—everything is in the machine. In science the significant change came about therefore as a result of a shift in emphasis from the uniformity of natural causes to the uniformity of natural causes in a closed system. This shift did not come because of newly discovered facts, but because of a shift in their presuppositions—a shift to the world-view of materialism or naturalism."[33]

Consequently, my line of reasoning is that although the church is in large measure aware of the prominence of empiricism in our modern culture, she seems to be either dangerously credulous concerning the goals and consequences of scientism or simply unwilling to accept that secularists are relentlessly and systematically advancing the acceptance of an evolutionary

---

32. Schaeffer, *Complete Works*, vol. 1, 229.
33. Ibid., 230.

materialistic explanation and guide for *every* area of society and life.[34] Their quest, if accomplished, not only results in a materialistic reduction of belief in the supernatural but the labeling of persistent other world beliefs as a psychological abnormality or deficiency. Their pursuit is not coexistence or separate domains of authority but rather the elimination of supernatural faith. Already the hostility to Christianity in American education and policymaking is painfully apparent.

Hostility toward and elimination of Christianity is the logical outworking of a secular materialistic worldview, something that was graphically displayed in the twentieth century in the Soviet Union. Concerning Communism Alister McGrath states, "Once materialism had been declared to lie at the heart of official Soviet ideology, a rigidly hostile attitude to Christianity and any other religion affirming and celebrating the spiritual dimensions of existence followed as a matter of course."[35] This once again highlights the truth that while the Christian worldview retains a prominent place for science, a liberal scientific worldview increasingly affords no legitimacy to Christianity.

In addition, in the United States, while the transition is not complete, it is very advanced, maybe to the point of no return without a national disaster of mammoth proportions, a national revival, or a great move of God in some other way. Robert Bork says that he and his friends came to the conclusion of what it would take to defeat modern liberalism, and they named four things which could produce the necessary moral and spiritual regeneration: "a religious revival; the revival of public discourse about morality; a cataclysmic war; or a deep economic depression."[36] Well-known British science commentator Brian Appleyard argues that "science does not coexist [with faith]. Faith has been and will continue to be eroded by science—it may work for you, but the numbers for whom it will work will tend to decrease. As a political and moral force, therefore, it will be weakened."[37] Bork noted optimistically, "Perhaps the most promising development in our time is the rise of an energetic, optimistic, and politically sophisticated religious conservatism."[38] However, as I write, the expansion of science as the final arbiter of what should and should not be continues unabated. What is not directly evaluated by mere empiricism is done so indirectly by the

34. I'm not using this term in a technical, philosophical way, but rather signifying the undue stress placed on that which can be experienced through the five senses as the source of truth and knowledge today.

35. McGrath, *Reenchantment*, 24.

36. Bork, *Slouching Towards Gomorrah*, 336.

37. Appleyard, *Understanding the Present*, 215.

38. Bork, *Slouching Towards Gomorrah*, 336.

widespread almost unqualified acceptance of studies, polls, and scientism-type thinking to resolve any and every issue.

McGrath sheds both historical and contemporary light on this subject when referring to Richard S. Westfall's demonstration of how nature began to be viewed out of the scientific revolution of the seventeenth century. One component is that of a machine, e.g., clock, so this passive matter behaved certain ways because of "mechanical laws," then referring to humans in similar terms, "levers and applied forces" referring to the muscular system, "hydraulic machine" referring to the circulatory system.[39] Of course now it is applied to all human behavior, actions, choices, thoughts, and often without so much as even the mildest demur. Another component of this new view is "a growing trend to accept the authority of experimental observations, and reflection upon them, in dealing with questions of science, rather than in turning to religious sources of authority . . . Nature was to be examined and explained on its own terms."[40] Much like Newton's interest in demonstrating that the laws of mechanics could explain the movements of planets, this viewing of the natural world as a machine is now applied to humans. Succinctly, McGrath notes, "Newton's followers saw the clock as a model for the solar system, [Thomas] Hobbes saw the new adding machines as models for the human brain."[41]

With regard to the desacralization and disenchantment of nature that results from materialism, McGrath notes, "Only the cruder forms of materialism that are mistakenly held to be the inevitable consequence of the natural sciences will lead to an impoverishment of the human sense of wonder at the beauty of nature."[42] Henry Morris says, "Science has to do with careful observations in the present. Unlike true science, both evolution and creation are, at best, historical reconstructions of the unobserved past since no one can empirically observe either. In reality they are complete worldviews, ways to interpret all observations in the present, and a basis for all of life's decisions. In previous years, 'science' was understood to mean 'the search for truth,' but many now limit that to a search for naturalistic explanations, even if that search leads to hopeless conclusions."[43]

Bork points out that faith is necessary to accept science as the final arbitrator of truth. "A belief that science will ultimately explain everything, however, also requires a leap of faith. Faith in science requires the unproven

---

39. McGrath, *Reenchantment*, 110.
40. Ibid.
41. Ibid., 117.
42. Ibid., 25.
43. Morris, "Things You May Not Know."

assumption that all reality is material, that there is nothing beyond or outside the material universe."[44] This faith is actually not a faith in science per se because it technically is a belief in naturalism. That is the belief that all that exists can be experienced through the five senses. Bork further comments referring to the ability for science to explain everything, "Perhaps that is right, though it seems counterintuitive, but it cannot be proven and therefore rests on an untested and untestable assumption. That being the case, there is no logical reason why science should be hostile to or displace religion."[45] I agree and would argue that while some scientists like Richard Dawkins are very vocal about their hostility toward religion, others simply are content to displace it inch by inch until it only occupies the private life of an individual.

My concern is that the vast majority of Christians can be or are unknowingly facilitating the very process that will ultimately cause Christianity to be regarded as the scourge of modern society, which will immeasurably complicate the task of evangelism. Of course, neither society's view of Christians, nor the difficulty of evangelism will alter the call of God upon His people, but the failure of stewardship may very well displease Him and make the task excruciatingly more difficult. This naiveté of Christians seems to be, at least in large part, due to the failure of pastors to equip the saints in their churches. Whether they have failed to carry out the mandate to equip the saints because of their own nescience, flirting with secularism, lack of opportunity to be thoroughly equipped, youthfulness, unwillingness to stay in their studies long enough to understand the issues themselves, or by defining ministry by numbers, trendiness, or some other kind of shallow relevance, each man must decide. What I do know is that much of what is heralded as cutting edge, communicative contemporary preaching actually invigorates the flesh, quixotically seeks to build lives upon hypnagogic clichés and reduces making disciples to making spiritual dolts who are absolutely incapable of recognizing much less stemming our Gomorrean slouch.

It is not my heart to be unduly harsh in considering my fellow pastors, for I well understand the pressures to succeed that we are under, and of course numbers and size define success in our society. The demands of modern-day ministry relentlessly draw the man of God away from his study and in-depth expositional teaching of the Scripture. The spiritual decline of the church is inevitable because of what Christians do not get—in-depth teaching from God's Word—and what they do get—the result of scientism through psychology, studies, and sociology peppered with biblical

44. Bork, *Slouching Towards Gomorrah,* 281–82.
45. Ibid., 282.

references, quips, and quotes. This type of exposé about the limitations of science and its transformation into full-blown naturalism can lead to conclusions that I am neither drawing nor implying. For example, it is not my contention to denigrate science, by which I mean the systematic study of the physical nature, interactions, and interrelationships of physical phenomena. That is science's legitimate domain. However, when science moves into seeking to explain all phenomena as *merely material,* or caused by the material, or allowing only material answers as *the* answers, then science, regardless how cleverly disguised, is actually transformed into naturalism or scientism.

This is where a large number of scientists and those teaching under the guise of science are today. These secularists masquerading under the camouflage of science unduly seek to marginalize supernatural religious beliefs in the marketplace of ideas while simultaneously expanding the domain of science. Those who argue that religion or belief in God have no place in state education, whether they are atheists or pastors, are promoting naturalism. Education, by its very nature, seeks to train people to be better people, citizens, and workers, and this is done by seeking to explain the purposes and values of life one should hold. Even the idea that education should produce good citizens is philosophical rather than scientific.

An example of how easily, and I might add readily, science is supplanted by naturalism can be seen in the following example. A more liberal state board instituted a definition of science in 2002 stating, "Science is the human activity of seeking natural explanations of the world around us."[46] This is more in line with naturalism than true science. In 2005, the board changed that reference to: "Science is a systematic method of continuing investigation that uses observation, hypothesis testing, measurement, experimentation, logical argument and theory building, to lead to more adequate explanations of natural phenomena."[47] The current board also added a qualifying sentence to an introductory paragraph that suggests a self-existing universe: "Although science proposes theories to explain changes, the actual causes of many changes are currently unknown (e.g., the origin of the universe, the origin of the fundamental laws, the origin of life and the genetic code, and the origin of major body plans during the Cambrian explosion)."[48] In addition, the board added information to better describe the core postulates of evolutionary theory and relevant information about its mechanisms. According to a board press release, "Biological evolution postulates an unguided natural process that has no discernible direction or

---

46. Patterson, "Evolution supporters likely to regain grip."
47. Ibid.
48. Ibid.

goal," and "the sequence of the nucleotide bases within genes is not dictated by any known chemical or physical law."[49] Of course the idea of "unguided" is a philosophical statement and "no discernible direction or goal" is as well.

In addition, I do not mean that there are not still many religious people in America in every strata of society. The number of people who, according to polls and church attendance, express a belief in God is significant, as is the number of teachers who silently refuse to teach certain claims of scientism in their class. What I do mean to emphasize is that there has been, over the last several generations, the loss of value, reliance upon, or place for opinions based upon religion or faith in the marketplace of ideas. This is true even for Christians.

Sociologist Alan Wolfe notes how modern day Christians blend into the landscape, and to reassure his liberal friends he states, "There is, then, no reason to fear that the faithful are a threat to liberal democratic values."[50] This loss is systematic, unabated, and inevitable in a scientific liberal culture, a culture that is identifiable by widespread and influential transforming of science into scientism. In fact, it is scientism that actually constructs the scientific liberal culture. Robert Bork notes two unchanging thrusts of liberalism, liberty and equality and he goes on to say, "What distinguishes . . . different stages of liberalism . . . is not any difference in liberalisms but a difference in the admixture of other elements that modify or oppose it."[51] I would add that the most successful attempt at secularizing society is through making science *the* source of public knowledge. That this secularization has significantly marginalized religious faith seems evidentially undeniable.

Some will point out major political shifts that were influenced by religious faith that are accepted by society and secular government, like the Civil Rights movement. While this is true, it is only because it coincides with the liberal view that, scientifically speaking, there is no reason that blacks, Hispanics, etc. should not have rights like everyone else. They would argue, and rightly so, from the Bill of Rights and the Constitution, and from sociology and other sciences, but not from the religious perspective of Martin Luther King and Christians. These from the Christian perspective believe it should be because all were created equal, as stated in the Bible, and the Declaration of Independence, which serves as the impetus for the Constitution. Note when these movements are dealt with by secularists, in large part, they blame the plight on religious oppression and credit the liberation to liberalism and secularism. In addition, some religious opinions and

49. Ibid.
50. Wolfe, *Transformation*, 255.
51. Bork, *Slouching Towards Gomorrah*, 57.

influence are allowed because they simply cannot purge the public square of them at this time, but they are working on it. Other religious opinions happen to coincide with their views.

As Christians, if we have any understanding of the prominent place that Christianity had in the history of our country, we are appalled to watch faith, religion, and particularly Christianity being further and further removed from the marketplace of ideas and made solely a private matter. This is quite baffling to most. How could we have changed so much? At this point of evaluation, it is important to remember my encapsulating concept, which I believe helps to make sense out of the secularization of America. It is that in God's world, there is room for science as well as faith and disbelief. But in a purely scientific world, if science is going to be the sole or primary mode of thinking and knowing for public discourse or policy, there simply is no viable public place for God or faith in him. God must and shall be consigned to superstition, tradition, psychological phenomena, societal immaturity, myth, fairytale, or simply the unknowable.

The move from ivory tower philosophical commitment to naturalism to mainstream acceptance has been through the philosophy of progressive education, and the vehicle for widespread dissemination is state-controlled education. Through government education, by which most Americans are educated, these ideas have influenced most people who then go into the marketplace with the idea that God really does not belong there but rather in the privacy of one's own life. God, or the belief in God, should have no bearing on public debate or policy because it is not knowable by science, and science is the arbiter of not only what works and what does not, but also what is publicly knowable. What is forgotten is the history of America and asking who made science the final arbitrator of everything. What needs to be shouted from the rooftops is that the Declaration of Independence is premised upon the existence of God, without which we have no unalienable rights. Neither science nor scientism could have given us the Declaration of Independence, the unalienable rights described therein, and neither can they protect or sustain them. Without religious knowledge being suitable for publicly imposable knowledge, America as we know her will perish.

Calling Christians to understand these subterranean shapers of our culture is critical for us to be what God wants us to be. I am not arguing for a movement to change the culture, but rather a movement to change the church and Christians so that God can use us most effectively. For example, the call for Christians to be Christian lawyers is not with the idea that our civil and criminal laws will be thoroughly biblical, although that would be best, but it is rather that the Christian lawyer can live out his faith and demonstrate the Christian life and mind in his area of expertise that sets the glory of God before the eyes of men. The same would be true of every Christian in every vocation.

6

The Peril of Trusting Science Too Much
The Strengths and Weaknesses of Science

THE FOUNDERS OF PROGRESSIVE education did not intend for science to merely dominate progressive education, but by progressive education they meant that science was the sole source and basis for education—real knowledge. That distinction with all of its consequences seems quite mysteriously to elude most Americans, who realize that Christianity has been displaced in public education, but are for the most part baffled as to why that happened. The transition from classical to progressive education was a shift from science being part of a good education to seeking to make science the only basis and source of knowledge in education. Therefore, if some knowledge, or a subject, does not come from scientific studies, i.e., empirical studies, then it is marginalized and placed in a separate category like philosophy, history—although they do still use the sciences. Consequently, if you want your opinion to be respected in shaping the future, you had better be in the sciences or call your endeavor scientific. Thus, the quest of areas such as psychology and sociology are to be classified as science, and they are not satisfied with soft science labels. This transformation resulted in shifting from science being taught in school to scientism or naturalism being the basis for all public discourse and education.

Bork asked why the west has become so quickly secularized, and then notes the underlying force as "the advance of egalitarianism and individualism together with the progress of technology."[1] Of course, the fundamental basis, which has provided fallow ground for those ideas, along with the es-

---

1. Bork, *Slouching Towards Gomorrah*, 281.

sential simultaneous erosion of the role of religion, is viewing all of reality through the lens of science—scientism. But why has science become the final arbitrator of truth in our society? Reasons can be given in two categories—some based on the nature of man and the others based on the nature of science.

The nature of man

The first man and woman were created in the image and likeness of God (Gen 1:26–27), and man was given dominion over all of the rest of creation (Gens 1:26, 28) and charged to cultivate and tend the earth (Gen 2:15). This is as lofty as it gets on planet earth. Man, if you will, was given attributes of God (not becoming God) and delegated authority by God over his creation. The image of God means that man and woman were created with a correspondence to God, an affinity with God. Man will always seek the transcendent, not merely to shield himself from the evils of earthly life, not as Marx and Lenin taught "opium of the people" or a primitive evolutionary survival instinct, survival gene, some mere psychological misfire or some other unreal idea as the Enlightenment has perpetuated, but because we were created in God's image.

Since the nature of man is at the center of all societal determinations, I provide the following working definition of man.[2] Man was created in the image of God, which means at least this: man is the product of special creation by God, which included God's bestowal of some of his divine attributes (Gen 1:26–28, 5:1). This did not make man God or a god, but rather the unique image bearer of God. Infants have these attributes in essence—infant form—and nurturing is to develop this essence as well as the child's physical being.

This image consists of at least righteousness; holiness; right relationship with and true understanding of God, man, and the rest of creation; sacredness of all human life; "otherwise" choice (libertarian free will and the ability to act contra-instinctually); a sense of justness (now often evidenced by humans' quest to justify self); moral and spiritual consciousness; extraordinary rationality (including self-awareness and intricate abstractional ability); relational complexity (need to love and be loved involving more than being instinctually relational); compassionate and merciful

---

2. I use this as a working definition since it includes aspects necessary to a thorough understanding of the image of God in man that others may rather classify as being consequences of the image of God rather than a component of the definition. I am fine with that distinction with regards to a technical definition.

dominion (ability to exercise delegated authority); creation of other image bearers (procreation); redeemability; ability to exercise trust (seen within the Trinity and essential to all higher-level relationships); and creative ability (e.g., ability to transform matter into wealth for survival, pleasure, or beauty as seen in creation and creative production beyond necessities in the garden).[3]

While some of these are similar to attributes of angels and animals who are created by God but are not created in His image, other attributes are either *essentially* dissimilar or dissimilar by an *unattainable* degree. Attributes that are essentially dissimilar are therefore undeniably not from anyone or anything other than the direct creation of God (e.g., Darwinian descent). Some that are not possessed by angels include redeemability, relational complexity, and procreating image bearers. Also, creative ability may not be possessed by angels or may not be possessed in the same degree and complexity as man. Animals do not include those attributes as well as righteousness; true understanding of God, man, and creation; a sense of justice; morals; rationality; spiritual consciousness; compassion; libertarian and contra-instinctual choice; and creative ability. Although man was created in the image of God, man sinned (Gen 3:1–6), and the image of God in man was changed. The following seeks to explain how the image was changed.

The narrow sense of the image of God includes righteousness, holiness, and right relationship with God. In the narrow sense, the image of God was destroyed. These attributes of the image did not remain in any sense after the fall of man. If man was to ever possess them again, God would have to recreate them through a redemptive and creative act, which He now offers though grace-enabled faith in Jesus Christ (2 Cor 5:17; Col 3:9–10).

The extensive sense of the image of God includes the rest of the attributes of the image of God. In this extensive sense, the image was not utterly destroyed in the fall and therefore still exists in man (Gen 9:6; 1 Cor 11:7; Jas 3:9); however, these attributes are severely corrupted and beyond human repair. Consequently, these still exist in man albeit in disfigured, diminished, and perverted form.

In these areas, we still imitate God, albeit in a very diminished and distorted way. For example, in the area of cognition, Plantinga reminds us that, "We resemble God not just in being persons, who can think and feel, who have aims and intentions, who form beliefs and act on those beliefs, and the like; we resemble God more particularly in being able to *know* and

---

3. Matter becomes a resource when it comes in contact with humans; before such creative contact it is just raw matter.

understand something of ourselves, our world, and God himself."[4] Now this cognitive ability is corrupted, not totally reliable, and can be used for evil, but it is still real and not imaginary. The same can be said of the other extensive attributes of the image of God. Therefore, fallen man still bears the image diminutively and correspondingly manifests the attributes of the image. Redemption in Christ is the only path to full restoration of the image of God (John 3:16; 2 Cor 5:17).

Man being thusly created in the image of God distinguishes him from the animal world. Man does share some physical characteristics with the animal world since both were made by the same creator, and animal and man's physicality were both made from the earth. Likewise, animals have other similarities like being social, but with animals that trait is merely instinctual. Man is volitional, rational, moral, spiritual, and in authority over God's creation, and this is not based on instinct but because he has been created in the image of God; therefore, man is different than the animals not merely in degree, but in kind.

In addition, there is simply an unbridgeable chasm between the truth of man's lofty creation and the evolutionist's view of man as merely the unintended product of natural forces, which makes him a cog in the completely natural world, with no free will, purpose, intrinsic value, or goal above that of an ant.[5] Although man started in this lofty position, being created in the image of God, when man and woman chose to listen to the temptation Satan proposed, they fell and became sinners, not merely in practice, but in their very nature. The image of God was not eradicated, making them animals, but it was marred and corrupted, making them incapable of experiencing their intended relationship with God and rightly fulfill their assignment from God.

This first temptation involved two parts. The first part was to trust someone else and therefore distrust God, which of course is the nature of all temptations even to this present hour. The second part of the temptation was not only believing that God's warning of death was not true, but also being tempted by the words of the great deceiver to believe that the real reason God was keeping them from eating was "For God knows that in the day you eat from it your eyes will be opened, and *you will be like God, knowing good and evil*" (Gen 3:5). (italics added) Now, subsequent to the

---

4. Plantinga, *Where the Conflict Really Lies*, 4.

5. Beyond a compatibilist redefinition of free will, which only results in defining determinism in a way that includes responsibility, but every sense of origination and otherwise choice is lost. For a fuller explanation see "The Fall of Angels and Man Two Views: Calvinism and Non-Calvinism," http://www.ronniewrogers.com/2013/10/09/the-fall-of-angels-and-man-two-views-calvinism-and-non-calvinism/.

fall, there is not only the potential to believe this and therefore be tempted, there is the driving predisposition to believe it, and therefore the desire to prove and demonstrate that man is not only godlike, he is his own God. Science, along with its worldview of evolutionary naturalism, has proven to be the most systematized and plausible argument for this view that seems to have ever been devised.

The strengths of science

Science has several positively understood characteristics that make it seem to be the reasonable replacement for Christianity. Let me mention eight.

First is the reality that science works. Brian Appleyard says, "Technology was, above all, the ultimate, unarguable assertion of science's one big claim: it works. From Newton onward science poured out its laws and technology turned them into steam engines, factories, cars and rockets. And the engines moved and the rockets went up. It works."[6] Jawaharlal Nehru, the first prime minister of India after the British colonists left, said, "It is science alone that can solve the problems of hunger and poverty, of insanitation and illiteracy, of superstition and deadening custom and tradition . . . the future belongs to science and those who make friends with science."[7] No one in the western world can deny that science has made our lives better. Who would dare return his electric refrigerator for an icebox, or give up the polio shot and risk that dreadful disease, or return to merely landline phones? Science affects our lives at every turn, and for the most part, we like it because it works, meaning it does what it says it can do. It can and has devised a better mousetrap.

Second is that science seems to be impartial. In referring to the battle between the progressives and the academic curriculum proponents, Ravitch mentions that science played a key role. "In the early decades of the century, science had a dazzling allure because it appeared to provide an impartial means of settling disputed matters."[8] Today, if science says it, it must be true because scientific conclusions are the result of supposedly unbiased and observable processes, even though this is not always the case.

Third, science is the universal language. An experiment performed in Oklahoma, which is then repeated in Japan, will, if it is a sound theory, yield

---

6. Appleyard, *Understanding the Present*, 66.
7. Ibid., 4.
8. Ravitch, *Left Back*, 66.

basically the same results. There simply is no Japanese science or Oklahoma science. There is just science. It is universal. It is something that everyone can see.

Fourth, it has an unquestionable obviousness about it. In other words, if someone makes a car battery that starts better and lasts longer, one would be senseless not to buy it if the price were the same. All things being equal, if a new medicine has been proven to fight a particular disease better, if it is there in black and white for anyone to see, then it would be foolish not to use it. Thus, it has a self-evident undeniableness.

Fifth, it seems to engender a tolerant society. This is because no scientific claim can boast of being universally true forever. By the very nature of science, it is open-ended. Consequently, when a scientist, or a person basing his conclusion upon science, speaks in a manner consistent with the evidence, he must do so tentatively, speaking in probabilities rather than certainties.

Sixth, science seems to be able to explain or offer plausible answers for everything. This includes every being, existence, process, and behavior, even offering an explanation for evil or good.

Seventh, science advances. Science seems to get better, correcting its own errors and producing better, more efficient products. There is just something in man that sees perceived improvements or progress as always better.

Eighth, science affords man a way to explain his existence. This permits man to have come into being without having been created by God and therefore accountable to God, which is of course the quest of man since the fall.

When you combine the nature of man and the nature of science, it is easy to see why science's popularity and power is ever advancing. Postmoderns may balk at that idea, but they do make toast in the morning before they drive to their air-conditioned offices. As one might imagine, these positives of science are not without inherent negatives and dangers, and this is particularly true in light of man as a fallen sinner who desires to replace God.

Weaknesses of science

As noted above, science has some very positive traits, but it also has weaknesses. Let me note six essential weaknesses that over time have had a deleterious impact upon the world of man, morals, faith, and hope, and therefore the church.

First is the weakness inherent in the reality that science works and is effective. The negative within that strength becomes more and more accepted over time, regardless of the disclaimers to the contrary. Science has an inherent message that what works better—more efficiently—is better, right, or good. This is particularly pronounced in a scientific liberal culture. This mindset is developed with regard to technology, but is not contained there. In reality, the effectiveness of something does not mean that it is right. Can does not equal should. Hitler had an efficient way of eliminating Jews, but it was not right. Eve had the ability; she could reach and eat the fruit of every tree, but her dexterity was not the determiner of right, and wrong. That man is able to perform an abortion and do it efficiently, does nothing to determine the rightness of the act. If one thinks as a progressive (where God's existence is uncertain or culturally unimportant), then the rightness of an act is determined by the scientific theory of open-endedness.

Although science claims to separate itself from values, it vociferously promotes the value that science is the best source of knowledge. Moreover, most people will assume that the ability to do something that is not obviously evil, means one should, and that the most effective way is the right way. For example, if this training helps my son get a better job, then he should have that training. However, this view presupposes that education is to be vocationally driven, and the question of whether education should be vocationally driven is a matter of debate; further, in what regard is this the best job—pay, environment, advancing the kingdom, helping fellow man, or other perks, , must be determined. Once the criteria for determining what the best job is and why, that criteria, e.g., pay, must be evaluated by whether it is right or wrong. Science's success in some areas has given it unearned authority in others. Science says here is a problem that we can answer, not whether something is right or wrong, nor even the best answer for the long term. This is often seen when a scientist in one area is accepted as an authority in another area—even though he has no training or expertise in that area—simply because he is a scientist.

Second is the weakness inherent in the reality that science is impartial and objective. This is derived from the nature of the scientific method of hypothesis, examination, observation, replication, and potential falsifiability. However, science is not immune to corruption. To quote Kohn, professor of Virology notes, "Breaches of ethics as encountered in scientific research cover a whole spectrum ranging from outright fraud and conscious falsification, through plagiarism and concealment of information, to minor infractions such as 'grantsmanship' and negligence."[9] The reality is that while the scientific method may be impartial and objective, humans conducting the experiments are not. This was more fully addressed in *Underestimating the biases in science* in chapter 2 of this book.

Third is the weakness inherent in the reality that science is the universal language. While it is true that there is not different science for different nationalities, races, or locations, the truth is that the same can be said for Christianity. But the problem is that not everyone accepts the claims of any one religion. For example, since the founding of the United States until post 1960s, if a politician or someone mentioned God, virtually everyone knew that it was the God of the Bible to whom he referred. That the Ten Commandments were good for society, because they came from God was generally accepted. This can be further generalized to include Europe—although the evanescing of such began earlier in Europe. The downside of science as the universal language, which will have a damning impact upon man, is that when science becomes the lingua franca, teaching history is devalued because it is not necessary or plays very little role in the advance of science. Appleyard notes, "A computer scientist need never have heard of Newton, he need only know of a thin film of recent knowledge to be able to master his art. Scientific progress is so radical that, at every stage, it is able to throw away almost all the baggage of its own history."[10]

The practical reality of science becoming the arbiter of all truth is that history is lost in history, and men begin to evaluate good and bad, right and wrong, benefit and harm, without the wisdom of the past, which decontextualizes the discussion and therefore leaves it open to demagoguery, fear mongering, or promising the moon when only a piece of cheese will eventuate. In many ways, science has become the unrivaled arbitrator of the future direction that should be taken, as well as the interpreter of the present. However, without history, there really is no sense of community because science is incapable of providing continuity from one generation to the next, connecting, or giving a sense of belonging to something bigger than the moment. With science, everything, and I do mean everything, is up for grabs.

It is common to hear expressions like "world community" based on common scientific values or knowledge, or communication based upon modern technology, but really the community is only for today. In reality, family, until the unbiquitousness of science, meant more than someone you

9. Kohn, *False Prophets*, vii.
10. Appleyard, *Understanding the Present*, 223.

are presently involved with in marriage. It included from whence you came and where you were going and why. Further, modern historical revisionists and multiculturalists actually divide the community into tribalism. The destruction of patriotism, devaluation of religious faith, and acceptance of the world community over nation and state by giving up anything that is seen as exclusivistic truth does not create family or community, but rather apathy and passive resignation. Bork says, "We no longer have a common moral culture and our religion, while pervasive, seems increasingly unable to affect our behavior."[11] With the disintegration of one language, and the devaluing of a common religious basis, we are losing the ability to communicate with each other as a historical people and are therefore subject to the latest poll and invention.

Science does not create one large community, but rather a multi-community world based upon their particular branches of science. It becomes so specialized and the jargon so esoteric that the average person cannot understand much of what is being said, and the specialist is convinced that no one outside of the scientific community can really understand, but actually even scientists have great difficulty communicating among themselves. Jerry Brotzge, a former member of the church where I pastor, told me about an experience he had that illustrates my point. Jerry, who has a PhD in meteorology from the University of Oklahoma, was a Research Scientist with the Center for the Analysis and Prediction of Storms (CAPS) and was the Director of NetRad Operations for the CASA Program. He was invited to an interdisciplinary symposium of scientists in Poland. He later told me that the conference was not that beneficial because the scientists were so specialized they could not communicate with one another.[12]

---

11. Bork, *Slouching Towards Gomorrah*, 64.

12. Jerry gives the following example as another illustration of the difficulty experienced by interdisciplinary scientists' communication. He said, "I work on an interdisciplinary, multi-campus project called CASA—Engineering Research Center for the Collaborative Adaptive Sensing of the Atmosphere. It's a ten-year research center funded by the National Science Foundation, with the end goal of producing small, inexpensive, low-power radars. The project includes computer scientists, mechanical and electrical engineers, meteorologists, and social scientists. During the first several years of the project, few of the disciplines could communicate. We each had our own vocabulary—sometimes even the same word had different meanings, depending on the discipline. We each had our own way of 'thinking' and approached problems differently. After much effort—multiple in-person meetings and daily/weekly phone conversations—we eventually learned how to communicate, but it wasn't easy. It required a concerted, focused effort and lots of time. Today, to move forward in science often requires these multidisciplinary collaborations. Overall, this seems to be a good thing—the results are something that could not be accomplished without this cross-discipline work. That being said, it requires more time, work, and lots of patience. There

Science as *the* source of truth guarantees that there is no connection to the past, for the past is merely an antiquated phase in the march of Darwinism, as one day we will be regarded as well. Because science deals only with the material aspect of reality, when it is expanded into other areas where there is an integration of material and immaterial, e.g., the nature of man, it becomes excessively reductionistic, defining man and his interactions based on what can be observed. It then trains him with that understanding of the world and thereby educates men and women not to their highest intellectual, spiritual, and moral capacity but according to the lowest common denominator. Man is simply matter, and therefore, as an overdeveloped piece of slime, has no elevated status—what is pejoratively referred to as speciesism—consequently what he learns is based on nature, what is valued is based on nature, what he should do is based on nature, rather than based on being created in the image of God.

For example, the state and the scientist have no problem saying that smoking causes cancer; therefore, it should be decreased or eliminated, and the state will be proactive in bringing about that goal. Notice the key component is that it is a physical issue—it harms people biologically. However, when the breakdown of the family creates more government dependence, crime, unstable families and troubled children, they are far less willing to take decisive steps if those steps involve spiritual or biblical teachings, e.g., monogamy, heterosexual marriage and parenting. This is true even when the evidence confirms that these relational breakdowns have disastrous physiological and psychological consequences. They are unlikely to support religion even when studies show the positive influence religion has on peoples' lives.[13] This is due in significant part to the fact that science is the final arbitrator, and the material or natural is all that we can really know as a society.

Moreover, if man is merely a product of matter or nature, he has no libertarian free will with otherwise choice, which is essential to answer the question of ultimate culpability.[14] Therefore, based on a merely scientific view of man, evil acts are not evil (in any sense other than a human construct), i.e., wrong, or sin, but merely an illness, disease, sickness, or mistake. Consequently, crime or violations are not the result of evil choices but the product of medical or psychological dysfunctions. Hence, criminals are treated medically rather than by an objective morality. This is the

---

is debate now within the scientific community about whether or not such collaborative projects are worth the money/effort."

13. Colson and Pearcey, *How Now Shall We Live*, have statistics and studies in these areas. See chapters 32 and 36.

14. Neither determinism nor compatibilism adequately address this.

foundational idea in the trial where Vermont Judge Edward Cashman sentenced Mark Hulett to 60 days in prison for raping a six-year old girl over a four-year period.[15] "The judge did this because he believes the criminal, 34-year-old Mark Hulett cannot get rehab in prison. And Judge Cashman believes punishment alone is not appropriate for child rapists . . . The Rutland Herald, which editorialized, 'Cashman issued the [60 day] sentence precisely to protect children. It was the only way to provide Hulett the treatment he needs in a timely manner in order to deter him from committing similar offenses in the future.'"[16] We are significantly, although not completely, advanced in moving from defining these kinds of issues according to the medical model rather than the moral model. Even Christians speak of things as medical issues when the Bible clearly places in the moral category—alcoholism, adultery, gluttony, etc., (1 Cor. 6:9–10).

Why should humans, who are, according to Molecular Biologist Dean Hamer, chief of Gene Structure at the U.S. National Cancer Institute, "a bunch of chemical reactions running around in a bag," have the right, responsibility, or capability to determine what is the good of society or anything else?[17] Why should any bag of material reactions listen to any other bag of material reactions or believe that bag A has better reactions than bag C because bags of reactions may demonstrate that this kind of reaction causes bags to live longer but it cannot tell you they should. It is the end of compassion as well. Why build hospitals to save meaningless, determined bags of material reactions, and if some bags do this, it is not compassion—a free choice—it just is.

It is contradictory. If scientific naturalism is true and nature is all there is; religion is merely a necessary adaptive trait of evolution like an expression of need, want, or a quest for power or survival, and only what can be empirically measured is real. Then one needs to ask, why trust the scientist? If naturalism is true, scientists are not free moral agents making impartial volitional studies, but rather they are just a part of the machine, dispensing ideas and formulas that they must produce as their part in the evolutionary dynamism. Colson states this rather succinctly, "Christians ought to argue that scientific naturalism is incoherent and self-contradictory, for scientists must exempt themselves from the very framework they prescribe for everyone else. All human beings are reduced to mechanisms operating by natural causes—*except* scientists themselves. Why? Because to carry out their experiments, they must assume that *they*, at least, are capable of

---

15. O'Reilly, "Vermont's Shame."
16. O'Reilly, "Some Vermont Media is Sympathizing."
17. Beauregard and O'Leary, *The Spiritual Brain*, 35.

transcending the network of material causes, capable of rational thought, of free deliberation, of formulating theories, of recognizing objective truth. They themselves must form the single glaring exception to their own theory. This is the fatal self-contradiction of naturalism."[18]

C.S. Lewis responded to Professor Price's scientific arguments against the reality of religion based on Price's naturalism, "He spoke as he did because the matter of his brain was behaving a certain way . . . what we call his thoughts was essentially a phenomenon of the same sort as his other secretions—the form which the vast irrational process of nature was bound to take at a particular point of space and time . . . he was deluded."[19] Lewis goes on to point out that, if naturalism is true, then thoughts, ideas, insights, being the determined product of non-intentional natural processes are nothing more than a hiccup or sneeze.[20]

The assertion is that science, as the universal language that trumps all other claims to knowledge, is the only source of public truth is not only self-defeating, as just demonstrated, but is also extraordinarily discouraging and pessimistic. This is because true science has been conflated with naturalism, and naturalism is pessimistic. Lewis notes, "Now most assuredly if naturalism is right then it . . . overthrows all our hopes: not only our hope of immortality, but our hope of finding significance in our lives here and now."[21] With naturalism, we are merely consigned to survive; it is not a choice, and no one knows why except that is what genes do. Man is determined, not to survive, but to fight to survive. British scientist and former professor at Oxford University, Richard Dawkins believes that our genes create humans, and "their preservation is the *ultimate rationale* for our existence."[22] It is crucial to note that his statement is philosophical or religious rather than scientific; of course most students would never grasp that Dawkins had moved from science to faith. In a conversation with Bryan Appleyard, Richard Dawkins said, with regard to the pessimism of hard science, "I don't feel depressed about it . . . but if somebody does that's their problem. Maybe the logic is deeply pessimistic, the universe is bleak, cold and empty. But so what?"[23] Ultimately, once one gets beyond the naturalist rhetoric, this is the *raison d'être* of human existence. There is none!

18. Colson and Pearcey, *How Now Shall*, 421.
19. Lewis, "Religion without Dogma" in *God in the Dock*, 136.
20. Ibid., 137.
21. Ibid., 135.
22. Dawkins, *The Selfish Gene*, 20.
23. Appleyard, *Understanding the Present*, 168.

Scientists like Francois Jacob, professor of Cellular Genetics at College de France and a member of the French Academy, who in 1965 shared the Nobel Prize in Medicine for his work in genetics, rejects the idea that science is limitless in its explanatory powers. . "It [science] limits itself to clearly defined questions . . . It knows today that its answers can only be partial and provisional. In contrast to science, other explanatory systems—magic, myth, religion—endeavor to be universal."[24] He later states,

> But clearly some questions have nothing to do with science. There is a limit to scientific investigation. Science declines to answer questions like, what is the meaning of life? How did everything begin? What is our purpose on earth? Faced with such questions, science has nothing to say. An entire domain is totally excluded from all scientific inquiry—that which concerns the origin of the world, the meaning of the human condition, the "destiny" of human life . . . Each of us, sooner or later, asks them. But these questions, which Karl Popper calls "ultimate," are a matter for religion, for metaphysics . . . Science cannot answer them.[25]

This is true science, and Jacob is precisely correct. However, and quite unfortunately, scientism expands every day right along with the legitimate progress of science. Science, in education and otherwise, is seeking to answer *all* questions, even about the genesis of man and the genesis and reality of faith, existence of God, etc. Morals are defined by what works for the progress of good as defined by science rather than derived from God. Appleyard states:

> First Copernicus had turned us into a cosmic speck, secondly Darwin had robbed us of any privileged position in creation, and, finally, he, Freud, had shown that man was not even master of his own mind." He states elsewhere, "For we too must be made of numbers and these numbers must be subject to the same iron logic of cause and effect. We do things because of other things and we are joined to the whole universal chain of causality. Free will is an illusion born of our ignorance. Science tells us that we can know everything and, therefore, that we can be utterly imprisoned.[26]

---

24. Jacob, *Of Flies*, 129.
25. Ibid., 148.
26. Appleyard, *Understanding the Present*, 72, 62.

Some scientists are at least honest about their duplicity. David P. Barash writes: "I suspect that we all—even the most hard-headed materialist—live with an unspoken hypocrisy: even as we assume determinism in our intellectual pursuits and professional lives, we actually experience our subjective lives as though free will reigns supreme. In our heart of hearts, we *know* that in most ways that really count (and many that don't), we have plenty of free will, and so do those around us. Inconsistent? Yes, indeed. But like the denial of death, it is a useful inconsistency, and perhaps even one that is essential."[27]

Fourth is the weakness inherent in the reality of its undeniableness. This is not necessarily a negative of science per se, but rather with the nature of man. The obvious efficiency of science, its accomplishments, and the benefits that we experience every day predispose modern man to be more than willing to give the benefit of the doubt to science. The comments given all too often by university professors about how science has disproved or undermined the intellectual legitimacy of the supernatural, or made it less than *real* knowledge, must be addressed by pastors in order to equip young Christians to not only know what they believe but why they believe and how to defend Christian truth.

There is a general tendency among college students to presuppose the professor's claims are true because after all, he is a professor. Of course, the professor is often quick to say, one can still be a person of faith, but he is quite clear that this kind of faith knowledge has no place in education; faith is faith and science is *real* knowledge—knowledge suitable for education and the public mind. Why? Because science is objectively knowable and successful; it works. Scientists said they could solve problems in manufacturing and productivity, provide safer automobiles and better medicines, and they did; therefore, categorizing faith knowledge as less than scientific knowledge must be true as well. To wit, the common assumption is, where science speaks, the only legitimate counter is more science even when the subject extends beyond the empirical. Science's obvious positive contributions to the ease and pleasure of modern life incline the average person to conclude that, if allowed enough time, scientists will answer all—or at least all that need to be or can be answered—the questions of life, which is at the heart of Enlightenment and Darwinian thinking.

Science is antagonistic toward external authority and any rules set over science. Science therefore seeks to be the final authority. Scientism, which is diaphanously veiled as science, seeks to be the unrivaled authority of the

---

27. Beauregard and O'Leary, *The Spiritual Brain*, 231.

day and constructs the rules of modern society in domains outside of the legitimate sphere of science proper. Accordingly, science's obvious success, prestige, and recognition produce a wittingly or unwittingly implicit bias toward science and away from that which challenges or bridles it in anyway. This transition reflects not only a shift in *what* twenty-first century Americans think but in *how* we think.

If science builds a better tire, all things—price, accessibility, etc.,—being equal, one would be quite unwise not to buy it. In like manner, (the supposed logic would follow) if psychology is a science as it is now considered, and it says that students learn better with child-centered curriculum, then that curriculum must be best. If scientists, including sociobiologists say that people are basically selfish because they are driven by selfish genes, then it must be right. Dawkins says regarding this, "I shall argue that the predominant quality to be expected in a successful gene is ruthless selfishness. This gene selfishness will usually give rise to selfishness in individual behavior . . .. Much as we might wish to believe otherwise, universal love and the welfare of the species as a whole are concepts that do not make evolutionary sense."[28] Most never pause to consider, is this really science? Has science overstepped its legitimate bounds? Can science really ascribe volitional qualities—selfishness—to material objects like genes? When science says students learn better under a scientific progressive model, do they mean they learn more, or do they learn more of what the pedagogues want them to learn? Because they do not seem to be learning more about such subjects as grammar, history, literature, or the founding and governing of America.

The reality is that the advantage or application of science in one area does not necessarily transfer to another. However, when the empirical is extolled, religion is privatized, and the practical significance of the immaterial is depreciated, the move from science providing the answer for how to make a better battery to providing the answer for the significance of human existence, morals, thought, and faith is a small subtle step for most. Most people have never heard of, much less understood, a distinction between science and scientism, science and scientific naturalism, science and epistemic naturalism, or science and methodological naturalism, and that obfuscates the grievous danger by which we as a society and church are presently being engulfed.

Fifth is the weakness inherent in the claims that it engenders tolerance. Today there is an overarching societal sin, and that is intolerance. To state that you know the absolute truth, for all people everywhere and for

---

28. Dawkins, *The Selfish Gene*, 2.

all time, is viewed as the height of arrogance. What is seen as intelligent, socially acceptable, and mature is uncertainty, tentativeness, nuance ad infinitum, and contextualized values. Granted, there are many times that these considerations are appropriate. But to grant that uncertainty has its place at times while at other times certainty is attainable, is quite different than saying that absolutes have no place or do not exist which is known philosophically as relativism. Although I do recognize the pervasiveness of relativism in our society, I do not regard today's relativism as philosophical relativism but rather the consequence of accepting science as the arbitrator of all truth in all areas.

As I stated before, tentativeness and non-absolutism are essential to legitimate science. That is what science is. It is the study of parts with partial knowledge. It is based on what can be observed with the knowledge that there may be the existence of something that we do not know about yet that will ultimately undermine some of the claims or falsify the conclusion of any and every scientific discovery regardless how much evidence there is at the present, e.g., a Newtonian view of the world being displaced by an Einsteinian view.

True science cannot say that it has the final answer to anything. It cannot say this is the rule from now on. Even in the area of scientific laws the scientist cannot rightly use law to mean that such and such *has* to happen. If he does, he has overstated his case and gone beyond the realm of science. He can use law to mean that such and such has happened with regularity or that the same cause and effect have a high statistical probability.[29] This use of law does not exclude anomalies, nor is it invalidated by them, at least to a certain point. In other words, it never tells us what *must* happen but rather what will possibly or probably happen, and when applied to humans, it cannot tell us what an individual or group must do, but rather what a certain group will probably do. Science can tell us what works in the material world, but it cannot tell us if something is right regardless how well it works.

When we have over one hundred years of progressive education, considered by progressives to be scientific education, science becomes the *way* of thinking; hence, relativism and tolerance are more by-products of scientism than an overtly adopted philosophical system. When scientific thinking is applied to every domain of existence—scientism—then tentativeness or relativism is the accepted expression du jour. As stated earlier, this is why education resists and rebels against starting with rules, be they rules of grammar, which are essential to phonics, moral standards over

---

29. One scientist, Dr. David Schmidt, with whom I met for many weeks, would not use the term laws but only the term regularities because the implication of the term law was *must happen*.

values clarifications, or anyone outside of science determining the best education based on other grounds. Everything, even such realities as human value, life, love, parenting, morals, and purpose is just another experiment, which is neither right nor wrong, and is determined apart from any belief in absolutely sure wisdom from the past.

In part, they are not trying to correct the errors of the past—except religious superstitions and anything else perceived to stand in the way of science—nor are they trying to prove they are right for all time because in a scientific liberal culture that is unnecessary and practically impossible. Rather, all they must demonstrate is that this idea works better than other competing ideas in advancing science and that no one can say we should or should not pursue it based on some ancient religious or moral authority. Additionally, the short-term argument is often difficult to refute because philosophy, religion, or non-material views of man are taboo; by the time the long-term consequences have shown their earlier answers and conclusions to be wrong, science has another answer for the present dilemma, and the cycle continues.

This scientistic thinking (elevation and expansion of rationalism and empiricism) has largely contributed to the popular acceptance of the dynamic reading of the U.S. Constitution, the Bible, and every other standard bearing document. For they consider everything to merely be a scientific experiment and therefore subject to revision. This has led, albeit at times unwittingly, to the antipathy of many state educators, scientists, lawmakers, and judges toward the presence of religion in any aspect of public life or debate. Why? Because religion is not science, and science is the genesis and guardian of public knowledge; hence, religion must be merely private. Scientism teaches us to apply "If it works for you"—like a new radio or pain pill—"it is ok, but don't force it upon me" to every area of life. That is to say, my experiments have not led me to conclude that your religion, maybe any religion, is right. My experiments have not led me to conclude that marriage is for life, stealing is always wrong or does not work, or that homosexuality is wrong, ad infinitum.

The clash between scientism and religion has begotten several showdowns in American culture. In my estimation, it appears that on a cultural level, scientism is winning. This is not to say anything about the truthfulness or value of faith, Christian faith, in which I believe. It is to say that scientism is on the march and is squelching religion on its way to unrivaled supremacy. Charles Colson writes, "The standard assumption is that science constitutes objective knowledge while religion is an expression of subjective need. Religion, therefore, must accommodate its claims about the world to

The Peril of Trusting Science Too Much   167

whatever science decrees."[30] Appleyard, in referring to the debate between religion and science, argues that there is usually a compromise in which science walks away with the upper hand. He uses the debate over experimenting on embryos in which a committee in Britain decided that it could be done up to the fourteenth day of development. That is when "it is said, that the 'primitive streak' appeared, and the embryo ceased to look like a random clump of cells. But this is, of course, no answer at all. The committee simply looked at the hard religious argument, then at the hard scientific evidence and drew a convenient and temporarily convincing line between the two. *And even that line was scientifically determined since it was the scientists who told the committee about the primitive streak.*"[31] (italics added)

The whole idea of saying that one knows truth is viewed as anti-educational. In a televised debate with Alan Keyes, Alan Dershowitz argued that he did not believe in God, while maintaining that people who do not believe in God can establish and do what is right, and there is no need to invoke God for us to be a moral society. He said repeatedly in one form or another, all we have to do, is do what is right. That became his mantra for refuting the idea that we need God to know right and wrong. All we need to do is what is right, he would say. The question from the audience for Dershowitz was this, "What makes something right?" Following is his response.

> It's a question I'm actually writing a book about. It's called "Doing Right." In my book, I reject natural law. I also reject simple legal positivism. If something is right, you have to struggle over that. It's very, very difficult. There are no simpleminded answers. It's not because God says so. Certainly I don't hear the voice of God. I don't believe any human being has ever heard the voice of God. But what is right is very difficult. What's right is what experience has taught us over generations is right. In my book, I say it's much easier to know what's wrong than to know what's right. We know what absolute evil is. We've seen it. We've seen it in the name of Secularism: Nazism. We've seen it in the name of atheism: Communism. We've seen it in the name of religion: the inquisitions and the crusades. *We know what evil is. We know what wrong is. Right is a process.* Right-ing is a process. A process of eternal search, beginning from the first human beings, moving through the Greek philosophers, through religious leaders, through civil leaders. *I don't know what's right. I know what's wrong.* But I have something else to tell you folks. *You don't know what's right.* The minute you think you know what's

---

30. Colson and Pearcy, *How Now Shall*, 419.
31. Appleyard, *Understanding the Present*, 219.

right, the minute you think you have the answer to what's right, you have lost a very precious aspect of growing and developing. *I don't expect ever to know precisely what's right, but I expect to devote the rest of my life to trying to find out.*[32] (italics added)

With regard to Dershowitz's argument, let me say a couple of things. First the atheist's ability to establish a moral standard or "do what is right" is not the question. Even thieves and terrorists can establish a moral standard. The question is, can they demonstrate *how* they establish an objective moral standard, and the answer is no. Moreover, they cannot establish *the* moral code, which can be done only by God. More to the point, this is a law professor at Harvard no less, and yet, he says he does not "know what's right," nor does he "ever expect to."

In light of his admittance that he does not know right, one may fairly and even quite urgently ask, what is he teaching—merely what works, the efficient? Why would one devote his life to something that apparently does not exist and that he will never know? If in knowing truth, what is right, we lose "a very important element of growing and learning," then why would we ever pursue it, at least with any intention of finding it because finding it has such a negative impact upon growing? If you do not know what truth is, then how do you know that you have not been shown it and rejected it? Further, does his understanding of truth mean that ignorance is growing? He is very adamant that he knows what is evil, wrong, but how pray tell can someone know what is wrong—the holocaust—if he does not know that preventing or stopping a holocaust is right? Dershowitz says experience teaches us right from wrong, but really it only teaches us what works—and what works or fails is always determined by the worker or powerful—and what does not work is based upon the goal of those who evaluate the experience. It can tell us how many thought something was right, but not what is right. This is the impoverishment and peril of scientism.

Dershowitz's argument is fatally flawed. Knowing what is right helps learning, and only knowing all right stops one from growing and developing, which is true of only God.

Sixth is the weakness inherent in the reality it advances. Maybe the significance of this is partly because we have been influenced by the very nature of science as demonstrated in areas like tolerance and relativism. Being created in the image of God would seem to carry with it the desire to improve and advance (Gen 1:27–28; 2:15), but with science defining the terms, advancing is what science says is advancing. Science has created a

---

32. Dershowitz and Keyes, "Organized Religion Debate."

culture where change is essential and not changing or clinging to the past in any way is harmful because that is not what science does nor what a scientific liberal culture esteems. An advance in science is an advance in culture, which if rejected is to go backward, an anathema to science and scientific liberals. Simply put, it is good to be progressive and thinking as a Neanderthal to conserve unflinchingly anything except the value of science.

Even in evangelical circles, churches are regularly evaluated by whether or not they are progressive enough, rather than whether they are faithful to true teaching from God. Because science created a culture where progress is viewed as inherently good, and therefore status quo or looking back to a better day or, at times, even to what God has actually said is injurious if it does not result in humanly esteemed progress. Religion is viewed as suspect, stifling at best, or irrelevant and evil. In addition, some of the dogmas and beliefs of religion "have been rendered incredible by the progress of science."[33] For example, the idea of repentance has become vastly unacceptable because it entails a spiritual problem, a solution that lies beyond man, and a commitment to a standard that does not change; to which one must turn *back* if he wants to live a meaningful life.

Of course, what is frequently missing in this discussion is what is meant by progress. Who determines what is progress, and how do we know that we are progressing? While most would agree that we have progressed technologically, in other areas like sanctity of human life, marital stability, and morals, we have regressed. Without absolutes, progress is reduced to meaning things are going in the way a particular person or group thinks they should. It still is therefore undecided, at least as a culture, what progress is. While the internet is clearly a mark of technological progress, it has also made immediately accessible the dungeons of lure for even the most fleeting fleshly whispers of child and man alike, and has thereby concomitantly contributed to the moral erosion of our culture. Moreover, biblically speaking, it is clear that we are spiritually and morally regressing into paganism, e.g., New Age, polytheism, normalizing homosexuality and idolatry. In large measure, culture has moved sin from the moral model to the medical so that it is no longer something from which to repent, but merely a sickness to be treated. Furthermore, when people in an SLC speak of progress, they most often mean moving away from past traditions, beliefs, and absolutes derived from God and particularly Christianity. Progress for the

---

33. Lewis, "Religion without Dogma" in *God in the Dock*, 129. This is one of Professor Price's points that science is proving religion to be "hard to believe." Lewis answers all four of his points. My purpose in mentioning it is to demonstrate that the nature of science is progress, and it is so strong that it engenders faith in its triumphing future over every rival.

promoter of scientism means the advancement of scientific understanding and prominence with the concomitant marginalizing of religion.

It is important to remember that many progressives and scientists are adamant against religion having any place in education except for comparative religion classes and the like.[34] This is because they deem progressive education to be scientific and they disdain any constraints that religion might bring to bear on the unbridled scientistic experiment.[35] When the need for moral restraints in science is suggested, some scientists argue that scientists often put moral regulations on themselves.[36] Of course, this is not the point because science is not sufficient to determine right and wrong. Further, scientism, which seeks to have science dominate public discourse in every area, is inherently anti-supernatural religion. It seeks the total abolishment of supernatural religious influence from public and private domains.

Appleyard insists that science does not coexist with religion (except for the religion of naturalism), and predicts with regard to making decisions, that the line will be drawn closer to science.

> Now, given the seductive effectiveness and persuasive power of science, over time it is clear that this line will tend to move further and further over to the scientific lobby. The pressure on the other side will be decreased as science continues to conquer because of its corrosive and restless refusal to coexist. . . . All moral issues in a liberal society are intrinsically irresolvable and all such issues will progressively tend to be decided on the basis of a scientific version of the world and of values. In other words they will cease to be moral issues; they will become problems to be solved. *The very idea of morality will be marginalized and, finally, destroyed.*"[37] (italics added)

An example of this is seen by the shift in our society to view criminal acts according to a medical model—they are sick and need treatment—rather than the moral model—they chose to do evil and must be punished. It should be noted that the moral model does not exclude the idea of rehabilitation but rather believes that punishment is not only right but also part of correcting the behavior and thinking of the criminal.

---

34. McGrath, referring to a 1996 professional study, says "Some 40% of working natural scientists hold religious beliefs." McGrath, *Reenchantment*, 67.

35. See McGrath, *Reenchantment*, 61–70 for a historical summary of this conflict.

36. This is a claim often made by the scientific community, and scientists that I have talked with have mentioned this to me as well.

37. Appleyard, *Understanding the Present*, 220.

Stephen J. Gould cloaked his antagonism by saying, "Science and religion cannot conflict because they deal with different things: Science is about facts, while 'religion struggles with human morality.'"[38] Unfortunately many Christians and pastors have accepted this distinction, which eventuates in the practical political triumph of scientism, and religion becoming merely private pietism. Some are more forthright about the place of science being the basis of a worldview. Richard Dawkins states, "Darwin made it possible to be an intellectually fulfilled atheist."[39] Biologist William Provine of Cornell University declares, "Darwinism is not just about mutations and fossils; it is a comprehensive philosophy stating that all life can be explained by natural causes acting randomly—which implies that there is no need for the creator. And if god did not create the world, he notes, then the entire body of Christian belief collapses."[40] It is important to note that even the word random, when used to mean that there is no intelligent organizational involvement, carries a philosophical presupposition that is beyond the scope of science. Random is merely an informational word that seeks to describe how things appear to have happened, but cannot tell us that nothing was involved in orchestrating the events because that is simply beyond the scope of science.[41]

38. Colson and Pearcey, *How Now Shall*, 91.
39. Dawkins, *Blind Watchmaker*, 6.
40. Cited in Colson and Pearcey, *How Now Shall*, 91.
41. I am indebted to David Schmidt, a neurophysiologist research scientist, for this insight into the nature of randomness. He helped me to understand that this is actually an informational word rather than an actual state of affairs. In other words, it is a word used to explain information that we come in contact with, but it does not mean random in the sense that there is no intelligent precipitator. He used an example of a coat being thrown onto a chair. Hence, the coat seems to be randomly thrown onto the chair, but actually, if it is traced back and studied closely, one would find that the muscles, dexterity, height, etc., of the player played a role in how the coat landed. In a more technical sense, one could do this with other supposed random happenings purported by evolutionists.

7

A Call for an Equipping Model of the Local Church

Restoring the Spiritual Vitality of the Local Church

IN ORDER TO SIMPLIFY the contrast between the *equipping* model of the local church with other less biblically grounded models, I use three terms to distinguish the various genres of churches today. I use *traditional* to refer to an array of church models that, for various reasons and in varying degrees, commonly consider certain traditional practices or beliefs as biblically superior to more contemporary approaches. That is to say, they claim the supremacy of past practices and beliefs because they consider them to be the most biblical. *Contemporary* is used to encompass various models that include a common commitment to contemporize church ministry without compromising the message of the gospel.[1] Each of these genres has styles that are more or less consistent with the biblical model. Equipping is the term that I use to describe the biblical model based on Eph 4:11–16 and Matt 28:18–20. Even the equipping model consists of varying styles of churches. See my book, *The Equipping Church: Somewhere Between Fundamentalism and Fluff*, for a full development of the equipping model and its contrast with both the traditional and contemporary models.

---

1. I recognize that each approach, such as church growth, emergent, etc., probably dislikes being grouped together, but I do so for the sake of simplicity, allowing me to focus more on clearly contrasting modern and traditional approaches with the biblical model as it is laid out in the New Testament.

Modern society is not a group of isolated entities, but rather it is better to see it as Pitirim A. Sorokin described it, a supersystem. Sorokin's fundamental axiom was that "every vigorous culture is integrated; he calls this a *sociocultural supersystem*.[2] The various aspects of culture—the arts, entertainment, and systems of truth, law, ethics, medicine, religion, politics, and economic and family life are all interconnected. Developments in one invariably influence the others; problems in one cannot be addressed or corrected without sooner or later affecting all of the others."[3]

This is at the heart of what I have been contending: scientizing state education eventually begins to define public debate and policy in every area of society. Consequently, pastors must reject the traditional and contemporary models of the church because they are not reflective of the biblical model and because neither is capable of equipping Christians to live out their faith in a modern scientific liberal culture. The traditional is in retreat. The contemporary is the avant-garde, but both are ineffective at transforming culture. Historically, cultural transformation occurred when Christians lived out their faith in every area of society, like in ancient Rome, the Reformation, the founding of America, and actually the entire western world.[4] Sorokin laid out three kinds of culture, not phases a culture goes through, but descriptive titles that speak of the dominant characteristics of a culture. The three cultures are Ideational, Idealistic, and Sensate. Below are some ideas and examples illustrating the differences in each of the cultures.

> Ideational. "Sees spiritual truth and values as virtually the only truth and values worthy of the name. God and the divine world are the highest and truest realities; the good is what God wills... willing to sacrifice pleasures and immediate goals for the sake of its high principles."[5]

A. Truth depends on God.

2. Sorokin wrote *The Crisis of our Age* in 1941, reissued unchanged in 1956, and again reissued unchanged in 1992. "Virtually every detail of Sorokin's predictions have been fulfilled except the main one—his expectation that our culture will finally find the way out of its system-wide crises and instead of a fiery *dies irae* (day of wrath) will experience a new dawn," Brown, *Sensate Culture*, 7. Compare this with other futurologists and he towers above all of them, not to mention that they were almost to the person very pessimistic and Sorokin was not—he believed in God, ibid.

3. Ibid., 8.

4. Although much of it is now in a precipitous downward slide into secularism, this does not change the historical cultural transformation.

5. Brown, *Sensate Culture*, 9.

B. Art—paint with a view toward God, spiritual. There is no effort to portray figures realistically because that would distract from God—pre-Renaissance. This is not primitive art, but the artist wants admirers to focus on the supernatural truth of the art and not the physical image.

C. Faith and the afterlife are everything.

Idealistic. "Rates spiritual truth and values above all others, but it also appreciates the realities and values of the sensory world and does not treat them as meaningless or nonexistent."[6] America at its founding was idealistic!

A. Spiritual truths are the highest, but recognize the reality and value of the material world and the senses.

B. Art still portrays and points to God and the supersensory reality of God, but it also portrays the material world and the reality of the sensory world; however, it portrays only the most sublime and noble aspects. It does not show the ugly and the vulgar; it portrays the beauty of the world to remind the viewer of God or to call people to aspire to the noblest of human life. Examples of such can be found in the narrative of older WW I & II movies, John Wayne, and comedies like Ozzie and Harriet.

C. Faith and the afterlife are everything along with living in the real world that God created.

Sensate. "It is interested only in those things, usually material in nature, that appeal to or affect the senses. It seeks the imposing, the impressive, the voluptuous; it encourages self-indulgence."[7] America today is sensate!

A. Truth is what can be empirically verified, experienced with the five senses. Religious truth is in a separate realm, religious truth is not connected with reality; consequently the distinction between scientific truth and religious truth.

B. Art—Ruben's fleshly nudes are unambiguously sensate. They attract the viewer not to the contemplation of any spiritualized human ideal

6. Ibid.
7. Ibid.

but to the excitement the flesh can offer. Aims to stimulate, excite, and attract, and draw the viewer and listener into the real world of sensory satisfaction rather than lift the individual above the sensory world to spiritual fulfillment. Nudity of a sensate culture is virtually indistinguishable from pornography.

C. The replacement of the Ed Sullivan show with shows such as Jerry Springer
D. You only go around once in life
E. Eat drink and be merry for tomorrow you may die.

Again, these are not three stages that every culture must pass through. One can go from a sensate to an ideational or idealistic, or from an idealistic to a sensate and back again. Christians transformed Rome from a sensate to an ideational. America has descended from an idealistic to a sensate culture. It is possible, by the grace of God, that it can be turned back. More importantly, the church that is being swept along in the sensate tide can become a holy communion of transformed lives that have the spiritual gravitas and depth to transform her environment.

It is not coincidental that our educational system and public culture has and is being scientized and our culture is progressively more and more a sensate culture. While other cultures were sensate without the influence of modern science, it seems clear that modern science has been the driving force in moving America from an idealistic to a sensate culture. In our present scientific liberal culture, with the exception of widespread privatized faith, the material universe is the source of all knowable knowledge. Ethereal reality is no longer prioritized or even believed in a publicly meaningful way. To an alarming degree, the evangelical church's desire to reach the culture and be accepted by the culture has resulted in her becoming so infected by scientism that now much like the liberal church, she accepts the sensate, scientistic culture while hanging on, in varying degrees, to some of the wisdom and truth of God. However, the present-day biblical knowledge of far too much of the professing evangelical church is puerile and clichéd, which is the fuel for the demise of public Christianity. Pastors must disregard the pressures of modern society if they are to have any chance of regaining a biblically literate and mature church. The issues of our day, as in any day, revolve around man's view of the nature of God and man. This is at the heart of personal and societal transformation, which pastors must understand and explain to their flocks in a way that trains believers to live, think, and engage in a scientific liberal culture.

In this kind of society, the esteem and place for clergy is lowered and limited. Commenting on the move toward a more secularized model of the church, David Wells says, "The new direction should be understood mainly as a psychological reaction to the growing irrelevance of the minister in society."[8] I would add that even seeking significance from a lost culture is evidence of how sick the church really is. As I noted in my book on church discipline, one of the reasons that church discipline is in such disfavor in the church is that it is contrary to the American mind, which equates success with growth.[9] "In 1966, according to a Harris poll, 41 percent of the public expressed great confidence in the leadership of the clergy. This figure dropped steadily to just 16 percent by 1989—the lowest rating given for the leaders of any of the major institutions, including medicine, the military, government, and the press."[10]

George Barna's research says, "The early returns from a year of research show the leading influencers in American society to be movies, television, the Internet, books, music, public policy and law, and family. The Christian church, his research shows, is not among the top dozen influences these days."[11] I would add that public progressive education should be added as the leading influencer because it creates a new way to think that is welcoming to the other contemporary influences; moreover, it is actually hostile to influences from Christianity. The significant influence from progressive education is more subtle than a blockbuster movie or blaring music, but that only adds to its pervasive and decaying impact upon society, like arsenic in a good drink.

I believe that we are still in the process of deciding what type of culture and church we will have and what type of message we will preach. Will our culture be one of freedom of religion, and the church a place where essential truths of Christianity are learned to be lived out, or will our culture be governed by the tyranny of scientism, which relentlessly proceeds to remove Christianity from public culture? As proposed earlier, since the Enlightenment, this is the raging battle of our day. Summarily stated, in a culture under God there is room for the supernatural and the study of the natural, i.e., science, and a place for both in public debate. But in a purely scientific liberal culture there is *no* place for supernaturalism as a meaningful reality in public life. The advent of postmodernism does not change the nature of

---

8. Wells, *No Place for Truth*, 219.
9. See my book *Undermining the Gospel*.
10. Wells, *No Place for Truth*, 256.
11. Barna Group, "Barna Responds to Christianity Today."

this duel because it is in fact, along with enhanced relativism, a product of scientism.

Bernard Ramm, commenting on this says, "Some scholars did not believe that the Enlightenment was fatal for Christianity. If Christianity were restated in light of the progress of the Enlightenment, then Christianity *could still be believable.*"[12] (italics added) He notes that Friedrich Schleiermacher was the first one to attempt this. In other words, Schleiermacher's goal was not to annihilate Christianity, to undermine it, but rather it was the noble goal of evangelism, reaching his culture in a meaningful way. He began to emphasize Christianity as an experience with God, not doctrines and confessions. Experience rather than propositional truth became the test of Christianity. This shift from faith being what one believed to a subjective experience is referred to by Ramm as "a Copernican revolution in theology."[13] Schleiermacher discounted belief in not only doctrines, angels, and the preexistence of Christ, but miracles as well. Religion lost its supernatural basis and he preached, "Religion is a part of the fabric of the universe and is therefore as natural to man as the air he breathes and the water he drinks. Omit the scandal of the miraculous and nothing stands in the way of the intellectual's return to the Christian faith."[14] Some of these same ideas can be found woven into the thoughts of the writings of the some of the contemporary churches today, some explicit but mostly implicit.

Schleiermacher was seeking to be relevant to his scientific culture. The death knell was to try to make Christianity acceptable to not only a natural man, but to a culture that accepted the scientific method as *the* source of truth rather than *a* source, nature is all there is. As a result of these foundational ideas, true Christianity was deemed unacceptable. What is important to note is his goal was to reach his culture with a relevant and believable message—from their standard of truth—based upon the internal subjective experience.

The liberal pastor Harry Emerson Fosdick wrote in the 1920s, "The sermon is uninteresting because it has no connection with the real interest of the people . . . The sermon must tackle a real problem," meaning a felt or immediate need in people's lives.[15] Doctrine was not relevant to that pursuit but people-centered preaching was and psychology began to be mainstreamed in the pulpits of the land on a massive scale. It is important

---

12. Ramm, *Evangelical Heritage,* 75.
13. Ibid., 76.
14. Ibid., 78.
15. Cited in MacArthur, *Rediscovering Expository Preaching,* 6.

to remember that modern psychology, being a science, is unjustifiably reductionistic concerning reality and the source of problems and their cures.

We often hear things like "Unchurched people today are the ultimate consumers. We may not like it, but for every sermon we preach, they're asking, 'Am I interested in that subject or not?' If they aren't, it doesn't matter how effective our delivery is; their minds will check out."[16] Two things need to be noted; first, notice that this is in fact the same philosophy that drives child-centered education, where the child's wants and interests determine the curriculum rather than there being certain truths that must be learned by everyone. Second, once again there is a confusion of the nature of the church in contradistinction from the world and an unwarranted conflation of the lost with believers in which the lost always are dominant. These always fail to note that the message born-again believers will be interested in may very well be quite different from what would hold the attention of the lost or be appropriate for them. That is why the Bible makes it clear that the church service is primarily for equipping the followers of Christ, and evangelism is to take place in the world. This does not preclude a real sensitivity to the presence of lost people in the church services as well as always including enough gospel truth to be saved by.

According to Barna, "One-third of the nation's Protestant congregations are headed by pastors who claim to be seeker-driven."[17] Whether these follow in the direction of Schleiermacher and Fosdick in denying the central teachings of Christianity or others who simply undervalue the importance of such topics because they fail to see them as relevant, both hold to the same pedagogical philosophy and both leave a generation of Christians who cannot distinguish truth from error much less communicate it; thereby, placing the future church in peril. Of course, some of the emergent church is taking this to a whole new level with their metaphorical analysis of Scripture, deemphasizing propositional truth, categorizing all certainty as mere modernity, and making fallacious and insubstantial arguments that would not have been convincing to anyone were it not for the recasting of the American mind by progressive education.[18] Peter Wagner, commenting on the church growth movement, to which he is committed, says, it "is deeply rooted in theological traditions, but it does not study theology for theology's sake."[19] As just mentioned, we now have the movement known

---

16. Ibid.

17. Barna Group, "A Profile of Protestant Pastors."

18. See my article "Velvet Elvis Revisited" October 3, 2007, http://www.ronniewrogers.com/2007/10/03/velvet-elvis-revisited/.

19. Wells, *No Place for Truth*, 255.

as the emergent church taking the church growth's emphasis on cultural relevance and marginalizing doctrine to the point of obscuring the truthfulness of the truth of Scripture for those whom they seek to reach.[20]

David Wells contrasts the church model, based on the Reformation and Puritanism, with its modern day evangelical descendants. While he contrasts the reformation model with the contemporary, and I am contrasting the equipping model with the contemporary as well as the traditional, his analysis is equally applicable to the comparison that I am making.

> The difference between the two models is not that theology is in one but not the other. Theology is professed and believed in both. But in the one, theology is the reason for ministry, the basis for ministry; it provides the criteria by which success in ministry is measured. In the other, theology does none of these things; here the ministry provides its own rationale, its own criteria, and its own techniques. The second model does not reject theology: it simply displaces it so that it no longer gives the profession of ministry its heart and fire.[21]

As a result, the offspring of church growth emphasis often has an unwillingness to speak the absolute truths of Scripture even in love.

The biblical church paradigm of the equipping model has been displaced by a market driven, methodologically neutral (theoretically but not actually so), growth evaluated paradigm.[22] The idea that churches should grow, meaning numerically, because healthy things grow, is merely a trite American saying that seems to lend biblical justification to what churches do to grow. I do not know of one place in Scripture that exhorts, encourages, or teaches that the church is to be evaluated based on size or whether it grows numerically or not. There have been and are situations in America and around the globe where faithful servant's churches are not growing *because* they are being faithful to the Word. I have yet to hear these growth

---

20. Francis A. Schaeffer coined the term "true truth." He said, "People today live in a generation that no longer believes in the hope of truth as truth. That is why I use the term "true truth" in my books, to emphasize real truth. This is not just a tautology. It is an admission that the word *truth* now means something that before . . . would not have been considered truth at all. So I coined the expression "true truth" to make the point, but it is hard to make it sharp enough for people to understand how large the problem is." Schaeffer, *Complete Works,* vol. 1, 312–13. The most prominent parts of the emergent church make biblical truth what they believe, but not necessarily objective truth for all to believe, or knowable truth about certain realities.

21. Wells, *No Place for Truth,* 255.

22. In my book *The Equipping Church: Somewhere Between Fundamentalism and Fluff,* I demonstrate how methods do in fact affect what will and will not be preached in churches.

models pushing, with the same passion, the practice of things that are emphatically commanded in Scripture like church discipline (Matt 18:15–18), teaching all that Christ commanded (Matt 28:18–20), and studying to show themselves approved workmen (2 Tim 2:15). To avoid being misunderstood, my disavowal of numerical size or growth as a barometer of biblical faithfulness is not an approval of churches that are not growing because of an unfaithfulness to the Scripture. Rather it is only to disavow the idea that numerical growth or church attendance sufficiently relates to biblical fidelity to be the standard.

The concepts promoted by much of contemporary evangelicalism are precisely the same as those that come out of progressive education like learning must be fun and learning must be immediately and practically relevant, leaving the academic side of Christianity and theology to the scholars in the academy, which is precisely some of the same essential building blocks as progressive education. The progressive focus is on what helps you vocationally, in this life, in the here and now, and the same is true of the seeker church, which results in Christian education, equipping, and ministry operating at the lowest common denominator. Wells notes that theology for many today is merely a tool and "the skills and techniques requisite for the management of the church determine what theology should be studied, not the importance of the truth itself."[23]

The gulf between seminary and church is vast, and the chasm between pastor and people is enormous as well. Christians do not have to have another way of presenting the gospel, a tract, etc., but they need to understand the Bible and the culture in a substantive way and then have the courage to engage the culture with the truth of the Word in their life situation, as a missionary. This is in stark contrast to the doctrinally minimal approach of much of the contemporary church. By substantive, I mean being able to speak out of a deep and full knowledge of Scripture, which requires time in studying truth for the sake of studying and knowing truth. This is something that the modern model does not do, nor even understands the need to do. Many do not even know they are not involved in deep study because they compare themselves only with something shallower than themselves and have no historical gauge for informative comparison.

The equipping model requires an unwavering commitment to study. The traditional model can be characterized by deep study of Scripture, although sometimes detached from the world we live in, but it can and does frequently become caught up in the business of the church and simply re-preaches what everyone already knows and believes. However, the

---

23. Wells, *No Place for Truth*, 255–56.

contemporary model has displaced serious and thoughtful study of the truth, which is essential for a more profound understanding of God, man, and this world; rather it is built largely upon the leader's ingenuity, creativity, personality, managerial skills, or communicating the message that meets the most obvious needs of practical life.

Pastors using the contemporary model seem to spend far more time studying methods, trends, and polls—learning by science—than studying God's truth for the sake of knowing God's truth. Of course science can tell you only what behavior people exhibit and what they say they feel, but never really why they feel, what to substantively do about it, or what is the real truth about God and man (Jer 17:9–10; 1 Cor 2:10–16; Heb 4:12). A man of God must be dedicated to study daily, where God leads, even though he often does not understand why, and may even study subjects that are over his head, with no opportunity even to communicate the knowledge, much less have an avenue for applying the knowledge in a practical way. Then and only then is he following God and positioning himself for knowing God on a significantly deeper level and thereby becoming capable of leading others into the deeply satisfying and maturing knowledge of God.

One thing that stands out to me is that you can usually judge a man's depth and direction of study by how he preaches. If he has been preaching for ten or twenty years, and his messages have the same substance they did years earlier, then it is pretty easy to surmise that his study is not very substantive and challenging but more geared toward the status quo or pedagogy. If you listen to a man preach and he is consistently shallow, it is a pretty good guess that his preaching simply reflects the level of his study. It is through study that the man of God prepares himself and is able to equip the saints to know and serve God. If his study is shallow, superficial, geared merely toward the obvious, so will be his preaching and church. It is by deep, meditative study and dissemination that God brings maturation to the body and unleashes the vision of himself to and through his church.

The equipping model of the local church requires always studying deeply in Scripture, theology, and other areas that have to do with framing the modern mind and heart. I believe the man of God must read broadly in order to have a grasp of the multifaceted world, in which we live to be able to protect, purify, and prepare the church to honor God. If a preacher is reading only best sellers, which is most likely what his congregants are reading, one may rightly ask, why do they need him? If they can glean from the Scripture they get from the pastor teacher, it seems clear that he is not fulfilling his calling, and they do not need him, spiritually speaking. Francis Schaeffer says, "Today we have a weakness in our educational process in failing to understand the natural associations between the disciplines. We tend to study all our disciplines in unrelated parallel lines. This tends to be true in both Christian and secular education. This is one of the reasons why evangelical Christians have been taken by surprise at the tremendous shift that has come in our generation. We have studied our exegesis as exegesis, our theology as theology, our philosophy as philosophy; we study something about art as art; we study music as music, without understanding that these are things of man, and the things of man are never unrelated parallel lines."[24]

The study habit I am advocating is based on the pastor's desire and willingness to be alone with God, not for minutes, but hours a day over the course of his life. This includes reading and studying subjects and books that are difficult, or topics that the pastor will not always be able to immediately or fully understand, things that are eternally important. If preachers are not constantly studying things that challenge them spiritually and intellectually, then it is disingenuous for the preacher to challenge the church to study the deep things of God and spend time with him. Oftentimes, pastors are studying books that are written for the masses or that reconfirm rather than broaden and deepen his understanding. If we fully understand every book that we read or read only what we like to read or read only for immediate gratification or dissemination, then we are not learners, but rather we are idolaters and we are our own idol. We should study the Scripture deeply because of the value of knowing God more deeply, which only happens in the context of knowing his self-revelation more deeply. He is worthy of such devotion, and we are needful of such revelation. In addition, there are a few practical reasons for studying deeply that stand out as well.

First, because people are admittedly receiving and processing more information today than ever before, and much of it contrary to God's truth; why would any pastor think we need shorter messages if his real heart is to train followers of Christ to think and live biblically? Just the sheer volume of information that has to be processed on a daily basis demands more teaching of Scripture, not less. Today there are more cults, false teachers and teaching, secular ideas, philosophies, and critical issues requiring biblical understanding than at any time in American history. How can any serious pastor or thinker say we need shorter, shallower, and fewer messages? James warned his listeners, "But prove yourselves doers of the word, and not merely hearers who delude themselves" (Jas 1:22). Today the question is, are they even getting an opportunity to hear the Word? Sure they are hearing clichés, verses quoted without due attention to authorial intent, or a string of disjointed verses strung together to give the lost a sense that God is there

---

24 Schaeffer, *Complete Works*, vol. 1, 211.

for them in whatever they are doing, but they are not hearing the Word of the Lord. Generational infection is a potential reality in any generation, but in modern America it is more pronounced than ever before. Three factors have caused this.

One, progressive education is an educational philosophy that simply devalues knowing history beyond what is immediately necessary.[25] Progressives today view history as serving no immediate utilitarian purpose for most pupils. For them there is no or very little required historical understanding that is necessary for American children to learn. The multiculturalists distort it, and scientism relegates it to curiosities or mere academics or of limited value to the professional historian because science is the source of truth, and history plays only a minuscule role at most in the success of the next experiment.[26] The philosophy of public education engenders this cultural mindset, and the fact that most Americans are educated in the public educational system or private progressive schools assures that it pervades every area of American culture, even the church. Those who refuse to be defined by that which emanates from this intellectual sachet are summarily deemed biological rogues. For today, science, not Christianity, determines what is normal and what is not.

Two, the media churns out tomes of information that masquerades as sufficient knowledge, seemingly satiating the human need for knowing, or at least preoccupying the population to the point of intellectual mummification. Three, many pastors, especially those who pursue seeker sensitive or emerging ministries, seem to disdain history as much as the progressives, that is if their messages are any indication of their appreciation for history—titillating historical quips and quotes notwithstanding. This is, of course, in accord with their progressive views and probably their education. Their desire to know or speak about history is limited to only that which has an immediate utilitarian purpose and will captivate the guest. This is true whether it is secular or biblical history. Biblical history and context is simply too cumbersome. Remember that immediacy reigns, and what is important is what will help me *now*.

---

25. Ravitch, *Left Back*, 127–129. Because "it [history] didn't seem to have a social purpose," ibid., 127. "History in the schools should be selected on the basis of 'the pupil's own immediate interest' and 'general social significance.'" US Bureau of Education, *Social Studies in Secondary Education*, 37.

26. Like trying to depict Japan as "victimized" and "defend[ing] their unique culture against Western imperialism," Schmidt, *The Menace*, 22. In a 1995 exhibit of the Enola Gay at the Smithsonian, WWII veterans and others objected to the distortion. These distortions are common, in part because they see America as evil, 164, antichristian, 155, Schmidt, *The Menace*.

One time, while on a writing leave of absence, Gina and I attended what is known to be a good church. The message was out of Neh 1:1–4. While the pastor did mention that Judah had been in Babylonian captivity, he moved almost immediately from Nehemiah's brokenness and distress, resulting in weeping, mourning, praying, and fasting for days over hearing about the broken walls in Jerusalem, to God's concern over the broken walls in the lives of the listeners. It seems, at least it should have been established what led them into captivity, what is fasting, and why was the wall really significant—not to mention was it real or metaphorical—and if so, how so. Or was Nehemiah suffering from depression and was he always crying—maybe that could be next week's message—how to deal with depression. The application from Nehemiah is indeed rich, but the rapid trek to application, which ignores history, is typical of the progressive pastor. Rather than being a part of transforming our culture, they are in fact, catering to its anti-biblical presuppositions, and in that sense, are wittingly or unwittingly co-laborers with them.

I do believe in reaching people where they are and simplifying the message and the language to make the gospel clear. However, any time the church is viewed as the primary place of evangelism, equipping the saints suffers and so does fulfilling the command to make disciples, Matt 28:19. The local church is the place to deal with biblical and moral issues more thoughtfully and thoroughly, and this by the shepherd and other studied teachers. This simply cannot be done with merely utilitarian, psychotherapeutic twenty-minute messages that are intended to offend no one either by its content or depth. Perish the thought that preachers would preach in contemporary and traditional models in a way that make people have to think, and think hard, and be exposed to biblical knowledge and thinking in a host of areas. Furthermore, people cannot really substantively learn from televised talking head shows, where often the host interrupts, and the loudest wins. I thank God for those who represent Christ in such forums, and although Christians who are seeking to develop a Christian worldview may leave feeling encouraged and learning maybe a point or two, they do not gain the depth of knowledge that is essential to being a mature Christian.

While people do think when presented with sound bites, movies, pictures, and other mediums, and these can be used to communicate Christianity, they are woefully inadequate for transmitting the essential teaching and truths of Christianity from one person to the next, much less one generation to the next. They are inadequate for communicating certain truths and for communicating them substantively. Christianity is a linear subject. It is the story of God and God's love for mankind that spans time and eternity, and to reduce it to mere quips, sayings, principles, mores, and guidelines is to necessarily leave it distorted. The story does contain sayings, principles, and the like, but Jesus was not a philosopher. He is the long promised Savior, and the Bible is his story of love. For example, the teaching about marriage and family in Eph 5:22–6:4 is not principles for marriage. It is the outworking of God's redemption described in chapters 1 through 3 and is wrought by the power of the Holy Spirit in his people's lives. It may have practical or sentimental esteem by the lost, but it has no real value because they have neither the heart nor the capacity to live the life commanded in this passage.

Second, returning to reasons to study deeply, there are many concepts in Christianity that take diligent study over an extended period to be able to understand. Often these truths are woven throughout Scripture. While today these are deemed too abstract or not understandable and irrelevant to the masses, some of these are the most significant truths that a person could ever learn—about God, holiness, the Trinity, the theanthropic Christ, redemption, sin, love, purpose, destiny, and a host of other truths that are essential and cannot be fully grasped without consistent diligence in studying the Word of God. One pastor recently quipped that humility is not thinking lower of yourself, but thinking less about yourself. Of course that may be a memorable sound bite, but it hardly does justice to the biblical meaning of humility.

Third, Christianity is historical. It is something that claims to transpire, in large part, in space-time history. Therefore, if that is true, there should be empirical corroboration of its claims. Moreover, to de-historicize Christianity actually destroys the meaning of Christianity. Paul says to the Corinthians, "And if Christ has not been raised, your faith is worthless; you are still in your sins" (1 Cor 15:17). It is not the principle, spiritual idea, or encouragement of an ethereal resurrection that Paul is referencing; it is an actual, bodily rising of Jesus from an actual space-time earthly death. To de-historicize Christianity by merely preaching application and principles is to obfuscate the uniqueness of Christianity and thereby pantheonize Christianity. Then Christianity becomes a choice among a myriad of choices, based on total subjectivism, which in fact is not Christianity at all.

Fourth, pastors determining what messages they should preach based upon merely the felt needs of people is an idea riddled with inadequacies. It actually reduces Christianity to something so anemic that any resemblance to biblical Christianity is merely coincidental.[27] No lost sinner ever really feels, on his own, like seeking God (Ps 14:1–3, Rom 3:11), or wakes up feel-

---

27. Joel Osteen, senior pastor of Lakewood Church in Houston, Texas is a prime example of this. He uses Scripture, but his message is not one of sacrifice, humility, following God at all costs, God's intrinsic worthiness, or future hell for all who do not repent, but one of God wanting all to have a great day, be positive, get along, etc.

ing a need to hear about hell, judgment, understanding the Trinity, how Israel was unfaithful to God, that they are too in love with themselves, or that they need to live a life of sacrifice. It is the man of God exposing them to the full counsel of God that births the awareness of those desires and adequately addresses them. It is undeniable that some of the essential truths of Christianity are not fully experienced in this life, e.g., the indisputable presence of the Trinity, heaven, hell, sinlessness, etc., but that in no way diminishes their importance and relevance to daily decision making.

Recently, I felt led to preach on the Unpardonable Sin (Matthew 12:22–32). I dare say I cannot think of anyone who has expressed a felt need to hear this message; however, two comments illustrate how God used it. A young mom told me that it was not the message she came to church to hear, but, much to her surprise, God used it mightily in her life. She described it as scary, unsettling, and wonderful. God ministered to her spiritually through that message. A missionary couple just happened to be there that Sunday. They, with tears, expressed to me how God had used the message to remind them why they needed to leave their children and grandchildren to go back to the mission field and share the gospel with Muslims.

If Christianity could be reduced to proverbs, then God would have merely given us a book of proverbs; if Christianity could be adequately learned without serious study and teaching, then the Holy Spirit would not have made those the emphases in the pastoral epistles—and we would not even need a pastor teacher. If communication of Christianity could be adequately done through pictures and sound bites, then our missionaries would not have given their lives to develop languages in order to communicate Christianity to the pagans, but rather they would have honed their art skills and drawn more pictures on the wall. Our Founders and their successors would not have started almost all of the first 123 academic learning centers in America, not to mention all of the Christian schools and seminaries existing today.[28] Dr. Richard Land once said, "The battle for Christianity in the future will be fought with the mind."[29] I believe this is true and evangelical pastors not diligently training their own minds and the minds of those under their watch care are part of the reason so many young people distance themselves from Christianity and the church during college.

For years I have heard that people do not want the deeper things. That is surely true for some, but it is absolutely not true for all. That being the case, should not those who want to mature on the meat of the Word get that

---

28. Kennedy and Newcomb, *What If Jesus*, 52.

29. Dr. Land made this statement while teaching Systematic Theology at Criswell College ca. 1984 when I was in the class.

training from the shepherds? If we just cater to those who only want the surface, practical, and immediately applicable, then we are mere pragmatists ministering to the lowest common denominator. We become spiritual minimalists and produce spiritual minimalists. Further, I have found that believers do want to know and understand their faith, and some want to plumb the depths of the mind and heart of God. In the churches I have pastored, Christians have demonstrated a deep desire to understand their faith, answer questions in order to be able to live for God in a very confusing time, process worldly information from a biblical worldview, and engage their contemporaries with the truth of God in every area of life; these simply do not happen without real in-depth equipping.

I have heard and read some pastors who say that when you answer questions about such topics as predestination, hell, judgment, or the Trinity, you are answering questions the modern man is not asking. My response to that is, while that may be true of the modern lost man, it is not true of the followers of Christ. They do ask these questions. As a matter of fact, I am constantly answering these kinds of questions. Maybe it is not that they are not asking or do not want to know, but they are not asking some pastors because the followers do not believe their pastors know or they have been previously deterred from asking. Or maybe the sheer shallowness of the teaching suggests that those things do not exist. It is a crisis when our sermons at associational meetings and many conventions and conferences have no more depth to them than the latest newspaper articles, even though most who are there are dedicated, theologically trained Christians. In addition, lost people do ask about predestination, heaven or hell, etc., and they have opinions about them as well. Humanly speaking, it may be the lack of clarity on some of these issues—or the lack of mention—causing them to stay in their sin and reject the god of their imagination.

Our surveys have consistently demonstrated that the number one reason people come to our church is the in-depth teaching.[30] I receive this kind of feedback constantly. I received a card from a young lady in our church that said in part, "For the longest time in my walk with Christ, I yearned for deeper teaching and thought surely there was something more. . . . I prayed that in some way I could have something deeper . . . despite what others told me, I thought you and Trinity would be the same as before but I was wrong! God lavished His grace upon me with . . . deep teaching." She went on to mention after meeting with me about some questions she had, she then

---

30. We offer new members the opportunity to tell us why they came to Trinity Baptist Church, what they like most, and what they would change. While other things are mentioned, the number one comment is regard for the in-depth teaching and equipping from the pulpit and classes in the church.

studied books I recommended concerning the errors of the documentary hypothesis. Again, often Christians have questions, but are simply told to have more faith or are dealt with tritely, but the questions remain, and they rarely grow beyond those barriers. A former member, Ben Wilson, went to seminary and wrote me in an e-mail, "Many of the people in my Greek class are working men and women who are taking seminary courses because they want substantive teaching, and I guess they aren't getting that at church. It seems like church is the place where people get saved, and seminary is the place where people go if they actually want to be fed in their walks with God."[31]

Apologetics, which is intellectually stimulating as well as hard work, is critical to engaging our culture. It is a fallacious juxtaposition to ask should we seek to engage people with the simple gospel only, apologetics, or a loving life, because it is not either/or but all of the above working in concert. Truly loving people must include telling them the truth about Christianity in a clear and convincing way. The truth is that everyone engages in apologetics because once a Christian moves from sharing what they believe—their faith—to why they believe, they have ventured into the arena of apologetics.[32] Therefore the question is not whether we use apologetics, but the question is how well we employ apologetics. I do not believe that people are won to Christ through reason any more than they are won by a kind deed or godly life, but answering nagging questions that undermine the veracity and viability of Christianity are important in the process of witnessing and developing strong, mature Christians.

At the age of 81, atheistic British philosopher Antony Flew became a theist. This was due to some compelling evidences of a creator that he faced when he debated theists like Dr. Gary Habermas. First, Flew described himself as an atheist, then was "considering becoming a theist," then "he had become a theist while still rejecting the concept of special revelation," and then in response to Habermas's question "Tony, you recently told me that you have come to believe in the existence of God. Would you comment on that?" Flew answered, "Well, I don't believe in the God of any revelatory system, *although I am open to that.*"[33] (italics added)

Flew makes it clear in his book *There Is a God* that he did not change his mind from atheism to theism based on an experience but rather he says,

---

31. Ben Wilson, email message to author June 25, 2006.

32. This is not meant to be a formal or working definition of apologetics, but simply to emphasize the inescapableness of the need to know apologetics. It has been said that every believer is an apologist; the question is whether they are a good or bad apologist.

33. "Atheist Becomes Theist."

"In short, my discovery of the Divine has been a pilgrimage of reason and not of faith."[34] He further states that this was not really a paradigmatic shift for him because it was simply "a consequence of my continuing assessment of the evidence of nature."[35] He makes it clear that he followed the Socratic insistence that "We must follow the argument wherever it leads."[36] In other words, his migration from atheism to theism was one of following the evidence rather than a personal encounter with the divine.

Concerning Christianity he now says, "If you're wanting omnipotence to set up a religion, it seems to me that this is the one to beat!"[37] Just based upon evidence, he believes that Christianity is really the only religion that makes sense, and although he has not become a Christian or claimed to have had a spiritual experience, he now says, "Some claim to have made contact with this Mind. I have not—yet. But who knows what could happen next? Someday I might hear a Voice that says, 'Can you hear me now?'"[38] Anthony Flew died April 8, 2010. I had prayed on several occasions that he would receive Christ as his Savior before he died. I pray that he did. I would love to see him in heaven. Regardless, the value of apologetics in his life should not be missed or minimized.

Now if apologetics can be a tool in changing the mind of one who many said was the foremost philosophical atheist in the world, surely it must have everyday value. Equipping believers to engage a very intellectually complex and hostile environment from a biblical worldview requires training, and some of that training is intellectually challenging. Mark Coppenger notes, "Apologetics is an important handmaiden of evangelism. It can strip away smugness, loosen up hardened soil, embarrass treasured criticisms, and sow disarray in a pagan worldview. Of course, the critic will seldom admit on the spot that you've scored points, but his private reflections may be a different story."[39] Evangelicals' emphasis on piety and the personal walk with Christ is wonderful truth and reality, but we must not by that emphasis denigrate the intellect. Apologetics, its content, training, and clarity, are essential to engage large segments of our culture with the gospel. Coppenger is correct in noting one of the benefits of apologetics is that "it cultivates dialogical prowess for the public square."[40]

34. Flew, *There is a God*, 93.
35. Ibid., 89.
36. Ibid.
37. Ibid., 157.
38. Ibid., 158.
39. Coppenger, "Why the church needs apologetics."
40. Ibid.

A look at where the intellectual disputers of our day are coming from signals the urgency of embracing a more intellectual Christianity. "Evangelicals need more practice in responsible disputation. Consider this comparison: For every Cal Thomas and Richard Land, you have a dozen (current or lapsed) Roman Catholic commentators or columnists, such as Sean Hannity, Chris Matthews, Pat Buchanan, Bill Bennett, Bill Buckley, Bill O'Reilly, Andrew Sullivan, John McLaughlin, Anna Quindlen, Phyllis Schlafly, Michelle Malkin, Linda Chavez, Peggy Noonan, Mark Shields, Paul Begalla, Laura Ingraham and Robert Novak. And we may be on the brink of a Catholic majority on the Supreme Court, with justices Thomas, Kennedy, Roberts, Scalia and Alito. Also, note the many front-line Jewish commentators such as William Kristol, David Horowitz, Michael Medved, Mona Charen, David Frum and Al Franken. We Evangelicals seem to have some cultural and educational gaps to fill."[41]

To think of pastors, some of the most biblically trained people in the world and by in large the most biblically trained people that the majority of Christians come in contact with on a regular basis, becoming the masters of quips, quotes and clichés, which only keep people dumb, is unimaginable except for the stark reality that it is true of many. Some of them are the most recognized and esteemed in evangelicalism. Sometimes under the pressure unleashed by the idea that the pastor has to model everything or it will not happen coupled with recognition and accolades of success being inextricably tied to growth, the pastor forsakes his time-consuming call to study and equip for modeling everything else. Pastors must remember they cannot do everything—nor should they—and they cannot be the best at everything, but they can model following God's calling and support of what God is doing through others in the church.

The prevalence of psychology and sociology and their societal esteem has wrought a serious change of perspective regarding human inadequacies. According to many of the modern evaluations, people are actually good, they know the right thing to do, and good religious messages are simply a means of supplementing their sound ideas. People's problems are not sin or wrong absolutely, but are merely not beneficial, productive, or self-gratifying. If sin does play a part, it is that it diminishes self-fulfillment or self-esteem. Robert Schuller said of sin, "Reformation theology failed to make clear that the core of sin is a lack of self-esteem. . . . at the deepest level the heart of sin is found in what it causes us to do to ourselves."[42]

---

41. Ibid.
42. Schuller, *Self Esteem*, 98.

In the *Los Angeles Times* article, "Self-help's big lie," Steve Salerno explains, "Self-esteem-based education presupposed that a healthy ego would help students achieve greatness, even if the mechanisms necessary to instill self-esteem undercut scholarship. Over time, it became clear that what such policies promote is not academic greatness but a bizarre disconnect between perceived self-worth and provable skill."[43] Similarly, preachers have fallen for the idea that just focusing on the positive, the practical, what builds people up, will produce better Christians, but actually it produces a similar disconnect between perceived self-rightness with God and actual righteousness that is far more damning than the academic disconnect.

Noting the prevalent influence of psychology upon the culture and the church, and the reorienting of Christian theology into a more acceptable psychological framework, Mark Ellingsen says, "To practice Christian ministry is to be engaged in therapy. . . . so religion is now interpreted by more and more Americans as an exercise in enhancing self-fulfillment. This is hardly surprising, for as several analysts have noted, psychology directs clients to focus more on obligations to oneself than to others."[44] "This trend was noted as early as the mid-1960s by the eminent cultural analyst Philip Rieff. 'Any religious activity is justified only by being something men do for themselves, that is, for the enrichment of their own experience.'"[45] Compatible preaching causes the church to lose it prophetic voice and essential counter cultural mission of confrontation and transformation rather than accommodation.

The pastor must be aware of his cultural milieu. He must understand his church and the nature of the church as a regenerated body of believers. The way he leads, prepares, protects, and ministers to that new culture is adequately delineated in the Scripture. Further he must grasp the educational level and background of the people in his church and area. A thorough familiarity with the influences of the day like multiculturalism, tolerance, postmodernism, modernity, and progressive education is essential, and this not in order to accommodate but to penetrate evangelistically and protect the flock from becoming a culturally amalgamated citizenry rather than a body of believers under the authority of the Scripture.

---

43. Salerno, "Self-help's big lie." Salerno is the author of SHAM: *How the Self-Help Movement Made America Helpless*.

44. Ellingsen, *Blessed Are the Cynical*, 129.

45. Ibid.,

Appendix A

Signing of Stem Cell Executive Order and Scientific Integrity

President Obama issued an executive order lifting limits on federal funding for embryonic stem-cell research, which illustrates his elevation of science as the supreme guide of his administration. The President explained:

> This Order is an important step in advancing the cause of science in America. But let's be clear: promoting science isn't just about providing resources—it is also about protecting free and open inquiry. It is about letting scientists like those here today do their jobs, free from manipulation or coercion, and listening to what they tell us, even when it's inconvenient—especially when it's inconvenient. It is about ensuring that scientific data is never distorted or concealed to serve a political agenda—and *that we make scientific decisions based on facts, not ideology.*
>
> By doing this, we will ensure America's continued global leadership in scientific discoveries and technological breakthroughs. That is essential not only for our economic prosperity, but for the progress of all humanity.
>
> That is why today, I am also signing a Presidential Memorandum directing the head of the White House Office of Science and Technology Policy to develop a strategy for restoring scientific integrity to government decision making. *To ensure that in this new Administration, we base our public policies on the soundest science; that we appoint scientific advisors based on their credentials and experience, not their politics or ideology; and that we are open and honest with the American people about*

the science behind our decisions. That is how we will harness the power of science to achieve our goals—to preserve our environment and protect our national security; to create the jobs of the future, and live longer, healthier lives.[1] (italics added)

Those of us who are not scientific liberals are open to considering the science related to issues, but unlike a scientific liberal like President Obama, we are unwilling to grant that science does not have its own bias (ideology), and that science *alone* can answer the most pressing questions concerning human life. He has allowed science and science *alone* to define human life, which is the quintessential characteristic of a SL.

---

1. Obama, "Signing of Stem Cell Executive Order," par. 10–12.

Appendix B

Southern Baptist Convention Resolution on Removing Children from the Public School System

The resolution being promoted by Pinckney and Shortt for 2004, "the initial 'Be it resolved' clause proposes that messengers to the June 15–16 SBC annual meeting declare that the Southern Baptist Convention 'encourages all officers and members of the Southern Baptist Convention and the churches associated with it to remove their children from the government schools and see to it that they receive a thoroughly Christian education, for the glory of God, the good of Christ's church, and the strength of their own commitment to Jesus.'"[1]

The resolution was declined by the Resolutions Committee along with five other proposals on education. Consequently Pinckney offered a modified version from the floor which was soundly defeated. However, the defeat was not an endorsement by the convention of a particular form of education or an exoneration of public schools' increasing secularism, but rather it was an endorsement of parental choice in the matter of education.

Calvin Wittman, Resolutions Committee chairman, said, "The committee believes 'this is a responsibility that God has given to the parents of each individual child, and we encourage parents to exercise that God-given responsibility over their children.'"[2]

---

1. Toalston, "Education resolution."
2. Strode, "SBC calls for cultural engagement."

"The Southern Baptist Convention adopted resolutions on education in 1999, 1997 and 1996. In the '99 resolution, messengers made an appeal 'to all Southern Baptist churches to consider carefully . . . supporting educational programs that follow biblical principles, whether they are implemented in Christian, private, public, or home schools . . . In the '97 resolution, messengers affirmed 'the right of all parents . . . to teach their children at home,' while also affirming 'the godly teachers in public schools who stand on the front lines to teach and train children who cannot be, or whose parents choose not to home-school.' In the '96 resolution, messengers affirmed 'the thousands of excellent Southern Baptist public, private and home-oriented educators,' while encouraging legislators in all levels of government 'to develop the means and methods of returning education and funding choices to parents.'"[3]

John Revell, at the SBC executive committee, said the Southern Baptist Convention is "the largest non-Catholic Christian denomination in the world with over 16 million members."[4]

---

3. Toalston, "Education resolution."
4. August 5, 2004 by phone call.

Appendix C

Examination of the Challenge to the Claim That America Had a Significant Christian Population in 1776

Isaac Kramnick and R. Laurence Moore dispute these statistics (that the constituency of the United States in 1776 was by and large Christian, see section It is constitutionally compatible in chapter three of this book). The basis of their rejection is their claim that "the highest estimates for the late eighteenth century make only about 10–15 percent of the population church members."[1] They do not cite the reference for this statistic.

In response to their assertions, let me say:

First, they mistakenly confuse statistics regarding church membership with claiming to be Christians, which are two entirely different issues.

Second, concerning the same basic time frame, Winthrop S. Hudson points out, "The American people were not as 'unchurched' in 1800 as the statistics would seem to imply .The number of people attending Sunday morning worship in the 1830s was usually three times the membership of a church. Furthermore, churches customarily computed their 'constituency' (those nominally related but not members) as approximately twice the number of attendants."[2]

Another example of membership to attendees ratio can be found in the Danbury Baptist Association, who wrote Jefferson and "was an alliance

---

1. Kramnick and Moore, *The Godless Constitution*, 17.
2. Hudson, *Religion In America*, 129–130.

of 'twenty-six churches' ... By the turn of the century [1800], William G. McLoughlin reported 'a total of 1484 members, but this number could be multiplied by five to include all the nominal adherents of these churches.'"[3]

Mark Noll states, "Religion ... was an important element in the political strife of 1800."[4] "The presidential election of 1800 was a major religious event."[5] Charles F. O'Brien notes, "The traditionally sensitive relation between religion and politics in the United States has rarely been more evident than in the presidential campaign of 1800."[6]

Third, denominations like Baptists do not include the children of members as members until they personally profess their faith in Jesus Christ and are baptized.

Fourth, in *Religion and The Founding of the American Republic*, a Library of Congress Exhibition, it says, "Against a prevailing view that eighteenth-century Americans had not perpetuated the first settlers' passionate commitment to their faith, scholars now identify a high level of religious energy in colonies after 1700. According to one expert, religion was in the 'ascension rather than the declension'; another sees a 'rising vitality in religious life' from 1700 onward; a third finds religion in many parts of the colonies in a state of 'feverish growth.' Figures on church attendance and church formation support these opinions.

Between 1700 and 1740, an estimated 75 to 80 percent of the population attended churches, which were being built at a headlong pace." See Section II "Religion in Eighteenth-Century America," http://lcweb.loc.gov/exhibits/religion/relo2.html, dated 5–28-04. Finally, the first Great Awakening took place from about 1725–1770, right up to the time of drafting the Constitution, and one of the historical effects was a rise in church attendance and building new churches, see Hudson, *Religion in America*. Hudson says concerning the increase in members at this time, "The number in all denominations was large."[7]

---

3. McLoughlin, *New England Dissent*, vol. 2, 920, 986.
4. Cited in Parton, *Life of Thomas Jefferson*, 570.
5. Noll, *One Nation under God?*, 75.
6. O'Brien, "The Religious Issue in the Presidential Campaign of 1800," 82.
7. Hudson, *Religion in America*, 77.

Appendix D

The Letter of the Danbury Baptists to Thomas Jefferson

The address of the Danbury Baptist Association in the State of Connecticut, assembled October 7, AD 1801.
To Thomas Jefferson, Esq., President of the United States of America

Sir,
Among the many millions in America and Europe who rejoice in your election to office, we embrace the first opportunity which we have enjoyed in our collective capacity, since your inauguration, to express our great satisfaction in your appointment to the Chief Magistracy in the United States. And though the mode of expression may be less courtly and pompous than what many others clothe their addresses with, we beg you, sir, to believe, that none is more sincere.

Our sentiments are uniformly on the side of religious liberty: that Religion is at all times and places a matter between God and individuals, that no man ought to suffer in name, person, or effects on account of his religious opinions, [and] that the legitimate power of civil government extends no further than to punish the man who works ill to his neighbor. But sir, our constitution of government is not specific. Our ancient charter, together with the laws made coincident therewith, were adapted as the basis of our government at the time of our revolution. And such has been our laws and usages, and such still are, [so] that Religion is considered as the first object of Legislation, and therefore what religious privileges we enjoy (as a minor part of the State) we enjoy as favors granted, and not as inalienable rights. And these favors we receive at the expense of such degrading acknowledgments, as are inconsistent with the rights of freemen. It is not to be wondered at therefore, if those who seek after power and gain, under the pretense of government and Religion, should reproach their fellow men, [or] should reproach their Chief Magistrate, as an enemy of religion, law, and good order, because he will not, dares not, assume the prerogative of Jehovah and make laws to govern the Kingdom of Christ.

Sir, we are sensible that the President of the United States is not the National Legislator and also sensible that the national government cannot destroy the laws of each State, but our hopes are strong that the sentiment of our beloved President, which have had such genial effect already, like the radiant beams of the sun, will shine and prevail through all these States—and all the world—until hierarchy and tyranny be destroyed from the earth. Sir, when we reflect on your past services, and see a glow of philanthropy and goodwill shining forth in a course of more than thirty years, we have reason to believe that America's God has raised you up to fill the Chair of State out of that goodwill which he bears to the millions which you preside over. May God strengthen you for the arduous task which providence and the voice of the people have called you—to sustain and support you and your Administration against all the predetermined opposition of those who wish to rise to wealth and importance on the poverty and subjection of the people.

And may the Lord preserve you safe from every evil and bring you at last to his Heavenly Kingdom through Jesus Christ our Glorious Mediator.

Signed in behalf of the Association,

Neh,h Dodge }
Eph'm Robbins } The Committee
Stephen S. Nelson }[1]

---

1. Cited in Dreisbach, *Thomas Jefferson*, 31–32.

Appendix E

Jefferson's Reply to the Danbury Baptist Association

Messrs. Nehemiah Dodge, Ephraim Robbins, and Stephen S. Nelson
A Committee of the Danbury Baptist Association, in the State of Connecticut.

Washington, January 1, 1802

Gentlemen,—The affectionate sentiments of esteem and approbation which you are so good as to express towards me, on behalf of the Danbury Baptist Association, give me the highest satisfaction. My duties dictate a faithful and zealous pursuit of the interests of my constituents, and in proportion as they are persuaded of my fidelity to those duties, the discharge of them becomes more and more pleasing.

Believing with you that religion is a matter which lies solely between man and his God, that he owes account to none other for his faith or his worship, that the legislative powers of government reach actions only, and not opinions, I contemplate with sovereign reverence that act of the whole American people which declared that their legislature would "make no law respecting an establishment of religion, or prohibiting the free exercise thereof," thus building a wall of separation between Church and State. Adhering to this expression of the supreme will of the nation in behalf of the rights of conscience, I shall see with sincere satisfaction the progress of those sentiments which tend to restore to man all his natural rights, convinced he has no natural right in opposition to his social duties.

I reciprocate your kind prayers for the protection and blessing of the common Father and Creator of man, and tender you for yourselves and your religious association, assurances of my high respect and esteem.[1]

---

1. Bergh, *The Writings of Jefferson*, 16:281–282.

Appendix F

Comparison of Four Texts—Jefferson and Danbury Baptists[1]

Jefferson's "Bill for Establishing Religious Freedom" (1779)	Jefferson's *Notes on the State of Virginia*, Query XVII (1780s)	Danbury Baptist Association's letter to Jefferson (Oct. 1801)	Jefferson's letter to Danbury Baptist Association (Jan. 1802)
	But our rulers can have authority over such natural rights only as we have submitted to them. The rights of conscience we never submitted, we could not submit. We are answerable for them to our God.	Religion is at all times and places a Matter between God and Individuals	religion is a matter which lies solely between Man & his God

1. Dreisbach, *Thomas Jefferson*, 49. Fig. 3.3 "Comparison of Four Texts."

Appendix F

Jefferson's "Bill for Establishing Religious Freedom" (1779)	Jefferson's *Notes on the State of Virginia*, Query XVII (1780s)	Danbury Baptist Association's letter to Jefferson (Oct. 1801)	Jefferson's letter to Danbury Baptist Association (Jan. 1802)
no man...shall be enforced, restrained, molested, or burthened in his body or goods, nor shall otherwise suffer, on account of his religious opinions or belief		no man ought to suffer in Name, person or effects on account of his religious Opinions	
that the opinions of men are not the object of civil government, nor under its jurisdiction; that to suffer the civil magistrate to intrude his powers into the field of opinion and to restrain the profession or propagation of principles...is a dangerous fallacy, which at once destroys all religious liberty...; that it is time enough for the rightful purposes of civil government for its officers to interfere when principles break out into overt acts against peace and good order...	The legitimate powers of government extend to such acts only as are injurious to others. But it does me no injury for my neighbour to say there are twenty gods, or no god. It neither picks my pocket nor breaks my leg.	the legitimate Power of civil Government extends no further than to punish the man who works ill to his neighbour	the legitimate powers of government reach actions only, & not opinions. [Man] has no natural right in opposition to his social duties

Appendix G

Phrases That Relate to God or Religion in Our Five Most Significant Founding Documents

EXCERPTS FROM THE *DECLARATION OF INDEPENDENCE* (1776)

"When in the Course of human Events, it becomes necessary for one People to dissolve the Political Bands which have connected them with another, and to assume among the Powers of the Earth, the separate and equal Station to *which the Laws of Nature and of Nature's God* entitle them, a decent Respect to the Opinions of Mankind requires that they should declare the causes which impel them to the Separation.

We hold these Truths to be self-evident, *that all Men are created equal, that they are endowed by their Creator* with certain unalienable Rights, that among these are Life, Liberty and the Pursuit of Happiness –

That to secure these rights, Governments are instituted among Men, deriving their just powers from the consent of the governed.

We, therefore, the Representatives of the UNITED STATES OF AMERICA, in GENERAL CONGRESS, Assembled, appealing to the *Supreme Judge of the World* for the Rectitude of our Intentions . . . And for the support of this Declaration, with a firm Reliance on the Protection of *divine Providence*, we mutually pledge to each other our Lives, our Fortunes, and our sacred Honor. (italics added)

EXCERPTS FROM THE *ARTICLES OF CONFEDERATION* (1777)

ARTICLE III and Conclusion. The said States hereby severally enter into a firm league of friendship with each other, for their common defense, the security of their liberties, and their mutual and general welfare, binding themselves to assist each other, against all force offered to, or attacks made upon them, or any of them, on account of *religion*, sovereignty, trade, or any other pretense whatever. And Whereas it hath pleased the *Great Governor of the World* to incline the hearts of the legislatures we respectively represent in Congress, to approve of, and to authorize us to ratify the said Articles of Confederation and perpetual Union . . . In Witness whereof we have hereunto set our hands in Congress. Done at Philadelphia in the State of Pennsylvania the ninth day of July in the *Year of our Lord* One Thousand Seven Hundred and Seventy-Eight, and in the Third Year of the independence of America. (italics added)

EXCERPTS FROM THE *NORTHWEST ORDINANCE* (1787)

Article 1. No person, demeaning himself in a peaceable and orderly manner, shall ever be molested on account of his mode of worship or religious sentiments, in the said territory. Art. 3. *Religion*, morality, and knowledge, being necessary to good government and the happiness of mankind, schools and the means of education shall forever be encouraged. (italics added)

EXCERPTS FROM THE *CONSTITUTION OF THE UNITED STATES* (1787, 1791)

ARTICLE I, **Section 7, Clause 2.** If any Bill shall not be returned by the President within ten Days (*Sundays excepted*) after it shall have been presented to him, the same shall be a Law, in like Manner as if he had signed it, unless the Congress by their Adjournment prevent its Return, in which Case it shall not be a Law. **ARTICLE VI, Clause 3.** (Sunday was considered the Christian Sabbath, and held in such high esteem that it was distinguished from all other days in the President's calendar). The Senators and Representatives before mentioned, and the Members of the several State Legislatures, and all executive and judicial Officers, both of the United States and of the several States, shall be bound by Oath or Affirmation, to support this Constitution; but *no religious Test* shall ever be required as a Qualification to any Office or public Trust under the United States. (italics added)

At the end of the document before the list of signers: Done in Convention by the Unanimous Consent of the States present the Seventeenth Day of September in the *Year of our Lord* one thousand seven hundred and Eighty seven and of the Independence of the United States of America the Twelfth. (italics added)

BILL OF RIGHTS, ADDED DECEMBER 15, 1791

AMENDMENT I. Congress shall make no law respecting an establishment of *religion* or prohibiting the free exercise thereof.

Authorial Definitions

Church—Body of immersion baptized believers freely assembled and organized according to the complete New Testament in order to fulfill the mandate of Matt 28:18–20 by following the model of the local church ministry described in Eph. 4:11–16.[1]

This body operates under the leadership of one or more pastors, of which at least one is designated Pastor Teacher whose primary role is teaching and preaching through expositional and doctrinal studies (Eph. 4:11; 1 Thess. 5:12–13; Heb. 13:17). All of the pastors are charged with the responsibility to teach and equip the saints and therefore must be able to teach (1 Tim 3:2; 2 Tim 2:24, 5:17).[2]

Their teaching, spiritual lives, and leadership protects the body from spiritual untruths and error, dangers associated with isolation and anonymity, spiritual predators, spiritual malnutrition, living at the lowest common denominator on milk with little or no meat, superficiality, tangents, and cherry picking. Their teaching also prepares the body for: present and future ministry, greater challenges, more dangerous spiritual combat, and holy living while providing the members with ever increasing opportunities to minister and contribute to the body and the advancement of the kingdom.

---

1. A local church may be considered a New Testament church without fulfilling perfectly all of the New Testament criteria for the church in the same way one may be a Christian without following everything perfectly; however, to the degree that one fails to incorporate or intentionally neglects the corpus of New Testament teaching concerning this, it is to that degree failing to be a thorough New Testament church.

2. To preach and teach God's Word is the primary task of elders (1 Tim 4:6, 11, 13, 16; 5:17; 2 Tim 2:15, 24; Titus 2:1). It was for that purpose that they were given to the church (Eph 4:11–14). While all believers are responsible to pass on the truths they have learned in God's Word, not all have gifts for preaching and teaching (1 Cor 12:29, 2 Tim 2:14; Titus 1:9, 2:1). Those who aspire to pastoral duty, however, must be so gifted. See MacArthur, *Rediscovering Expository Preaching* for more on this topic.

The regenerate church body encourages and holds one another accountable to live lives reflective of regeneration through church discipline as prescribed in the New Testament, which elevates membership commensurate with the nature of the church.

Discipleship—Discipleship is a life characterized by devotion to learning the Scripture, living what you learn, loving God more worthily (Matt 22:37–39), and engaging the culture that God chooses for you by speaking in love the truth that you have learned (Eph 4:15).[3] Disciple-making is the direct and indirect intentional activity of leading people to a saving knowledge of Christ and then enabling them to follow Christ more faithfully. "Disciple-making, then, refers to a massive range of relationships and conversations and activities."[4]

Indirect disciple-making of others occurs when a disciple seeks to follow Christ. This indirect discipling influence flows from the life of every faithful disciple to those with whom he comes in contact. Additionally, there is to be a direct disciple making influence that results from intentionally engaging relationships for the primary purpose of teaching and training others to follow Christ more closely and to disciple others do the same.

Generational Infection—The process whereby each successive generation becomes adapted to accepting an idea or philosophy to a degree that the previous generation would not have entertained. This shift is not merely a change of *what* people think (the ideas), but *how* they think (say scientistically vs. classically), and the way that they think (unaware of their insufficient knowledge). This conceptual modification is a process, which is the real phenomenon underlying the more obvious epiphenomenal changes in cultural behavior, norms, and thinking.

The means for generational infection are processes like changing of educational philosophy, changing the vocabulary of a culture, deconstruction of accepted foundational ideas, and then rebuilding the same ideas and maintaining the same name, while imbuing them with new definitions. Some examples of this would be marriage, family, science, public education, separation of church and state, and the First Amendment.

The change is deceptive because it is both stealthy and gradual, and the generation being infected lacks sufficient relevant knowledge of history and or their worldview and therefore can make little or no substantive

---

3. From a message of mine delivered at Trinity Baptist Church, Norman, Oklahoma, 12/4/2005 entitled "Our Place in God's Plan of Loving the World," http://www.sermonaudio.com/sermoninfo.asp?SID=99617151348451.

4. Marshall and Payne, *The Trellis and The Vine*, 154.

comparison; they are unaware of the fundamental change in the philosophy on which their new ideas are based as well as the profound and the immense ramifications of such. Further, church leaders often fail to recognize and understand the process and therefore only address the epiphenomenal rather than the real phenomenon.

Therefore one generation incorporates certain proposals into their vocabulary and evaluative database, which sound consistent with what they believe about the world, but they are actually based upon an entirely antithetical worldview. This, albeit somewhat subliminally, erodes the uniqueness and distinctiveness of their worldview or the one that their parents are seeking to deposit into their lives. These changes are not necessarily readily apparent in their major beliefs or behaviors. Then this less distinctive worldview, which is more accepting of new ideas than their parents, is transmitted to the next generation, which in turn repeats the pattern.

Each successive generation becomes less capable of detecting contrary ideas than the previous generation.

Thus, generational infection is where fundamental beliefs and the coherency of one's worldview are eroded to the point where successive generations are willing to accept what previous generations rejected categorically because in accepting certain proposals, they also accept certain modifications of their philosophy of life even though they were either marginally or totally unaware of it. It is only detected by evaluating where a person is and who one is in light of more than one's own experience or culture because phenomenologically the two ideas may look very similar or compatible, but philosophically they are irreconcilable.

For example, a pastor attends seminary and becomes truly grounded in biblical theology. He truly understands the basis of his beliefs and is very careful in what he preaches and how he articulates both biblical truths and applications of them; however, as pastor his desire is to speak to the immediate needs of the people, and consequently he does not teach the theology of his beliefs (at least in any substantive way) but mainly the belief and the application. In place of theology, he emphasizes more culturally popular measurements like polls or studies.

Those under his teaching grow up believing the right things, but they do not have the deep theological understanding that the pastor has, but they, in varying degrees, assume that they do because surely their pastor taught them everything they need to know. His undue dependence upon culturally acceptable measurements to prove his point settles in upon the mind of the listener.

Out of his church come Christian leaders and influential lay people who see little need for formal theological training since they lack such and its importance was not modeled or taught to them. They begin to incorporate some things that are absolutely contrary to sound doctrine but they do not have the biblical acumen to recognize, which they in turn teach to a whole new generation, who are even further from the deep theological moorings of the former pastor, and the process repeats itself only now to a greater degree.

I would offer as examples, the move from historically doctrinal churches to churches in the church growth movement, and from there to the emergent church. Also, as seen in this book, public education is a glaring example of this shift.

Science Proper—Science is the systematic study of the physical nature, relationships, and interactions of physical phenomena.[5]

Evolution vs. Darwinism—Biologist Jonathan Wells offers some vital clarifications concerning evolution and Darwinism. He notes, "Evolution means change over time"[6] and of course no one doubts that. "But Charles Darwin claimed far more than any of these things. In the *Origin of Species* he set out to explain the origin of not just one or a few species, but all species after the first—in short, all the diversity of life on earth. The correct word for this is not evolution, but Darwinism."[7]

He then gives three distinguishing characteristics of Darwinism: "(1) All living things are modified descendants of a common ancestor; (2) The principal mechanism of modification has been natural selection acting on undirected variations that originate in DNA mutations; and (3) unguided processes are sufficient to explain all features of living things—so whatever may appear to be design is just an illusion."[8] Darwin's theory specifically "applies only to living things... [even though he] speculated that life may have started in 'some warm little pond' but beyond that he had little to say on the subject."[9]

---

5. This is my definition with advisement from scientists.

6. "Change over time . . . cumulative change through time . . . a change in gene frequencies over generations . . . Darwins' phrase 'descent with modification' is ok in a limited sense," Wells, *Politically Incorrect*, 1–2. "Even hypotheses that some closely related species (such as finches on the Galapagos Islands) are descended with modification from a common ancestor are not particularly controversial." Wells, *Politically Incorrect*, 3.

7. Ibid., 3.

8. Ibid., 2.

9. Ibid., 4.

Authorial Definitions 213

Scientism—The view that the assumptions and methods of physical and biological science are equally essential and applicable to every area of life because all of life is either physical or epiphenomenal (emanating from the physical), and that it is the only or at least most reliable form of knowledge for public considerations. Succinctly, scientism is naturalism enveloped in the cloak of respectable science. Epistemic Naturalism is the same thinking process.

Methodological Neutralism—I define methodological neutralism as the idea that the most effective method should be employed because methods are neutral and do not affect the message as long as the methods are not patently unbiblical. A method can avoid being patently unbiblical by not violating direct explicit commands of Scripture such as "thou shall not steal" or "thou shall not lie," and by being at least marginally or coincidently compatible with Scripture. The method does not have to be biblically driven. The mantra of methodological neutralism is "methods change but the message doesn't."

Scientific Liberal Culture (SLC)—An (SLC) is a society in which meaning, truth, morality, the definition, and understanding of life, what is normal and what is abnormal, what is good and what is not good, and what is suitable for politics, education, and public policy is ostensibly determined by science. Scientific thinking is the process for objectively knowing. An (SLC) seeks to explain or justify everything scientifically, which necessarily results in culture operating according to naturalism because true science is too limited for such a task.[10]

While individuals or groups may personally and privately operate according to their personal faith in the supernatural, that faith has little or no marketplace value. To put it another way, an individual *can at times* be permitted to publicly express his personal faith, or tenets of his faith, but such expressions have no value or place in establishing public policy, the public mind, or education because it is not imposable knowledge, whereas that which is labeled science is. At other times even the mere expression of religious faith elicits an invective response.[11]

---

10. Reductively describing humans as being merely physical is beyond the scope of science and is therefore a philosophical or religious assessment. Even the premise that what we can know about humans physically is what is in fact true about humans is not a scientific statement, but rather a philosophical one.

11. An example might be when a president speaks of his faith or God or when someone in public debate refers to his or her own faith.

Bibliography

Adler, Mortimer J., et al., eds. *The Annals of America*, vol. 3. Chicago: Encyclopaedia Britannica, 1968.
Allison, Jim. "A Big Fuss Over Nothing." The Constitutional Principle: Separation of Church and State website, http://candst.tripod.com/bigfuss.htm.
Appleyard, Bryan. *Understanding the Present: Science and the Soul of Modern Man*. New York: Doubleday, 1992.
"Atheist Becomes Theist." A Discussion between Antony Flew and Gary R. Habermas, February 1985. http://www.theroadtoemmaus.org/RdLb/21PbAr/Apl/FlewTheist.htm.
The Barna Group. "Barna Responds to Christianity Today Article." September 17, 2002. https://www.barna.com/research/barna-responds-to-christianity-today-article/.
———. "A Profile of Protestant Pastors in Anticipation of Pastor Appreciation Month." September 25, 2001. https://www.barna.com/research/a-profile-of-protestant-pastors-in-anticipation-of-pastor-appreciation-month/.
Barrow, John D. *The World within the World*. Oxford: Clarendon, 1988.
Beauregard, Mario, and Denyse O'Leary. *The Spiritual Brain: A Neuroscientist's Case for the Existence of the Soul*. New York: HarperOne, 2007.
Begley, Sharon. "DSM-5: Psychiatrists' 'Bible' Finally Unveiled." *The Huffington Post*, May 16, 2013. http://www.huffingtonpost.com/2013/05/17/dsm-5-unveiled-changes-disorders-_n_3290212.html.
Bennard, George. "The Old Rugged Cross." Words and music composed by George Bennard in 1913.
Bennett, William J. *The De-Valuing of America: The Fight for our Culture and our Children*. New York: Summit Books, 1992.
Bergh, Albert E., ed. *The Writings of Thomas Jefferson*, 19 vols. Washington, D. C.: The Thomas Jefferson Memorial Association of the United States, 1905–7.
Beth, Loren P. *The American Theory of Church and State*. Union, NJ: The Lawbook Exchange, 2002.
The Bible & Public Schools–A First Amendment Guide. New York: The Bible Literacy Project; Nashville: First Amendment Center, 1999. http://www.firstamendmentcenter.org/madison/wp-content/uploads/2011/03/bible_guide_graphics.pdf.
Boltz, Ray, and Steve Millikan. "Shepherd Boy." Copyright Gaither Music/Shepherd Boy Music 1988.

Bork, Robert H. *Slouching Towards Gomorrah: Modern Liberalism and American Decline*. New York: Regan, 1996.
Bradford, M.E. *A Worthy Company*. Marlborough, NH: Plymouth Rock Foundation, 1982.
Brady, Joseph H. *Confusion Twice Confounded: The First Amendment and the Supreme Court: An Historical Study*. South Orange, NJ: Seton Hall University Press, 1954.
Brown, Harold O.J. *The Sensate Culture*. Dallas: Word, 1996.
Bruno, Rosalind R. "School Enrollment." July 1995. https://www.census.gov/prod/1/pop/profile/95/p23-189.pdf.
Butterfield, L.H. "Elder John Leland, Jeffersonian Itinerant." *Proceedings of the American Antiquarian Society* 62 (Oct 1952) 155–242.
Carroll, Joseph. "American Public Opinion About Religion." The Gallup Organization, March 2, 2004, http://www.gallup.com/poll/10813/religion.aspx.
Carter, Stephen L. *The Culture of Disbelief: How American Law and Politics Trivialize Religious Devotion*. New York: Basic, 1993.
———. *God's Name in Vain: The Wrongs and Rights of Religion in Politics*. New York: Basic, 2000.
Citizens Commission on Human Rights (CCHR International). "The Difference between a Medical Diagnosis and a Psychiatric Diagnosis." http://www.cchrint.org/psychiatric-disorders/psychiatristsphysicians-on-lack-of-any-medicalscientific-tests/.
Colson, Charles, and Nancy Pearcey. *How Now Shall We Live?* Wheaton, IL: Tyndale House, 1999.
Commager, Henry Steele, ed. *Lester Ward and the Welfare State*. Indianapolis: Bobbs-Merrill, 1967.
Coppenger, Mark. "FIRST-PERSON: Why the Church Needs Apologetics." *Baptist Press*, December 27, 2005. http://www.bpnews.net/22359.
Cremin, Lawrence A. *The Transformation of the School: Progressivism in American Education*. New York: Knopf, 1961.
Crotty, James Marshall. "7 Signs That U.S. Education Decline Is Jeopardizing Its National Security." Forbes.com, March 26, 2012. http://www.forbes.com/sites/jamesmarshallcrotty/2012/03/26/7-signs-that-americas-educational-decline-is-jeopardizing-its-national-security/#3a1eecc55999.
Dawkins, Richard. *The Blind Watchmaker*. New York: Norton, 1986.
———. Review of *Blueprints* by Donald Johanson and Maitland Edey. *New York Times*, April 9, 1989.
———. *The Selfish Gene*. Oxford: Oxford University Press, 1989.
Dembski, William A. *Intelligent Design: The Bridge Between Science and Theology*. Downers Grove, IL: InterVarsity, 1999.
Dershowitz, Alan and Alan Keyes. "Organized Religion Debate." C-Span, September 27, 2000. Transcribed from https://www.c-span.org/video/?159474-1/organized-religion-debate.
Dewey, John. *A Common Faith*. New Haven: Yale University Press, 1934.
———. "My Pedagogic Creed," *School Journal* 54 (January 1897) 77–80. http://dewey.pragmatism.org/creed.htm.
Dewey, John, and Evelyn Dewey. *Schools of To-Morrow*. New York: E.P. Dutton, 1915.
Donahue, Michael J. "Intrinsic and Extrinsic Religiousness: Review and Meta-Analysis." *Journal of Personality and Social Psychology* 48 (1985) 400–419.

Dreisbach, Daniel L. *Thomas Jefferson and the Wall of Separation between Church and State*. New York: New York University Press, 2002.

Ellis, Albert, and Shawn Blau. *The Albert Ellis Reader: A Guide to Well-Being Using Rational-Emotive Behavior Therapy*. New York: Citadel Press, 1998.

Ellis, Albert. *Reason and Emotion in Psychotherapy*. New York: Lyle Stuart, 1962.

Ellingsen, Mark. *Blessed Are the Cynical: How Original Sin Can Make America a Better Place*. Grand Rapids, MI: Brazos, 2003.

"Establishment clause overview." First Amendment Center, September 16, 2011. http://www.firstamendmentcenter.org/establishment-clause/.

Fagan, Patrick F. "Why Religion Matters: The Impact of Religious Practice on Social Stability." *The Heritage Foundation* 1064 (January 25, 1996). http://www.heritage.org/Research/Religion/BG1064.cfm.

Feaver, J. Clayton, and William Horosz, eds. *Religion in Philosophical and Cultural Perspective: A New Approach to the Philosophy of Religion Through Cross-Disciplinary Studies*. Princeton, NJ: D.Van Nostrand Company, 1967.

Flew, Antony, and Roy Abraham Varghese. *There is a God: How the World's Most Notorious Atheist Changed His Mind*. New York: Harper One, 2007.

Ford, Paul Leicester, ed. *The Writings of Thomas Jefferson*, 10 vols. New York: G.P. Putnam's Sons, 1892–99.

Frances, Allen J. "DSM 5 Is Guide Not Bible—Ignore Its Ten Worst Changes, APA Approval of DSM-5 is a Sad Day for Psychiatry." Psychology Today.com, December 2, 2012. http://www.psychologytoday.com/blog/dsm5-in-distress/201212/dsm-5-is-guide-not-bible-ignore-its-ten-worst-changes.

Gaustad, Edwin. Historical Introduction to *The Bloudy [Bloody] Tenent of Persecution for Cause of Conscience*, by Roger Williams. 1644. Reprint, Macon, GA: Mercer University Press, 2001.

Gewehr, Wesley M. *The Great Awakening in Virginia, 1740–1790*. Durham, NC: Duke University Press, 1930.

Gould, Stephen Jay. *Ontogeny and Phylogeny*. Cambridge, MA: Belknap, 1977.

Graff, Henry F. *America the Glorious Republic*. Rev ed. Boston: Houghton Mifflin, 1990.

Gray, John. "The Closed Mind of Richard Dawkins." *New Republic.com*, October 2, 2014. http://www.newrepublic.com/article/119596/appetite-wonder-review-closed-mind-richard-dawkins.

Groves, Richard. Preface to *The Bloudy [Bloody] Tenent of Persecution for Cause of Conscience*, by Roger Williams. 1644. Reprint, Macon, GA: Mercer University Press, 2001.

Guinness, Os, and John Seel, eds. *No God but God: Breaking With the Idols of Our Age*. Chicago: Moody, 1992.

Hanegraaff, Hank. *The Face that Demonstrates the Farce of Evolution*. Nashville, Word, 1998.

Hart, Benjamin. "The Wall That Protestantism Built: The Religious Reasons for the Separation of Church and State." *Policy Review* (Fall 1988) 44–53.

Hawkins, Greg L., et al. *Reveal*. South Barrington, IL: Willow Creek Community Church, 2007.

Haynes, Charles, et al. *The First Amendment in Schools*. Alexandria, VA: ASCD, 2003.

———. *Finding Common Ground: A First Amendment Guide to Religion and Public Education*. Nashville, TN: Vanderbilt University Freedom Forum, 1994.

———. *Teaching about Religion in American Life: A First Amendment Guide*. Nashville, TN: Vanderbilt University Freedom Forum, 1998. files.eric.ed.gov/fulltext/ED439078.pdf.

Hobbs, Donald A. and Stuart J. Blank. *Sociology and the Human Experience*, 3rd ed. New York: John Wiley & Sons, 1982.

Hubbard, Ruth. *The Politics of Women's Biology*. New Brunswick: Rutgers University Press, 1997.

"The Huxley Brothers," *LIFE* magazine, March 24, 1947.

Huxley, Julian. *Religion Without Revelation*. New York: Mentor, 1957.

"Humanism and Its Aspirations: Humanist Manifesto III, a Successor to the Humanist Manifesto of 1933." 2003. American Humanist Association. https://americanhumanist.org/what-is-humanism/manifesto3/

"Humanist Manifesto I." 1933. American Humanist Association. https://americanhumanist.org/what-is-humanism/manifesto1/.

"Humanist Manifesto II." 1973. American Humanist Association. https://americanhumanist.org/what-is-humanism/manifesto2/.

"Is 'Secular Humanism' a 'Religion'?" Vine & Fig Tree website. http://vftonline.org/Patriarchy/definitions/humanism_religion.htm.

Jacob, Francois. *Of Flies, Mice, and Men*. Translated by Giselle Weiss. Cambridge: Harvard University Press, 1998.

Jefferson, Thomas. "First Annual Message to Congress, December 8, 1801." A Compilation of the Messages and Papers of the Presidents, Prepared under the direction of the Joint Committee on printing, of the House and Senate. Pursuant to an Act of the Fifty-Second Congress of the United States. New York: Bureau of National Literature, Inc., 1897. The Avalon Project at Yale Law School. New Haven, CT: Lillian Goldman Law Library, 2008. http://avalon.law.yale.edu/19th_century/jeffmes1.asp.

———. "First Inaugural Address, March 4, 1801." The Avalon Project at Yale Law School. New Haven, CT: Lillian Goldman Law Library, 2008. http://avalon.law.yale.edu/19th_century/jefinau1.asp.

———. "Second Annual Message to Congress, December 15, 1802." A Compilation of the Messages and Papers of the Presidents, Prepared under the direction of the Joint Committee on printing, of the House and Senate. Pursuant to an Act of the Fifty-Second Congress of the United States. New York: Bureau of National Literature, Inc., 1897. The Avalon Project at Yale Law School. New Haven, CT: Lillian Goldman Law Library, 2008. http://avalon.law.yale.edu/19th_century/jeffmes2.asp.

———. "Second Inaugural Address, March 4, 1805." The Avalon Project at Yale Law School. New Haven, CT: Lillian Goldman Law Library, 2008. http://avalon.law.yale.edu/19th_century/jefinau2.asp.

———. "Proclamation Appointing a Day of Thanksgiving and Prayer, 11 November 1779," *Founders Online,* National Archives, last modified December 28, 2016, http://founders.archives.gov/documents/Jefferson/01-03-02-0187. Original source: *The Papers of Thomas Jefferson*, vol. 3, *18 June 1779–30 September 1780*, ed. Julian P. Boyd. Princeton: Princeton University Press, 1951, 177–179.

Johnson, Phillip. *Objections Sustained: Subversive Essays on Evolution, Law & Culture*. Downers Grove, IL: InterVarsity, 1998.

———. *The Right Questions: Truth, Meaning & Public Debate.* Downers Grove, IL: InterVarsity, 2002.

———. *The Wedge of Truth: Splitting the Foundations of Naturalism.* Downers Grove, IL: InterVarsity, 2000.

"A joint resolution authorizing and requesting the President to proclaim 1983 as the "Year of the Bible." Public Law 97–280, 96 Stat. 1211, approved 4 October 1982. https://www.govtrack.us/congress/bills/97/sjres165/text.

"Joint Statement on Rights and Freedoms of Students." *Academe* 79:4 (Jul—Aug, 1993) 47–51.

Jung, Carl. *Modern Man in Search of a Soul.* New York: Harcourt, Brace, 1933.

Kafer, Krista. "How To Teach Religion in Public Schools." *The Heritage Foundation*, August 31, 2002. http://www.heritage.org/education/commentary/ed083102-how-teach-religion-public-schools.

Kennedy, D. James, and Jerry Newcombe. *What If the Bible Had Never Been Written?* Nashville: Thomas Nelson, 1998.

———. *What if Jesus Had Never Been Born?* Nashville: Thomas Nelson, 1994.

Kickbush, Peter. "Religious Expression in Public Schools." August 29, 1995. http://listserv.ed.gov/archives/edinfo/archived/msg00029.html.

Kohn, Alexander. *False Prophets: Fraud and Error in Science and Medicine.* Oxford: Basil Blackwell, 1989.

Kramnick, Isaac, and R. Laurence Moore. *The Godless Constitution: The Case Against Religious Correctness.* New York: W.W. Norton, 1996.

Lacey, A.R. *A Dictionary of Philosophy.* London: Routledge & Kegan Paul, 1976.

Larson, David B., and Susan S. Larson. *The Forgotten Factor in Physical and Mental Health: What Does the Research Show?* Rockville, MD: National Institute for Healthcare Research, 1994.

Leland, John. *The Writings of the Late Elder John Leland.* Compiled by L.F. Greene. New York: G.W. Wood, 1845.

Lewis, C. S. *God in the Dock: Essays on Theology & Ethics,* edited by Walter Hooper. Grand Rapids: Eerdmans, 1972.

Lipset, Seymour Martin. *Rebellion in the University.* New Brunswick, NJ: Transaction, 1993.

Little, David. "Roger Williams and the Separation of Church and State." *Religion and the State: Essays in Honor of Leo Pfeffer.* Waco, TX: Baylor University Press, 1985.

Little, Lewis P. *Imprisoned Preachers and Religious Liberty in Virginia: A Narrative Drawn Largely from the Official Records of Virginia Counties, Unpublished Manuscripts, Letters, and Other Original Sources.* Lynchburg, VA: J.P. Bell, 1938.

Lutz, Donald S. "The Relative Influence of European Writers on Late Eighteenth-Century American Political Thought." *American Political Science Review* 78 (1984) 189–197.

MacArthur, John, Jr., and The Masters Seminary Faculty. *Rediscovering Pastoral Ministry: Shaping Contemporary Ministry with Biblical Mandates.* Dallas: Word, 1995.

Marshall, Colin, and Tony Payne. *The Trellis and The Vine.* Kingsford, NSW, AU: Matthias Media, 2009.

McDowell, Josh. *The New Evidence that Demands a Verdict.* Nashville: Thomas Nelson, 1999.

McGrath, Alister. *The Reenchantment of Nature.* New York: Doubleday, 2002.

McLoughlin, William G. *New England Dissent, 1630–1883: The Baptists and the Separation of Church and State*, vol. 2. Cambridge, MA: Harvard University Press, 1971.

McNamara, Patrick. "The New Rights View of the Family and Its Social Science Critics: A Study in Differing Presuppositions." *Journal of Marriage and the Family* 47:2 (1985) 449–458.

Meek, Esther Lightcap. *Longing to Know*. Grand Rapids, MI: Brazos, 2003.

Morais, Herbert M. "Life and Words of Elder John Leland." MA thesis, Columbia University, 1928.

Morris, Henry. *Men of Science—Men of God*. San Diego: Master Books, 1984.

———. "Things You May Not Know About Evolution." *Institute for Creation Research*, no. 160, April 2002. http://www.icr.org/article/things-you-may-not-know-about-evolution.

Nash, Ronald H. "The Myth of a Value-Free Education." Acton Institute *Religion & Liberty* 1, no. 4 (1991). http://www.acton.org/pub/religion-liberty/volume-1-number-4/myth-value-free-education.

Nicholi, Armand M., Jr. *The Question of God: C.S. Lewis and Sigmund Freud Debate God, Love, Sex, and the Meaning of Life*. New York: Free Press, 2002.

Noll, Mark A. *One Nation under God? Christian Faith and Political Action in America*. San Francisco: Harper and Row, 1988.

Obama, Barak. "Remarks by Obama at Signing of Stem Cell Executive Order: Obama Lifts Ban on Federal Funding for Embryonic Stem Cell Research." March 9, 2009. http://iipdigital.usembassy.gov/st/english/texttrans/2009/03/20090309150227eaifaso.4777185.html#ixzz4Ytorq1SW.

Oppenheimer, J. Robert. *Uncommon Service*. Boston: Birkhäuser, 1984.

O'Brien, Charles F. "The Religious Issue in the Presidential Campaign of 1800." *Essex Institute Historical Collections* 107, no. 1 (1971) 82–93.

O'Reilly, Bill. "Some Vermont Media is Sympathizing with Judge Cashman . . ." *Fox News*, January 13, 2006. www.foxnews.com/story/2006/01/13/some-vermont-media-is-sympathizing-with-judge-cashman/.

———. "Vermont's Shame Continues . . ." *Fox News*, January 17, 2006. www.foxnews.com/story/2006/01/17/vermont-shame-continues/.

Parton, James. *Life of Thomas Jefferson: Third President of the United States*. Boston: James R. Osgood, 1874.

Patterson, James. "Evolution Supporters Likely to Regain Grip in Kansas Following Tuesday Primary Wins." *Baptist Press*, August 2, 2006. http://www.bpnews.net/23722.

Persons, Stow. *American Minds: A History of Ideas*. New York: Holt, Rinehart and Winston, 1958.

Plantinga, Alvin. *Where the Conflict Really Lies: Science, Religion, and Naturalism*. New York: Oxford University Press, 2011.

Plymouth Rock Foundation editors. *Biblical Principles concerning issues of importance to Godly Christians*. Plymouth, MA: Plymouth Rock Foundation, 1984.

Postman, Neil. *Teaching As a Conserving Activity*. New York: Delacorte, 1979.

Postman, Neil, and Charles Weingartner. *Teaching As a Subversive Activity*. New York: Delacorte 1969.

Potter, Charles Frances. "Letters to the Editor." *LIFE* magazine, April 14, 1947.

Ramm, Bernard. *The Evangelical Heritage: A Study in Historical Theology*. Grand Rapids, MI: Baker, 1973.

Randall, Henry S. *The Life of Thomas Jefferson*, vol. 3. New York: Derby and Jackson, 1857.

Randolph, John William. *Early History of the University of Virginia, as Contained in the Letters of Thomas Jefferson and Joseph C. Cabell*. Richmond: C.H. Wynne, 1856.

Rauch, Jonathan. *Kindly Inquisitors: The New Attacks on Free Thought*. Chicago: University of Chicago Press, 1993.

Ravitch, Diane. *The Language Police: How Pressure Groups Restrict What Students Learn*. New York: Alfred A. Knopf, 2003.

———. *Left Back: A Century of Failed School Reforms*. New York: Simon & Schuster, 2000.

Reagan, Ronald. "Remarks at an Ecumenical Prayer Breakfast in Dallas, Texas." August 23, 1984. https://www.reaganlibrary.archives.gov/archives/speeches/1984/82384a.htm.

Reiser, Oliver L., and Blodwen Davies. *Planetary Democracy*. New York: Creative Age, 1944.

Rogers, Carl. *Freedom to Learn*. Columbus, OH: Merrill, 1969.

———. *On Becoming a Person*. Boston: Houghton Mifflin, 1961.

Rogers, Ronnie W. *The Death of Man as Man: The Rise and Decline of Liberty*. 2011. Reprint, Bloomington, IN: WestBow, 2016.

———. *The Equipping Church: Somewhere Between Fundamentalism and Fluff*. Bloomington, IN: WestBow, 2016.

———. *Undermining the Gospel: The Case and Guide for Church Discipline*. Bloomington, IN: WestBow, 2015.

Rosenberg, Robin S. "Abnormal Is the New Normal: Why Will Half of the U.S. Population Have a Diagnosable Mental Disorder?" Slate.com, April 12, 2013. http://www.slate.com/articles/health_and_science/medical_examiner/2013/04/diagnostic_and_statistical_manual_fifth_edition_why_will_half_the_u_s_population.html.

Roth, John. *The Holocaust Chronicle: A History in Words and Pictures*. Lincolnwood, IL: Publications International, 2001.

Rousseau, Jean Jacques. *Emile*. 1762. Reprint, London, J.M. Dent & Sons, 1966.

Salerno, Steve. "Self-Help's Big Lie." *Los Angeles Times*, January 1, 2006. http://www.latimes.com/opinion/la-op-selfhelp1jan01-story.html.

Sampson, Robin. *What Your Child Needs to Know When*. Woodbridge, VA: Heart of Wisdom, 2001.

Savodnik, Irwin. "Psychiatry's Sick Compulsion: Turning Weaknesses into Diseases." *Los Angeles Times*, January 1, 2006. http://www.latimes.com/news/la-op-psych1jan01-story.html.

Schaeffer, Francis A. *The Complete Works of Francis A. Schaeffer: A Christian Worldview*. Westchester, IL: Crossway Books, 1996, c1982. Libronix electronic edition.

Schevitz, Tanya. "Cramped Speech at UC Berkeley / Teacher Warns 'Conservative Thinkers.'" *SFGate.com*, May 10, 2002. http://www.sfgate.com/education/article/Cramped-speech-at-UC-Berkeley-Teacher-warns-2838019.php.

Schmidt, Alvin J. *The Menace of Multiculturalism: Trojan Horse in America*. Westport, CT: Praeger, 1997.

Schuller, Robert H. *Self Esteem: The New Reformation*. Waco: Word, 1982.

Schutz, John A., and Richard S. Kirkendall. *The American Republic*. St. Louis, MO: Forum, 1978.

Shilling, Louis E. *Perspectives on Counseling Theories*. Englewood Cliffs, NJ: Prentice-Hall, 1984.

Shurden, Walter B. Foreword to *The Bloudy [Bloody] Tenent of Persecution for Cause of Conscience*, by Roger Williams. 1644. Reprint, Macon, GA: Mercer University Press, 2001.

Sims, Amy C. "Religion Gets Supersized at Megachurches." *Fox News*, February 3, 2004. http://www.foxnews.com/printer_friendly_story/0,3566,110240,00.html.

Skousen, W. Cleon. *The Making of America: The Substance and Meaning of the Constitution*, 2nd ed. Washington, D.C.: The National Center for Constitutional Studies, 1986.

Smith, Huston. *Why Religion Matters: The Fate of the Human Spirit in an Age of Disbelief*. New York: HarperCollins, 2001.

Smyth, Albert Henry, ed. *The Writings of Benjamin Franklin*, 10 vols. New York: Macmillan, 1905–7.

Snyder, K. Alan. "Who is Censoring Whom in Schools? Christians Should Be Concerned about What's in Textbooks Today." Editorial/opinion page. Marion, IN: *Chronicle-Tribune*, September 5, 1993. Cited on Snyder's blog, http://ponderingprinciples.com/writing/Who_is_Censoring.pdf.

"Some NEA Resolutions Passed at 2002 Convention in Dallas." *Education Reporter* no.199: (August 2002). http://www.eagleforum.org/educate/2002/aug02/NEA-Resolutions.shtml.

Spencer, Herbert. *Education: Intellectual, Moral and Physical*. New York: Burt, 1859.

Strickland, Charles E. and Charles Orville Burgess, eds. *Health, Growth and Heredity: G. Stanley Hall on Natural Education*. New York: Teachers College Press, 1965.

Strode, Tom. "SBC Calls for Cultural Engagement; Education Resolution Declined." *Baptist Press*, June 16, 2004. http://www.bpnews.net/18501/sbc-calls-for-cultural-engagement-education-resolution-declined.

Toalston, Art. "Education Resolution among Submissions to SBC Committee." *Baptist Press*, May 12, 2004. http://bpnews.net/18262/education-resolution-among-submissions-to-sbc-committee.

Torbet, Robert G. *A History of the Baptists*, 3rd ed. Valley Forge: Judson, 1963.

"Twenty Troubling Facts About American Education." Freedom Works, June 21, 1999. http://www.freedomworks.org/content/twenty-troubling-facts-about-american-education.

US Bureau of Education. *The Social Studies in Secondary Education*. Washington, D.C.: US Government Printing Office, 1916.

Vick, Kyle. "Soul as Theory." Paper presented at the Oxford Round Table on Religion and Science: Shaping the Modern World, Harris Manchester College, Oxford, England. July 27, 2010.

Vitz, Paul C. *Psychology as Religion: The Cult of Self-Worship*, 2nd ed. Grand Rapids, MI: William B. Eerdmans, 1977.

Warren, Rick. "Contemporary Approaches to Ministry, Evangelism and Organization—Reaching the Baby-Boom Generation." *Occasional Paper* 14 (December 1989). Home Mission Board, Southern Baptist Convention.

Wells, David F. *No Place for Truth: Or Whatever Happened to Evangelical Theology*. Grand Rapids, MI: William B. Eerdmans, 1993.

Wells, Jonathan. *The Politically Incorrect Guide to Darwinism and Intelligent Design.* Washington, D.C.: Regnery, 2006.

Wells, William V. *The Life and Public Services of Samuel Adams*, vol. 3. Boston: Little, Brown, 1865.

Wessler, Richard L. "A Bridge Too Far: Incompatibilities of Rational-Emotive Therapy and Pastoral Counseling." *The Personnel and Guidance Journal* 62 (1984) 264–266. doi:10.1111/j.2164-4918.1984.tb00200.x.

Wiebe, Ken F., and J. Roland Fleck. "Personality Correlates of Intrinsic, Extrinsic and Non-Religious Orientations." *Journal of Psychology* 105 (1980) 111–117.

Williams, Roger. *The Bloudy [Bloody] Tenent of Persecution for Cause of Conscience.* 1644. Edited by Richard Groves. Reprint, Macon, GA: Mercer University Press, 2001.

Wilson, Edward O. *On Human Nature.* Cambridge: Harvard University Press, 1978.

Wolfe, Alan. *The Transformation of American Religion: How We Actually Live Our Faith.* New York: Free Press, 2003.

"Yale Professors Edit Textbook Series on Religion in American Life." Yale News, September 7, 1999. http://news.yale.edu/1999/09/07/yale-professors-edit-textbook-series-religion-american-life.

Zachry, Caroline B. "Emotion and Conduct in Adolescence." New York: Appleton-Century, 1940.

Name Index

Appleyard, Brian, 37, 52–53, 143, 154, 157, 161–62, 167, 170

Barna, 178
Bellah, Robert, 100
Benson, Herbert, 131
Bork, Robert, 2, 52, 143–45, 147, 150, 158
Bradford, M.E., 84

Carter, Stephen L., 40, 42
Cashman, Edward, 160
Commager, Henry Steele, 73
Cremin, Lawrence A., 11, 73

Dawkins, Richard, 51–52, 133, 145, 161, 164, 171
Dewey, John, 5n10, 12, 14, 19, 21, 23, 24n69, 31, 72–73, 76–77, 109, 138–39

Einstein, Albert, 139
Ellis, Albert, 106, 140

Flew, Antony, 63, 188–89
Fosdick, Harry Emerson, 177–78
Frances, Allen J., 104–5

Gould, Stephen J., 56n75, 171

Hall, G. Stanley, 19, 26, 40, 76–77, 109
Hitler, 156
Huxley, Julian, 138

Jacob, Francois, 46n43, 132n114, 133n120, 162
Johnson, Phillip, 47–48, 51
Jung, Carl, 139

Keyes, Alan, 167
King, Martin Luther, 147
Kohn, Alexander, 55–56, 156
Kramnick, Isaac, 84, 119, 197

Land, Richard, 186, 190
Larson, David, 104
Leland, John, 117–18, 125
Lewis, C.S., 61, 161

Mann, Horace, 27
Marshall, John, 128
Marx, 67, 151
Maslow, Abraham, 139
Mayhue, Richard L., 11
McGrath, Alister, 143–44, 170n34
McNamara, Patrick, 101

Nehru, Jawaharlal, 154
Nicholi, Jr., Armand M., 131

Osteen, Joel, 29–30, 185n27

Pestalozzi, Johann Heinrich, 72–73
Plantinga, Alvin, 47, 152

Ramm, Bernard, 177
Rauch, Jonathan, 48, 56, 139
Ravitch, Diane, 3n3, 7–8, 15, 19–20, 44n36, 45, 77n54, 86, 90, 154

225

Reagan, 110
Rogers, Carl, 15, 44, 106, 139
Rousseau, Jean Jacques, 12, 14, 30, 45, 72–74, 77

Schaeffer, Francis, 72, 142, 179n20, 181
Schleiermacher, Friedrich, 177–78
Schmidt, Alvin J., 41, 53
Schuller, Robert, 28, 190
Smith, Huston, 41, 46, 48
Sorokin, Pitirim A., 173
Spencer, Herbert, 11, 68n21, 73–74, 77n54, 109
Story, Joseph, 128

Thomas, Cal, 190
Thorndike, Edward L., 8, 75–77, 101, 102n3, 109

Vitz, Paul C., 53–54, 86

Wagner, Peter, 178
Warren, Earl, 128
Warren, Rick, 16
Wells, David, 10, 28, 65, 176, 179–80
Wells, Jonathan, 38, 212
Whitlow, Sam, 22
Williams, Roger, 114–22, 127
Wilson, Ben, 188
Wilson, Edward O., 102
Wolfe, Alan, 41, 147

Subject Index

absolutes, xiii, 30, 37, 67–68, 70–71, 74, 97, 165, 169
apologetics, 188–89

Baptist, 31, 95, 114, 117, 120, 123, 125, 129, 195, 199
biases, 55–57, 103–4, 157
Bible, 7, 9, 11, 13, 17, 31, 60, 64, 68–70, 81, 83–84, 89, 103, 128, 133, 147, 157, 160, 166, 178, 180, 185
biblical, xiii–xiv, 1, 5–7, 14, 17–18, 21, 26, 28, 31, 36, 69, 101, 128, 145, 148, 159, 172–73, 175, 179–80, 182–85, 187, 189, 196, 211–12
biological, 34, 38, 41, 74, 100–101, 103, 108, 133, 146, 183, 213
biologist, 38, 56, 160, 171, 212

causality, 103, 162
chemical reactions, 160
child-centered, ix, 9, 18–19, 21–23, 30, 45, 77, 164, 178
Civil Rights, 86, 91n97, 147
classical, ix, xiii, 7–9, 12, 14–15, 18, 33, 37, 46, 150
Constitution, 68, 79, 82, 84–85, 92–93, 111, 113, 119–21, 125, 128–29, 147, 166, 198, 206
contemporary, x, xiv, 5, 10, 16, 18, 21, 23, 28, 75, 85–86, 88, 91–92, 98–100, 111, 133, 144–45, 172–73, 176–77, 179–81, 184
cultural milieu, 191

Darwinism, 38, 68, 102, 159, 171, 212
Declaration of Independence, 99, 113, 128–29, 142, 147–48, 205
discipleship, x, 17, 29, 210
DSM, 104–5, 107–8

Enlightenment, 33, 36, 65–67, 151, 163, 176–77
epistemology, 42, 48, 67
equipping, x, xiii–xiv, 5, 13, 25–26, 172–73, 178–81, 184, 187–89
ethics, 53, 55, 80, 136, 141, 156, 173
evolution, 38–39, 47, 50–52, 57, 67, 71, 101, 144, 146, 160, 212
experience, 2, 8–9, 12, 14–15, 17, 19–26, 28, 31, 42, 45, 53, 57, 77, 79, 87, 95, 103, 105, 110, 138, 158, 163, 167–68, 177, 188–89, 191, 193, 211

Fourteenth Amendment, 88, 112
free will, 35, 58, 151, 153, 159, 162–63
fun, 9, 17, 26–30, 180

generational infection, 2, 3, 47, 183, 210–11
guidelines, 45, 68, 86–87, 96, 184

happiness, 19, 73, 80–81, 126, 131, 138n9, 205–6
homosexuality, 79, 103, 129, 166, 169
Humanist Manifesto, 77, 137–38

image, 35, 102, 151–53, 159, 168, 174

227

imposable, 34, 37, 57, 63–66, 71, 142, 148, 213

law, 48–49, 62, 75, 80, 109, 111–14, 116–18, 122, 125, 147, 165, 167, 173, 176, 200–201, 206–7
Leadership Magazine, 10
look-say, 9, 20, 26, 68, 78

materialist, 163
mental discipline, 7–9, 12, 61, 76
methodological neutralism, 70, 213
minimalists, 187
mission, xiii–xiv, 61, 70, 186, 191
multiculturalism, 16, 41, 45, 86, 90, 191

naturalism, 34–35, 38, 41, 46–48, 49n50, 50–52, 56, 58, 62–63, 65–66, 68, 70, 74–75, 77, 94–95, 101–2, 110, 133, 136–39, 141–42, 145–46, 148, 150, 154, 160–61, 164, 170, 213
NEA, 88

Oxford, 52, 161

pedagogy, 10, 14, 16, 43–44, 69, 71–72, 95, 106, 181
philosopher, 11–12, 63, 65, 73, 77, 106, 185, 188
philosophy, 1–2, 4, 9, 18, 22, 31, 33–34, 37–38, 42, 46, 58, 62–63, 68–69, 71–72, 74, 76, 87, 92, 135, 137–38, 142, 148, 150, 166, 171, 178, 182–83, 210–11
preaching, xiii, 11, 13, 20–21, 23, 28, 30–31, 68, 78, 145, 177, 181, 185, 191, 209
predestination, 10, 187
progressives, 3n3, 5, 8–9, 12–16, 24, 28, 30, 33, 40, 50, 60, 62, 69, 72, 74, 77, 99, 130, 135–36, 154, 165, 170, 183
psychologists, 8, 15, 66, 104, 106
psychology, 5n10, 8, 11, 19, 34, 36, 38, 55, 74–77, 100–101, 104, 106, 110, 139, 145, 150, 164, 177–78, 190–91
Puritans, 82–83, 85

scientific liberal, 37, 55, 62, 64–66, 68, 99, 147, 156, 166, 169, 173, 175–76, 194, 213
scientific liberalism, 67–68
secular humanism, 137, 139
secularization, 61, 78, 147–48
Separatists, 82–83
sociologists, 66, 101, 104, 110
sociology, 11–12, 34, 38, 41, 74, 100–101, 103–4, 110, 145, 147, 150, 190
style, 15–16, 31
supernatural, 31, 33–34, 46, 48, 50, 66–67, 69, 71, 74, 95, 97–98, 103, 106, 136–41, 143, 146, 163, 170, 174, 176–77, 213
Supreme Court, 111, 112n23, 128, 137n4, 190

thinking, xiii, 1, 4, 15–16, 30, 35, 57, 61, 63–64, 66–67, 70, 74, 78, 84, 91, 96, 102, 104, 107, 144, 148, 163, 165–66, 169–70, 184–85, 210, 213
traditional, xiv, 17, 24, 54, 86, 100, 102, 172–73, 179–80, 184
Trinity, 25, 104, 152, 185–87
Trinity Decision, 128
tsunami, xiii, 61–62
two tables, 118

unchurched, 85, 178, 197
Unpardonable Sin, 186
utilitarianism, 12–13, 73

value-neutral, 53

weakness, 35, 94, 133, 156–57, 163–64, 168, 181
worldview, 2, 36–37, 60, 63, 66, 68–69, 71, 81, 85, 100, 129–30, 143, 154, 171, 184, 187, 189, 210–11

Scripture Index

GENESIS
1:26–28	151
1:26–27	151
1:26, 28	151
1:27–28	168
2:15	151, 168
3:1–6	152
3:5	153
5:1	151
9:6	152

EXODUS
20:1–11	117
20:12–17	117

NEHEMIAH
1:1–4	184

PSALMS
14:1–3	185
119:65	13

JEREMIAH
17:9–10	181

MATTHEW
5:13–16	121
10:16	121
12:22–32	186
18:15–18	180
22:37–39	210
28:18–20	xiv, 25, 172, 180, 209, 121
28:19	184

LUKE
9:23	29

JOHN
3:16	153
6:52–66	29
20:27	139n18

ACTS
20:27	10

ROMANS
3:11	185

1 CORINTHIANS
2:10–16	181
2:14	23
3:1–3	23
6:9–11	103
6:9–10	160
9:22	16
11:7	152
12:29	209n2
15:17	185

2 CORINTHIANS

5:17	152, 153

EPHESIANS

4:11–16	xiv, 25, 172, 209
4:11–14	209n2
4:11	209
4:15	210
5:22–6:4	185
6:1	102

COLOSSIANS

3:9–10	152

1 THESSALONIANS

5:12–13	209

1 TIMOTHY

3:2	209
3:15	59
4:6, 11, 13, 16	209n2
5:17	209n2

2 TIMOTHY

2:14	209n2
2:15	180
2:15, 24	209n2
2:24	209

TITUS

1:9	209n2
2:1	209n2

HEBREWS

4:12	181
13:17	209

JAMES

1:22	25, 182
2:18	130
3:9	152

1 PETER

2:11	83

2 PETER

3:18	25

www.ingramcontent.com/pod-product-compliance
Lightning Source LLC
Chambersburg PA
CBHW060601230426
43670CB00011B/1915